ACTRESSES AND SUFFRAGISTS

Women in the American Theater, 1890-1920

Albert Auster

PRAEGER SPECIAL STUDIES • PRAEGER SCIENTIFIC

New York • Philadelphia • Eastbourne, UK
Toronto • Hong Kong • Tokyo • Sydney

Library of Congress Cataloging in Publication Data

Auster, Albert.
    Actresses and suffragists.

    Bibliography: p.
    Includes index.
    1. Actresses—United States—Biography. 2. Women's
rights—United States. I. Title.
PN2285.A9   1984   792'.028'0922 [B]   83-19253
ISBN 0-03-069778-6

Photos: Courtesy of the Theatre Collection; the Museum of the
City of New York

Published in 1984 by Praeger Publishers
CBS Educational and Professional Publishing
A Division of CBS, Inc.
521 Fifth Avenue, New York, New York 10175 U.S.A.

56789   052   98765432

Printed in the United States of America on acid-free paper.

In memory of my father Lazar Auster (1905-1962)
and to my mother Mollie Auster and
to Dr. Kurt C. Rawitt

Acknowledgments

I wish to thank Professor Robert D. Marcus, formerly of the history department of the State University of New York at Stony Brook for his support of this project when it was a doctoral dissertation. I am also indebted to Dr. David Burner, Dr. Ruth Schwartz Cowan, and Dr. Michael Schwartz for their cooperation and criticism. In addition, I wish to thank Professors Herman Lebovic, Wilbur Miller, and Joel T. Rosenthal for their timely advice and assistance.

Thanks alone nor dinner at the "Canal House" could never repay the immense debt I owe Barbara Schlapp-Gilgoff. Her tireless and intelligent criticism and editing, as well as her emotional support, make her a true collaborator in this project in everything but its errors and mistakes, which are mine alone. A deep feeling of appreciation also goes to her husband Nathan Gilgoff and daughter Caitlin who had to do without a wife and mother while she helped me. Similarly, to Miriam Helbok, who typed a heavily edited manuscript skillfully and efficiently, another note of thanks.

I also wish to thank my editor Lynda Sharp for her faith in my work and her help in publishing it.

Contents

Chapter   *Page*

1   Introduction   1

2   Actresses and Feminists: An Overview   11

3   Women and the Growth of Show Business   31

4   The Actress: An Economic and Social View   49

5   Mary Shaw: The Actress as Clubwoman and Suffragist   67

6   Lillian Russell: "The American Beauty" as Feminist   91

7   Ethel Barrymore: "The American Girl" and Women's Emancipation   119

8   Conclusion   143

Bibliography   149

Index   165

About the Author   177

Chapter 1

Introduction

riting about actresses, dancers, and singers in her classic study *The Second Sex*, Simone De Beauvoir noted:

> For three centuries they have been almost the only women to maintain a concrete independence in the midst of society, and at the present time they still occupy a privileged place in it. They often skirt the sphere of gallantry and, like courtesans, they spend a great deal of their time in the company of men; but making their own living and finding the meaning of their lives in their work, they escape the yoke of men. Their great advantage is that their professional successes — like those of men — contribute to their sexual valuation; in their self-realization, their validation of themselves as human beings, they find self fulfillment as women.[1]

Other feminists certainly shared De Beauvoir's regard for actresses. In her two books on American career women in the pre- and post-revolutionary eras, Elizabeth Dexter included references to their achievements and their positions in society.[2] Similarly, Gerda Lerner paid tribute to their accomplishments by citing that "only in the performing arts has individual female talent had the same opportunity as male talent."[3]

Nevertheless, despite their accomplishments, only recently has there been any major attempt to examine the lives of American actresses and their influence on society. The most notable study, particularly in regard to the American theater, is Helen Krich Chinoy and Linda Walsh Jenkins' *Women in American Theater*.[4] Filling in the gap for the American theater left by Rosamund Gilder's pioneering study *Enter the Actress* (which concluded in the early nineteenth century with the English actress-manager Madame Vestris),[5] Chinoy and Jenkins have joined together a varied array of essays, both narrative and analytic, enumerating

1

the achievements and contributions of actresses, woman dramatists, critics, and feminist theater groups in the American theater right up to the present. While confirming the importance of women in American theater, the Chinoy and Jenkins book also serves to underscore the importance of the theater in American society.

Although confronted by social and ideological obstacles, the theater enjoyed slow but steady growth in the first three centuries of the American experience. One of its earliest devotees was George Washington, who, after seeing his first play in Barbados at the age of nineteen, noted in his journal: "Was treated with a play ticket by M. Carter to see the Tragedy of George Barnwell acted: the character of Barnwell and several others were well performed."[6]At Valley Forge, Washington permitted the Continental Army soldiers to put on a performance of *Cato* and, as President, kept a box at the theater.[7]

Besides the prominent attending the theater, the theater was also prominent in American events, most tragically figuring as the site of Lincoln's assassination. However, even before the murder of the President, the theater served as the occasion for violent nationalistic and almost open class warfare at the Astor Place riot of 1849 in which 31 died and 150 were injured.[8] Subsequently, it became an arena in the cultural struggle over realism when Shaw's *Mrs. Warren's Profession* was banned[9] and Synge's *Playboy of the Western World* caused a near riot.[10]

American writers and novelists were well aware of the importance of the theater in American life. An inveterate theater-goer himself, Mark Twain included scenes of theatrical life in his tour-de-force portrait of mid-nineteenth century America, *The Adventures of Huckleberry Finn*. In these episodes, Huck and Jim help those two poseurs, the Duke and the Dauphin, impersonate "David Garrick the younger" and "Edmund Kean the elder" before a frontier audience in a series of sketches from Shakespeare and a rollicking farce. Here, Twain captured the rough and ready qualities of their performances while reflecting the deep hunger of frontier audiences for entertainment.[11]

Similarly, Theodore Dreiser drew an illuminating and insightful portrait of the importance of late nineteenth century theater in his novel *Sister Carrie*. Besides filling the novel with descriptions of theatrical performances (most notably Carrie's amateur debut in a production of Augustin Daly's *Under Gaslight*),[12] he also called attention to the average man's love of basking in the limelight of the nineteenth century actor. Describing the salesman Drouet's reason for enjoying Rector's restaurant, he wrote: "When dining it was a source of keen satisfaction to him to know that Joseph Jefferson was wont to come into the same place, or that Harry Dixey, a well known performer of the day was then only a few tables off."[13]

Sociologists, too, perceived the importance of the theater in American life. While delineating the significance of new technological amusements like the movies in their classic study of social change in American life, *Middletown*, the Lynds did not neglect to mention the theater. In fact, the information they obtained about the theater indicates that it was carefully scrutinized for any negative effect it might have on the community.[14] According to the Lynds, a local performance of *Sappho* (a late nineteenth century French play translated into English) scandalized many, especially due to the last scene in which the hero picks up the heroine in his arms and carries her upstairs toward what everyone in the audience knew was the bedroom.[15] The Lynds reported that the local newspaper editorial "roasted" the play and admonished the manager of the local opera house that "[Middletown] has had enough of naughtiness on the stage. Manager W_____ will do well to fumigate his pretty playhouse before one of the clean instructive plays he has billed comes before the footlights."[16]

More recently, American cultural and intellectual historians began investigating and analyzing the effects of American theater on American culture and society. An early example of this type of research was Francis Hodge's *Yankee Theater*, which examined the way in which a number of American actors fashioned a "Yankee" character out of American sources between 1825 and 1850, and made of him the first identifiable American national type to achieve recognition as such both at home and abroad.[17]

Other studies, using popular theatrical forms like vaudeville, melodrama, and minstrelsy as their sources, showed how popular culture can give us insight into popular consciousness. The work of Albert F. McLean, Jr. in *American Vaudeville as Ritual*, David Grimsted in *Melodrama Unveiled*, and Robert Toll in *Blacking Up* also revealed that these popular cultural forms articulated ideas, values, and stereotypes that helped their audiences adjust to a society confronted by rapid industrialization, a developing democratic ethos, and racial and ethnic tensions.[18]

Historian John Higham relied, to a large extent, on popular culture as evidence for his thesis that the 1890s were a watershed in American history. He revealed that the 1890s saw a revolt against the intellectual, cultural and social rigidities inherited from the first three-quarters of the nineteenth century.[19]

Higham's interpretation represented a revision of the conventional historical notion which saw the 1920s as the major decade of modern cultural change. However, even before the publication of Higham's thesis, Henry May concluded that the major intellectual changes which came into mass consciousness after World War I occurred from 1912 to 1917. Subsequent investigations by James R. McGovern, James Burnham, and David Kennedy supported these conclusions by researching the areas of manners and morals and sexual liberation, and they confirmed the period from 1890 to 1920 as the source of major twentieth century cultural and intellectual change.[20]

The 1890's were correspondingly a period of preeminence for the theater in American society and culture. The rapid industrialization of the American economy, the increasing amounts of leisure time, and the weakening of clerical influence produced tremendous growth in the entertainment industry, and, by 1900, there were an estimated 3,000 theaters throughout the United States.[21] In that very year, 392 dramatic and musical comedy touring companies[22] traveled around the country, while as many as 8,000 to 10,000 variety acts toured the vaudeville circuits.[23] This phenomenal expansion made millionaires out of men like B. F. Keith, Charles Frohman, and Abe Erlanger, who created trusts which dominated the entertainment business in the same way that Standard Oil controlled the petroleum industry.[24]

The audience for the entertainment boom was not confined solely to the middle class, although they made up the majority of its attendance. Popularly priced theaters such as the Midwest Stair and the Havlin chain presented melodrama to the masses,[25] and the Loew's vaudeville circuit combined vaudeville and movies at low cost to attract the working classes.[26] Such was the power of the low-priced vaudeville and legitimate theaters that they could and did defy the power of the autocratic syndicates.

Just as the theaters prospered and audiences increased, the period from 1890 to 1920 was considered a golden age of players (if not plays). Although melodrama, historical epics, and the European translation still predominated and the American theater had yet to develop its own superior dramatic writing talent, it did produce an array of actresses and actors who were recognized at home and abroad as first rate. Indeed, some—Joseph Jefferson, Richard Mansfield, Edward Sothern, Mrs. Fiske, Maud Adams, and Madame Helena Modjeska—became legendary.[27]

In addition to its own actors and actresses, the American stage also played host to the most luminous stars of the European theater and music hall. Between 1880 and 1917, Sarah Bernhardt made numerous tours of America, appearing in everything from tents to barns.[28] The adulation accorded her was so great that quite ordinary people went out of their way to catch even a fleeting glimpse of her. One woman wrote:

> As we came up to the Forrest theatre, we saw quite a mob, and when we investigated we found that the "Divine Sarah" had played there and they were waiting for her to come out on her way back to her hotel. And although I never did such a thing before in all my life, I waited too—and although I was dog-tired, I thought she was the one person that a glimpse of would be some satisfaction.[29]

Similarly, Eleanora Duse appeared all over the country, as did Sir Henry Irving and his co-star, Ellen Terry. Lillie Langtry, Johnston Forbes-Robertson, Yvette Guilbert, and Marie Lloyd all met critical acclaim and drew large box-office receipts.

Everywhere, from Broadway (where 89 new productions opened in the 1899-1900 season alone)[30] to the vaudeville circuits (which featured playlets starring renowned actors and actresses like Maurice Barrymore, Denman Thompson, and the great Bernhardt herself), the legitimate stage or its echo proliferated.[31] One found frivolous musical comedy, light comedy, melodrama and the historical spectacle, as well as plays of moral uplift and educational value.[32]

Timothy Arthur Shay's *Ten Nights in a Barroom* became a staple of touring companies and practically a Women's Christian Temperance Union (WCTU) tract.[33] Following this example, Dr. Thomas Hepburn, a leader in the reform movement against the "crime of silence" which surrounded the problem of venereal disease, distributed 10,000 copies of Eugene Brieux's play *Les Avaries* (translated into English as *Damaged Goods*), which told of the terrible consequences that befall a marriage in which the husband has syphilis. Not only did Hepburn distribute the play, he even persuaded actor-manager Richard Bennett to produce it, and, after a few special perfomances, it opened to such commercial success that it spawned a whole genre known as "vice plays."[34]

One vice play, *The Lure* (a drama about white slavery) so moved the British suffragist Mrs. Pankhurst, who saw it one evening in New York, that she gave a short, spontaneous speech to the audience attesting to its veracity.[35] Mrs. Pankhurst's gesture is less important as a judgment on the worth of the play than as a symbol of the fact that the growth of the theater in America and its simultaneous use for educational and reform purposes coincided with the revival of the women's movement in the late nineteenth and early twentieth century.

The "New Woman," as she was referred to in this period, was a product of increased higher education, expanded leisure, and the growth of women in the work force. A major result of these changes was the resurgence of the women's suffrage movement as younger women joined veteran feminist leaders Susan B. Anthony and Elizabeth Cady Stanton in the final campaign to gain the right to vote. Although this phase of the struggle concentrated primarily on the issue of the ballot, the progress of the "New Woman" did raise questions about her relationship to both home and a career, as well as men and marriage.[36]

The theatrical world, too, became aware of changing feminine patterns. As early as the seventies and eighties, theatrical managers noted the increasing number of women who attended the theater, and a manager as prominent as Augustin Daly even declared that they constituted the majority of theater-goers. Another barometer of the change was the growth of the "matinee girl" phenomenon. These were young women and girls who often attended matinees unescorted, created idols of the leading men and women of the day, and made these performances virtually unchallenged citadels of female attendance, sentiment, beauty, style, and fashion. Social commentators and theater critics blamed them for the decline in both acting and playwriting, while doctors proclaimed their excessive playgoing caused nervous prostration in women.[37]

Nevertheless, public concern failed to dampen the "matinee girl" phenomenon or stem women's attendance at the theater. Moreover, as the women's movement gained strength, the theatrical profession congratulated itself on providing women with an equality they hardly knew elsewhere. The *New York Dramatic Mirror* said in an editorial titled "Women and the Stage":

> One phase of the question as to women and the stage will bear repeated reference and reiterated declaration. While women win distinction as befits their ability in literature; while a few of the gentler sex succeed — but none of them without some loss at least of self respect — in the journalism of the day; while occasionally the eye is saluted by the shingle of a woman M.D. whose practice necessarily must be special; and while the occasional woman not only creates a sensation for the public but also amazes her furtively glancing colleagues at bench and bar as a lawyer, the theatre alone of all the institutions of civilization offers to her sisters a field in which they may and do stand absolutely on an equality with men.[38]

Although the meaning of "absolute equality" is not spelled out, the editorial was substantially correct if it ascribed to women of the theater economic opportunities, as well as a social and sexual independence, enjoyed by few other women in the society. However, the editorial fails to convey that their position on the stage also gave actresses a great opportunity to aid in the struggle for women's rights and women's emancipation.

Using Gerda Lerner's distinction between "women's rights" (civil rights such as property rights, divorce, and the right to vote) and "women's emancipation" (the attempt to gain "freedom from oppressive restriction imposed by sex; self determination and autonomy"),[39] it is the thesis of this study that actresses both wittingly and unwittingly used the stage and the celebrity that some of them derived from it to raise women's consciousness in the struggle for women's rights and women's emancipation in the period from 1890 to 1920.

A number of articles have already shown how the plays of this period depicted the "New Woman"[40] and how cultural institutions like urban cabarets and nightclubs helped foster the new image for women and altered their relationship with men.[41] Furthermore, a recent study of the pioneers of the modern dance movement (Ruth St. Denis, Isadora Duncan, and Martha Graham) indicates the ways in which modern dance projected an alternative image of woman's body, health, and dress.[42] Similarly, a study of the movies by Robert Sklar points out how popular culture forms, symbols, and narrative undermined, rather than buttressed, established cultural values and norms.[43]

With these studies in view, this book will first examine the evolution of the theater in America, the part that women played in its development, and the first personal and political links between actresses and feminists. It will then trace the growth of the entertainment industry in nineteenth century America and the corresponding increase in the number of women and their influence in the show business. After looking at the economic and social lives of these women, this study will focus on the lives and careers of three actresses — Mary Shaw, Lillian Russell, and Ethel Barrymore — who exemplify the ways in which actresses participated in the struggles of the women's movement of the era.

In no way do these three actresses exhaust the list of women in the theater who supported the campaign for equal rights and autonomy for women in this period. Nevertheless, they do shed light on the means by which actresses aided those efforts, and they illuminate a profession whose contribution to those struggles has often been acknowledged but rarely discussed in depth. As prototypical figures, they confirm Simone De Beauvoir's analysis of the actress as one who "gives meaning to her own life by giving meaning to the world."[44]

NOTES

1. Simone De Beauvoir, *The Second Sex* (New York: Bantam Books, 1961), pp. 661-662.

2. Elizabeth A. Dexter, *Colonial Women of Affairs: Women in Business and Professions in America Before 1776* (Boston: Houghton-Mifflin, Co., 1931), and Elizabeth A. Dexter, *Career of Women in America, 1776-1840* (Francestown, N.Y.: Marshall Jones Company, 1950).

3. Gerda Lerner, "New Approaches to the Study of Women in American History," in Gerda Lerner, *The Majority Finds its Past: Placing Women in History* (New York: Oxford University Press, 1981), p. 7.

4. Helen Krich Chinoy and Linda Walsh Jenkins, *Women in American Theatre* (New York: Crown Publishers, 1981). Two noteworthy studies of British Actresses have been done by Christopher Kent, "Image and Reality: The Actress and Society," in Martha Vicinus, ed., *A Widening Sphere* (Bloomington: Indiana University Press, 1977), pp. 94-116. See also Michael Baker, *The Rise of the Victorian Actor* (London: Croom Helm, 1978), pp. 95-108.

5. Rosamund Gilder, *Enter the Actress: The First Women in the Theater* (New York: Theatre Arts Books, 1931).

6. Bernard Hewitt, *Theatre U.S.A., 1668-1957* (New York: McGraw-Hill Company, Inc., 1959), p. 32.

7. Ibid.

8. Richard Moody, *The Astor Place Riot* (Bloomington: Indiana University Press, 1958).

9. Glen Hughes, *A History of the American Theatre, 1700-1950* (New York: Samuel French, 1951), pp. 338-339.

10. "A Rousing Playboy Riot," *New York Drama Mirror*, Nov. 29, 1911, p. 7.

11. Mark Twain (Samuel L. Clemens), *The Adventures of Huckleberry Finn* (New York: Washington Square Press, 1962), pp. 173-196.

12. Theodore Dreiser, *Sister Carrie* (New York: New American Library, 1961), pp. 170-182.

13. Ibid., p. 44.

14. Robert S. Lynd and Helen M. Lynd, *Middletown: A Study in Contemporary American Culture* (New York: Harcourt Brace and Company, 1929), p. 268.

15. Ward Morehouse, *Matinee Tomorrow: Fifty Years at Our Theater* (New York: Whittlesey House, 1949), pp. 26-28.

16. Lynds, *Middletown*, p. 268.

17. Francis Hodge, *Yankee Theatre: The Image of America on the Stage, 1825-1850* (Austin, Tex.: University of Texas Press, 1964).

18. Albert F. McLean, Jr., *American Vaudeville as Ritual* (Lexington, Ky.: University of Kentucky Press, 1965). David Grimstead, *Melodrama Unveiled: American Theater and Culture, 1800-1850* (Chicago: University of Chicago Press, 1968). Robert C. Toll, *Blacking Up: The Ministrel Show in Nineteenth Century America* (New York: Oxford University Press, 1974). Another study of nineteenth century American popular culture that is particularly evocative is Neil Harris, *Humbug: The Art of P.T. Barnum* (Boston: Little, Brown and Company, 1973), also for a general history of popular culture see Russell Nye, *The Unembarrassed Muse: The Popular Arts in America* (New York: Dial Press, 1970).

19. John Higham, "The Reorientation of American Culture in the 1980's," in John Higham, *Writing American History: Essays in Scholarship* (Bloomington: Indiana University Press, 1970), pp. 73-102.

20. Henry F. May, *The End of American Innocence: A Study of the First Years of Our Time, 1912–1917* (Chicago: Quadrangle Paperbacks, 1964). May's ideas were supported by the subsequent work of James R. McGovern, "The American Woman's Pre-World War I Freedom in Manners and Morals," *Journal of American History*, LV (September, 1968), pp. 315-333, James C. Burnham, "The Progressive Era Revolution in American Attitudes Toward Sex," *Journal of American History*, LIX (March, 1973), pp. 885-908, David M. Kennedy, *Birth Control in America, The Career of Margaret Sanger* (New Haven: Yale University Press, 1970). These are some of the books and articles that revised the older interpretation of the twenties as the decade of the change in manners and morals. The latter are embodied in books and articles like Frederick Lewis Allen, *Only Yesterday: An Informal History of the Nineteen-Twenties* (New York: Harper Brothers, 1931), pp. 88-122; William E. Leuchtenberg, *The Perils of Prosperity, 1914–1932* (Chicago: University of Chicago Press, 1958), pp. 158-177; Kenneth A. Yellis, "Prosperity's Child: Some Thoughts on the Flapper," *American Quarterly*, XXI (Spring, 1969), pp. 44-63.

21. Abel Green and Joe Laurie, Jr., *Show Biz: From Vaude to Video* (Garden City, N.Y.: Permabooks, 1953), p. 26.

22. Jack Poggi, *Theater in America: The Impact of Economic Forces, 1870-1967* (Ithaca, N.Y.: Cornell University Press, 1966), p. 30.

23. Alfred L. Bernheim, "The Facts of Vaudeville," *Equity*, IX (January, 1924), p. 42.

24. Poggi, *Theater in America*: pp. 11-14.

25. Alfred L. Bernheim, *The Business of the Theater* (New York: Actors Equity Association, 1932), p. 106.

26. Bosley Crowther, *The Lion's Share: The Story of an Entertainment Empire* (New York: E. P. Dutton and Company, 1957), pp. 19-32.

27. Garff B. Wilson, *A History of American Acting* (Bloomington: Indiana University Press, 1966).

28. Henry Knepler, *The Gilded Stage: The Years of the Great International Actresses* (New York: William Morrow and Company, Inc., 1965).

29. Ruth Rosen and Sue Davidson, eds., *The Maimie Papers* (Old Westbury, N.Y.: The Feminist Press, 1977), p. 58.

30. Poggi, *Theater In America*, p. 47.

31. Green and Laurie, Jr., *Show Biz*, p. 74.

32. Hughes, *A History of the American Theatre*, pp. 300-379.

33. Joseph R. Gusfield, *Symbolic Crusade: Status Politics and the Temperance Movement* (Urbana, Ill.: University of Illinois Press, 1972), p. 32. See also Hughes, *History of the American Theater*, p. 188.

34. Burnham, "Attitudes Toward Sex," pp. 905-906. (See Note #20)

35. Agnes Repplier, "The Repeal of Reticence," *Atlantic Monthly*, LXVI (March, 1914), pp. 297-298.

36. Eleanor Flexner, *Century of Struggle: The Woman's Rights Movement* (New York: Atheneum, 1972). See also William O'Neill, *Everyone Was Brave: A History of Feminism in America* (New York: Quadrangle/New York Times Book Co., 1971), pp. 146-168; Andrew Sinclair, *The Emancipation of the American Woman* (New York: Harper Colophon Books, 1965), pp. 233-273.

37. David Carroll, *The Matinee Idols* (New York: Arbor House, 1972), pp. 9-24. See also "A Warning to Matinee Girls," *Morning Telegraph*, February 27, 1901, p. 6.

38. "Woman and the Stage," *New York Dramatic Mirror*, August 25, 1897, p. 12.

39. Gerda Lerner, "Women's Rights and American Feminism," in Gerda Lerner, *The Majority Finds Its Past*, p. 49.

40. Deborah S. Kolb, "The Rise and Fall of the New Women in the American Drama," *Educational Theatre Journal*, XXVII (May, 1975), pp. 149-160.

41. Lewis Allen Erenberg, "Urban Night Life and the Decline of Victorianism: New York City's Restaurants and Cabarets," 1890-1918 (unpublished Ph.D. dissertation, University of Michigan, 1974).

42. Elizabeth Kendall, *Where She Danced* (New York: Alfred A. Knopf, 1979).

43. Robert Sklar, *Movie-Made America: How The Movies Changed American Life* (New York: Random House, 1975).

44. De Beauvoir, *The Second Sex*, p. 662.

Chapter 2

Actresses and Feminists: An Overview

In his landmark 1901 novel *Sister Carrie*, Theodore Dreiser described Carrie's first experience as an actress:

> This new atmosphere was more friendly. It was wholly unlike the great brilliant mansions which waved her coldly away, permitting her only awe and distant wonder. This took her by the hand kindly, as one who says, "My dear, come in." It opened for her, as if for its own. She had wondered at the greatness of the names upon the billboards, the marvel of the long notices in the papers, the beauty of the dresses upon the stage, the atmosphere of carriages, flowers, refinement. Here was no illusion. Here was an open door to see all that. She had come upon it as one who stumbles upon a secret passage, and behold, she was in the chamber of diamonds and delight![1]

Carrie's brief moment of amateur theatrical triumph obviously opened up the possibility of a whole new world to her, one complete with wealth, mobility, and, though she didn't know it at the time, independence. By presenting the portrait of a seduced woman who does not suffer for (and even achieves success despite) it, Dreiser's novel launched an attack on American Victorian prudery and, accomplishing that, also showed an astute sensitivity to the theater's role in women's achievement of autonomy.

Carrie's vision and her future success in the theater underscore the way in which the theater has been a means by which some women have attained material wealth, mobility, and even social and political power ever since ancient times. Needless to say, it was not always an easy road. Though women in the Greco-Roman period had gained a certain level of political, social, and religious power, the rise of the Christian church effectively curtailed that. Indeed, during its medieval hegemony, the Church practically turned actors into outlaws and even barred them from Christian burial.[2]

Given this hostility to actors, it is ironic that the Church itself was to provide the first opportunity for a woman's involvement in drama. In the tenth century, the nun Hrothvithsa presented her plays before the Holy Roman Emperor.[3] Moreover, despite Church disapproval, the number of acting troupes grew, and by the sixteenth century actresses were regularly performing with commedia dell'arte groups all over the continent.[4]

It was not until after the Restoration, however, that the first actress appeared on the English-speaking stage. Although it is unclear who that woman was, there is very little controversy about the infamous reputation of the stage of that day or the notorious character of its actresses.[5] William W. Sanger's widely read mid nineteenth century *History of Prostitution* refers to the Restoration theater as a place that fostered lewdness by "depicting it in glowing and attractive colors."[6] His notions of actresses were just as damning, and he adds that those who were most successful were precisely those "who took the greatest liberties with the text and most improved on the lewdness of expression." Undoubtedly, one of the classic examples was Nell Gwynne, who rose from "orange girl"—a euphemism for a prostitute—to stage star, and then to king's mistress and a peerage.

Despite middle-class scorn of the profession, a number of actresses in the late eighteenth and early nineteenth centuries achieved great fame. In fact, the first "Divine Sarah," Mrs. Sarah Siddons, was such a source of national pride and adoration that Lord Byron proclaimed her the "beau ideal of acting,"[7] and William Hazlitt called her "Tragedy Personified."[8]

Besides such acclaim, the stage also offered women a means for supporting themselves and for gaining recognition. Aphra Behn, hailed in the twentieth century by Virginia Woolf as the foremother of women who earned their living by their wits, wrote both novels and plays, and she is generally credited with being the first English professional woman playwright.[9] Another woman, Madame Vestris, became the English-speaking world's first actress-manager with the opening of the Olympic Theatre in 1831.[10]

America proved a more difficult place for the theater. The "New Land" and its struggling settlements had very little time for leisure or amusements. In addition, the authority of Calvinist teachings against the sin of idleness and the lures of the devil precluded any professional entertainments. Nevertheless, this barren soil did produce some sketchily documented amateur theatrical performances, and there is a record of a production of the play *Ye Bare and Ye Cubb* in Accomac, Virginia, in 1665, for which three young men were haled before the court.[11]

The first professional troupe to make its appearance in America was led by Walter Murray and Thomas Kean, and made its debut in Philadelphia in 1749. However, very little is known of the composition, repertoire, organization, or finances of the troupe.[12] In contrast, the history and work of the Hallam company, which made its American debut in September of 1752 and dominated the American theater for the next twenty years, is comparatively well documented.[13]

Lewis Hallam Sr. was sent to the New World by his enterprising brother William when the latter's license to perform in London was cancelled. Gathering a small company which included his wife and children, Hallam first performed in Jamaica and then ventured north to the American colonies, performing in Williamsburg, New York, Philadelphia and Charleston from 1752 to 1755. On his return to Jamaica, Hallam died of a fever and his wife married David Douglass. Renamed the "London Company of Comedians," the Douglass-Hallam troupe returned to America in 1758 with Mrs. Hallam-Douglass as leading lady and her son as the leading man. Under Douglass's management, the group prospered, even venturing as far north as the Puritan stronghold of Boston, where it performed under the ruse of giving "moral dialogues." Rechristened the "American Company" when relations between England and the colonies grew embittered, the troupe traveled up and down the Atlantic seaboard until 1774, when performances were prohibited by the Continental Congress.[14]

Despite this pioneering effort, however, the title of "Father of the American Drama" goes to William Dunlop. Dunlop's theatrical career was a financial failure, but his writing and translation of over seventy plays, his importation of the continental melodramatic form in the plays of Kotzebue and Prixecourt, his management of New York's prestigious Park Theater, and his monumental three volume *History of the American Theater* and diaries entitle him to that honor.[15]

Dunlop's vision of drama as an indigenous vehicle for national uplift and progress fit in well with the post-War of 1812 desire for an authentic American culture. However, his theater did not root very deeply in American soil. As a matter of fact, American theater and culture in general were held in derision by most Europeans. Many would have agreed with the comments of Sidney Smith: "In the four quarters of the globe, who reads an American book or goes to an American play?"[16]

However, the career of Edwin Forrest answers that question. Born in 1806 to a large Philadelphia family of declining middle-class economic status, Forrest began his career on the stage in 1822 and, within four years, was generally acclaimed as America's first truly native theatrical star. Forrest excelled in Shakespearean roles like Othello, Macbeth, and Coriolanus, but his real popularity with American audiences rested on his portrayal of democratic heroes like Spartacus in *The Gladiator* and the doomed Indian chief Metamora in the play of the same name. This latter play served as a contribution to the writing of original American drama. In 1827 Forrest offered a $1,000 prize for the best original American play. Forrest continued the offer for four more years with mixed results to his repertoire, but inestimable encouragement to American playwrights and drama.[17]

Forrest's enormous popularity notwithstanding, his influence was not to everyone's taste. Writing in the *Brooklyn Eagle* in 1846, a young drama critic named Walt Whitman commented:

> We do not intend the following reflections—which started during the view of Mr. Forrest's performances—to bear directly on that actor. Mr. F. is a deserved favorite with the public—and his high talent in his profession. But the danger is that as he has to a measure become identified with sort of an American style of acting, the crowd of vapid imitators may spread quite all the faults of his style, with none of its excellencies. Indeed, to all candor, all persons of thought will confess to no great fondness for acting which particularly seeks to "tickle the ears of the groundlings."[18]

This particular penchant for playing to the passions of his audience involved Forrest in one of the most serious controversies of his life—the famous Astor Place riot of 1849.[19] William Macready was the most successful English actor of his day and Forrest's chief rival. Not physically as well endowed as Forrest, but possessed of both good voice and taste in repertoire and interpretation, he had succeeded in elevating the standards of the English stage. Though dissimilar in acting style, physical prowess and taste, Forrest and Macready were similar in their extreme sensitivity to criticism and their competitiveness. When Forrest toured England between 1843 and 1845, he had been cordially received by Macready, although the latter, as he confided to his diaries, neither liked Forrest nor approved of his acting style. This surface amiability became strained when British critics attacked Forrest, for which he blamed Macready. Relations between the two broke down altogether when Forrest greeted Macready's performance of Hamlet one evening in Edinburgh with a quite audible and public hiss.[20]

When Macready toured America in 1849, this public demonstration of disapproval prompted a heated exchange of letters between the two in the newspapers. The matter finally came to a head in April of that year when both played in New York at the same time in the same role. A working-class mob, already stirred up by class antagonisms and further agitated by appeals to xenophobic nationalism, attempted to storm the theater and prevent Macready's performance. This action was repulsed by troops and police who had been called out to protect Macready and his audience of upper-class New Yorkers. The ensuing battle left 31 dead and 48 severely wounded. Though Forrest did not agitate the mob directly, the consequences of the petite insurrection showed how deeply the theater had become entwined with the politics of American society. Indeed, the stage had become a symbolic battleground for the class tensions that were convulsing ante-bellum America.[21]

The riot took place at a time when the United States was deep in the first throes of industrialization, and even contemporary accounts see it as a consequence of class tensions. The *Philadelphia Ledger* lamented, "There is now in our country, in New York City, what every good patriot has hitherto considered it his duty to deny—a high class and a low class." The newspaper also added, "the B'hoys of New York and the 'upper Ten' are as divided as the white and red roses of York and Lancaster."[22] In addition, *The Home Journal* commented, "Let but the more passive aristocratic party select a favorite and let there be but a symptom of a handle for the B'hoys to express dissent and the undercurrent breaks forth like an uncapped hydrant."[23]

Needless to say, this struggle was not directly over wealth, but over the nature of American culture. From this point on, the theater in America became as divided in the types of entertainment it offered the different classes as those classes had been segregated by sectioning off theaters into pit, boxes, and galleries.

Foremost among these popular entertainments was the minstrel show, the first indigenously created American professional amusement, wherein white actors played black men. Though black characters were found on the American stage even before the minstrel show, they did not come into their own as the centerpiece of a separate theatrical form until T. D. Rice first jumped "Jim Crow" in 1829, subsequently creating a separate song and dance act in 1832. Rice's act stimulated a number of imitators, and, in 1843, Dan Emmett and a group called the Virginia Minstrels performed a whole evening of Negro imitations.

With the advent of companies like The Christy Minstrels and others, minstrelsy came to dominate American popular entertainment from 1850 through 1870. In those years it took on a ritualized form the audience knew and loved. The show began with the entire company sitting around the master of ceremonies (referred to as the interlocutor) who traded straight lines for jokes with the end men, known as Mr. Tambo and Mr. Bones. Interpolated throughout this first part were songs and dances, followed by an olio in which the various members of the company performed their specialties.[24]

Through the stereotyping of the black characters in minstrelsy, the white audience was made to feel superior, and this helped to reinforce the prevailing American ideology that was loosely Jacksonian in its emphasis on themes such as expansion, anti-monopoly, and white supremacy. In addition, the minstrel show laid heavy stress on nostalgia for the vision of the settled, permanent world of the plantation and "Ole Massa." This vision had particular appeal to the diverse and formerly agrarian population who were caught up in the convulsive changes brought about by industrialization and urbanization. Finally, the ritualized format of the show appealed to an audience of diverse cultural backgrounds, giving them a common cultural denominator and also providing them with forms of humor, sentiment and characters which many of them had been deprived of in the transition from a rural to an urban environment.[25]

Ironically, although it celebrated home and family within the matrix of the plantation and was especially respectful of the black mammy, the minstrel show totally excluded women performers. However, this did not mean that American women had ceased to play an important role on the stage.

In the colonial period, it had been the first Mrs. Lewis Hallam who had served as the connecting link between the Hallam and Douglass Companies. Moreover, it was her daughter-in-law, Mrs. Lewis Hallam Jr. (nee Sarah Tuke) who precipitated the first major theatrical crisis in American history. Due to the tensions between her elderly husband, Lewis Hallam Jr., and his young partner, John Hopkinson (which she exacerbated), the matter had to be placed before a community committee to be settled. Their quarrels resulted in demonstrations at the theater by partisans from each side, and this eventually resulted in the break-up of the company which had been the oldest and most successful in America.[26]

During the Revolution; Mercy Otis Warren, daughter of a prominent Massachusetts family and wife of the paymaster of the Continental Army, wrote plays which raised the major issues of the revolutionary period.[27] Although more a propagandist and a pamphleteer than a great dramatist, her literary career did draw praise from Thomas Jefferson, who wrote: "I have long possessed evidence of her high station in the ranks of genius."[28] Similarly, in the same period, Sussana Rowson pursued a career as playwright and actress, although she is better known for her sentimental Richardsonian novel, *Charlotte Temple*.[29]

Nevertheless, it was not until the 1840s that America was to produce its first great native and internationally acclaimed actress. Of Pilgrim ancestry, Charlotte Cushman sought employment on the stage as a result of the straitened financial condition of her merchant father. Cushman began her career as an opera singer, but, failing in that, she turned to acting and toured steadily after her debut in 1835. After appearing with Macready in his 1843 American tour, she became his protege, with Macready exercising enormous influence on her professional life. At his urging she went to London, appearing both with him and then separately as Lady Macbeth, Queen Elizabeth, Bianca, and Meg Merrilees. In these roles, she received the praise that made her a star.[30]

More than just a fine actress, Cushman had a profound influence on the professional and artistic character of the American stage. Writing a reminiscence about her, the nineteenth century drama critic of the *New York Tribune*, William Winter, said:

> Miss Cushman was not an egotist. She thought of her duty as an intellectual leader and exemplar: and in all she undertook she wrought benefit of society. She not only acted great parts, but in acting them, she gave something to her auditors. She imparted to them a conception of noble individuality and an incentive to noble behavior. She told them that they also were of an immortal spirit; that it was their duty to live pure lives: to endure with fortitude and to look forward with hope and trust. She did not fill their minds with images of decadence and promptings of degeneracy, recklessness and failure. She was a minister of the beautiful; and therefore she was a benefactor to her time and to all times that were to follow. It is difficult to convey an adequate sense of the mental, moral and artistic superiority that she exemplified, or the inspiring influence she exerted.[31]

Part of that influence was felt by younger actresses. Clara Morris, billed in the 1880s as "America's Greatest Living Actress," attested to Cushman's influence in her autobiography. Faced with the decision of whether to give up the stage for marriage or struggle along with her as-yet-unsuccessful career, Cushman saw her perform, and her praise inspired Morris to go on.[32] In a like manner, Cushman came into the life of Mary Anderson, later beloved of American audiences and often referred to as "our Mary." When Anderson needed encouragement and support to overcome her mother's objections to the stage, it was Cushman who gave her that much needed nurturance.[33]

Because of her talent and high professional standards, Cushman's popularity in America equaled that of Forrest, and her exemplary life blazed a trail for women on the American stage. It was to this that she alluded two years before her death in her final curtain speech at Booth's Theater in New York on November 7, 1874. She said:

> I found life sadly real and intensely earnest, and in my ignorance of other ways of study resolved to take therefrom my test and watchword—to be thoroughly in earnest, intensely in earnest, in all my thoughts and actions, whether in my profession or out, it became my one single idea. I honestly believe that therein lies the secret of my success in life. I do not believe any great success in art can be achieved without it.[34]

In a similar way, the career of Anna Cora Mowatt lifted the social and literary reputation of the theater. Born to a large well-to-do New York family, Anna Cora Ogden married lawyer James Mowatt at 15, and, after the decline of her husband's fortune, she attempted to help him with a series of public readings. These readings, however, were cut short by ill health, and during her recuperation she decided to pursue a literary career. In a burst of creative energy between 1844 and 1845, she wrote and saw produced her social satire, *Fashion* — which is considered to be one of the few really good American plays of the nineteenth century. Subsequently she decided to go on the stage herself. This decision shocked her social circle, but undoubtedly aided in breaking down some of the still pervasive and active prejudice of many Americans against the stage. After her debut in 1845, Mowatt toured both America and England as a leading lady for nine successful seasons.[35] Among the most memorable of her reviews is Edgar Allen Poe's judgment that "the greatest charm of her acting is its naturalness. She moves, looks and speaks with well-controlled impulsiveness as different as can be conceived from the the customary rant and cant — the hack conventionality of the stage."[36]

Although Cushman and Mowatt did not totally erase American prejudice against the stage, their careers and personal examples did raise its professional and artistic standards. More importantly, they provided models for a career that women, and not only men, could pursue.

Despite the successes of Cushman and Mowatt, the advance of women on the American stage was not an unbroken triumph. Mid-century estimates were that still over 70 percent of Americans disapproved of and had probably never attended a theatrical performance.[37] This prejudice was not alleviated by the career of Adah Isaacs Menken. Menken's performance of the wild ride in the melodrama *Mazeppa* (presumably in the nude) called down upon her not only the wrath of the ministerial population, but even secular voices like Horace Greeley. In a scathing editorial in the *New York Tribune*, Greeley wrote, "It is to be deplored that a woman whose sole claim to questionable fame is her nightly appearance in the nude before depraved audiences should be hailed as an artist."[38] Unfazed, Menken fought back with advertisements challenging Greeley to watch her perform. Notoriety seemed hardly to bother the New Orleans-born Menken, and she was quick to appreciate the value of her beautiful face and voluptuous figure. She turned the wild ride of *Mazeppa* into a vehicle which garnered her international celebrity.

As a matter of fact, Menken paid little heed to the cries of the scandalized over her personal, as well as professional, life. She married four times, had numerous affairs, and was even known to smoke cigars in public. What the conventional thought about her mattered little since she saw herself as a poet and a bohemian. She chose her friends among literary men and women like Walt Whitman, Charles Dickens, Algernon Swinburne, and Alexandre Dumas, père, and George Sand.[39]

Menken met George Sand during her tour of the continent. Though their relationship was brief and nothing remains of their correspondence, their friendship was important because of the link it indicates between women of the theater and literature. Indeed, Sand seems to have been

Menken's close and influential friend. Sand served as godmother to Menken's son, whose given name was Louis Dudevant (after Sand's real name) Victor Emmanuel Berkeley, and it was at her urging that Menken was herself baptized. In addition, there was even a report that Sand was writing a play for Menken. Unfortunately, Menken's early death ended the relationship.[40] Nonetheless, even though their friendship did not make a literary stir, it does point to a delicate network of literary and dramatic connections which brought feminists and actresses together. Although these ties are too filled with elements of "la vie bohème" to have had much of an impact on society at large, they were a beginning.

It was another relationship between an actress and a woman writer—that of Fanny Kemble and Catherine Sedgwick—which suggests the broader implications of such associations. Born in 1809, Fanny Kemble was of the blood royal of the British stage, for she was the niece of John Phillip Kemble and Sarah Siddons. Making her debut in 1829, Kemble gained wide acclaim for her "Juliet." Following in the footsteps of a long line of English actors, she and her father made a tour of America in 1832, and, along with the President, the Chief Justice of the Supreme Court, and the American literati, she made the acquaintance of the Sedgwick family.[41] It was not long before she was referring to the eldest daughter of that family—Catherine—as "my best friend in this country."[42]

Catherine Sedgwick was as well known as Kemble. Daughter of a former Massachusetts congressman and justice of the Massachusetts Supreme Court, she was descended from the Dwight family and was a writer of international reputation. Her initial work, *New England Tale* (1822), followed by *Redwood* (1824) and *Hope Leslie* (1827), established her reputation as a novelist of profound didactic concerns. Among her most important notions was the idea of a woman's sphere, a sphere bounded by home and children that she along with other women writers like Catherine Beecher, Sarah Josepha Hale, and Lydia Sigourney saw as the new moral base for an American society undermined by industrialism. Their idea was that by establishing a sphere based on feminine attributes of piety, purity and submissiveness, and dedicated to domesticity, women would wield a kind of moral hegemony over America.[43]

At the time of her first meetings with Sedgwick, Kemble was probably not given to that kind of speculation. Indeed, Fanny had fallen in love. The man she married, Pierce Butler, was the scion of a rich aristocratic Southern plantation-owning family. It was a match that Catherine Sedgwick did not approve, and she wrote a friend expressing a "thousand fears."[44] She considered Fanny "a captivating creature, steeped to the lips with genius. A complex being made up of glorious faculties, delightful accomplishments, immeasurable sensibilities—and a half hundred faults." Her thoughts about Pierce Butler were less kind. She wrote that he was "a gentlemanly man with good sense and an amiable disposition, but so infinitely inferior to her that the experiment of marriage might be dangerous."[45]

Sedgwick's fears were hardly groundless. The marriage began to founder when Fanny's boredom and isolation came into conflict with Pierce's demands that she play a more wifely role and his family's disdain for her former career. Their relationship worsened when Fanny's journal of her American trip was published a year after their marriage (1835),[46] further rubbing salt into the wounds of Americans still smarting from the comments of Mrs. Trollope. Pierce then took Fanny south to spend a year on his plantation. That year, recorded in Fanny's *Journal of a Residence on a Georgia Plantation* (1838-1839) only confirmed Fanny's abolitionist feelings, which were supported by the Sedgwick family.[47] Letters from Catherine filled with stories like that of a black woman's remark when her wicked master died that, "Massa, pray God to forgive him! Oh, how he prayed. And I'm afraid God heard him, for they say he is good," were repeated by Fanny, and prompted Butler to forbid her to have any communication with the Sedgwicks.[48] In fact, it was a letter from the Sedgwicks that brought about a final break between Fanny and Pierce in 1843. In 1846, Fanny left Butler, and, after a widely publicized divorce trial in 1849, Butler gained custody of their two daughters.[49]

The Sedgwick family's support sustained Fanny in this difficult period, and their abolitionist sentiments contributed to her eventual decision to publish her *Journal* in 1863.[50] There is also further evidence of Fanny's agreement with Catherine on women's issues. A lifelong feminist, Catherine was never a suffragist. Likewise, although Fanny felt that women should have all rights, and she was even friendly with English suffragist Frances Cobbe, she resisted the attempts of suffragists to win her to their "platform."[51] In a letter to her lifelong friend Harriet St. Leger, her thought is tinged with some of Catherine's idealism. She wrote, "I do rejoice at it [a new law on woman's right to hold property enacted by the Massachusetts legislature]. Legislate, make laws for justice for women, in all such matters you cannot do too much, for you will never do enough to counteract natural law, by which women are constituted and constitute themselves the *subject* of man."[52]

The relationships of Kemble and Sedgwick and, to a lesser extent, George Sand and Adah Isaacs Menken, are indicative of the fact that women in the early nineteenth century who were pursuing careers in literature and drama were coming together in alliances that were intellectually and emotionally supportive. Nevertheless, as yet, these connections did not have other than personal ramifications. However, with the advent of the women's rights movement, these friendships and associations would take on a more active political role.

While women like Cushman and Mowatt were making their entree into the American theater, and Lydia Sigourney, Sarah Josepha Hale and others were carving a niche for women in literary circles, middle-class women in America were experiencing a drastic change in status. The rough equality that had existed in a frontier society where women were valued for their contribution to household production had given way to a world in which production now took place outside the home in the factory. As industrialism and urbanization expanded, the productive role of middle-class women was undermined. They responded by carving out a role for themselves as guardians of the nation's culture and by transforming the home into the moral center of the society. Many extended this role from the family to the society at large through charitable organizations and eventually into abolitionism and the temperance movement.[53] Eventually, women like Lucretia Mott, Elizabeth Cady Stanton, and Susan B. Anthony began to organize for women's rights as a result of their efforts in these movements.[54]

When Mrs. Stanton and Mrs. Mott found themselves excluded from the 1840 world anti-slavery convention in London, they decided to organize and fight for their own rights. In 1848, at Seneca Falls, a small group of women adopted a "Declaration of Sentiments" (patterned after the Declaration of Independence) which delineated the grievances of nineteenth century American women. In later years, so much of the energy of the women's movement was concentrated on the suffrage issue that it is easy to forget that in its earliest decades the women's rights movement addressed itself to problems that ran the gamut from property rights, to dress reform, and to the general tyranny of men over women.[55] In fact, it was the plight of an actress, Abby Sage Richardson, that enabled women's rights activists to publicly raise the issue of divorce for the first time.

After a brief flurry of debate in the public prints between Horace Greeley and Henry James Sr., and then Horace Greeley and Robert Dale Owen, Elizabeth Cady Stanton raised the issue of divorce at the 1860 Woman's Rights Convention.[56] It was Mrs. Stanton's and Susan B. Anthony's advocacy of this radical position and their more militant stance on suffrage that split the women's rights movement. In 1869, Stanton and Anthony formed the National Women's Suffrage Association, and the moderates led by Henry Ward Beecher and Lucy Stone organized the American Woman's Suffrage Association.[57]

In November of that same year, Daniel MacFarland, a lawyer, low-level Tammany functionary and failed speculator, killed Albert D. Richardson, the well-known and widely acclaimed *New York Tribune* journalist. The cause of the murder was the relationship between Richardson and MacFarland's former wife, Abby Sage. MacFarland had married Abby

Sage, a former factory girl turned school teacher, in 1857. Although their marriage produced two children, it was not a happy one and tensions rose between them due to MacFarland's drinking and business failure, in contrast to Mrs. MacFarland's success as a writer (she published in places like *The Atlantic Monthly*) and her elocutionary talent which allowed her to give very successful public readings. Eventually, Abby decided to go on the stage, and, appearing under the name of Mrs. Cushing, she played with Edwin Booth. In 1867, Abby left MacFarland and secured an Indiana divorce. Nonetheless, MacFarland still felt that Abby was his wife, and, when he heard of her relationship with Richardson, he shot him. In a deathbed ceremony performed by Henry Ward Beecher, Abby married Richardson.[58]

The murder trial of Daniel MacFarland was the *cause célèbre* of the day, with entire transcripts of the trial published daily in the newspapers. In addition, because Mrs. Richardson was the recipient of condolence letters from Vice President Schuyler Colfax, Eldridge P. Gerry (a grandson of the signer of the Declaration of Independence), Horace Greeley and Henry Ward Beecher, the case took on wider political ramifications. It was the defense's contention that Mrs. Richardson's stage career, combined with her association with "Free Love and Fourierism" advocates like Greeley, that unbalanced MacFarland and made him innocent by virtue of "temporary insanity."[59] These issues helped convince the jury, and, in less than two hours after a six-week trial, the jury acquitted MacFarland. It was a verdict, according to the newspapers, that made the "welkin ring with cheers" and "strong men weep like women."[60]

On the other hand, the decision outraged feminists. Even before the trial, Elizabeth Cady Stanton wrote Susan B. Anthony, "You ask me what I think of the Richardson affair. I rejoice over every slave that escapes from a discordant marriage. My opinion is that a woman has the right to choose between a base petty tyrant and a noble magnanimous man."[61] On the final day of the trial, Mrs. Stanton addressed a women's suffrage meeting, saying:

> No matter what the character of the husband — though a bloated drunkard and a diseased libertine, leaving his wife and children to poverty and rags, to suffer hunger in a New York garret, victims to his daily outbreaks of brutality and passion, or his stolid indifference or neglect — let him in fact, be and do as he chooses, no other man shall have mercy on these helpless ones, and the woman shall continue to be his wife as long as she lives, though her flesh crawl and her soul sickens every time he enters her presence.[62]

Following the decision, over two thousand feminists gathered at New York's Apollo Hall to denounce the verdict and petition the governor to confine MacFarland to an insane asylum. At this meeting, Stanton gave a resounding speech calling for more liberal divorce laws.[63]

Unfortunately, within two years the "Woodhull affair" and the Beecher-Tilton divorce case set back the cause of liberalizing divorce laws. Nevertheless, the Richardson-MacFarland case indicated a developing close relationship between feminists and actresses. Evidence of this was the introduction by the defense of letters from Laura Calhoun, a journalist, a feminist, and a friend of Mrs. Richardson. The defense used the letters to indicate the corrupt influences surrounding Mrs. Richardson. However, they also show the support and encouragement that Mrs. Richardson received. In a letter dated 1866, Mrs. Calhoun wrote Mrs. Richardson:

> I hope that you will study toward the stage, if not for the stage this summer. That goal seems inevitable, and so desirable if you cultivate your great gifts at all, that when ever I think of you, I wish you were in your rightful place. The Diana in the beautiful art, and worthy to be its prophet. My own dreams of serving it will ever be hopes now, but whenever I see brave young feet set toward it, and thoughtful brows bent thitherward, I say "God Speed," from my inward soul.[64]

In other letters, she cited the examples of "Cushman and Mowatt," cheered Mrs. Richardson's engagement with Booth, and commented that "Now, if ever, women of power are needed on the stage."[65]

To women like Mrs. Calhoun, the popular prejudice against the stage and popular amusements seemed hardly to exist. Furthermore, to feminists, the stage was doubly to be honored because it was one arena in which men and women had achieved professional equality. Indeed, it was about the same time as the MacFarland-Richardson affair that a well-known actress of the day, Olive Logan, began to argue the equality of men and women in the theater, thereby adding the lustre of her name to the women's rights movement.

Logan, a third daughter in the family of actor Cornelius Logan, debuted at the age of five and toured until age eighteen. In 1857, she married a French journalist and moved to Paris, where she was received at court by the Empress Eugenie. After her marriage broke up in 1864, Logan returned to the United States and resumed her stage career. She also supplemented her stage appearances by writing, and her play *Surf* was a popular hit for Augustin Daly's company in the post-war period. Encroaching deafness forced Logan to quit the stage, but she made a quick and rather painless transition from acting to a lecturing and writing career.[66]

Logan's lectures, which included a witty piece on women's suffrage, brought her to the attention of women's rights activists like Elizabeth

Cady Stanton, Anna Dickinson, and Susan B. Anthony. After hearing one of Logan's lectures, Miss Anthony invited Logan to speak before the Equal Rights Convention of 1869.[67] Sharing a platform with Frederick Douglass, Henry Ward Beecher, Lucretia Mott, and Miss Anthony, Logan said:

> I stand here tonight full of faith, inborn faith, in the rights of women to advance boldly in all ennobling paths, and full of faith in her right to do with her hands all that she is able to do, and what her brain and intellect are equal to, and reject all the drudgeries that men dislike and thus think and say women are particularly made to do, I have full faith in her right to enter the arena of politics and set something right in politics which is now all wrong.[68]

Logan's equal rights speech, her advocacy of suffrage, her writing in *Revolution*, and her lectures before women's rights groups gained the attention of women's rights activists and sympathizers throughout the nation. They were pleased by the adherence of so well-known a woman to their cause. As one admirer wrote in *Revolution*:

> It is only wonderful to me to see a lady who has led the life of Olive Logan—a pet of society and a fashionable belle at the gay, fascinating and dangerous French court—one who has all her life been associated with the very wealthy and surrounded by the flattery and adulation of courtiers and statesmen—one who has breathed the perilous atmosphere of theatrical life for years without soil to her glorious womanhood—I say it is only wonderful to me that any woman who has led that life is free to live it still—should turn her back on it and engage with tact and culture in advocating the humdrum reforms of the day.[69]

Although Logan allied herself with the women's rights movement, her major concern was still the theater. The issue that most concerned her was the question of what was then called "The Nude Drama," even raising the issue in her equal rights address. Referring to a woman who had written her about the possibility of the stage as a career, she commented in her speech:

> What was that woman to do? She appeals to me what would I advise her to do; asks if I would advise her to go on the stage. Alas! No: I cannot advise any woman to go upon the stage with the demoralizing influences which seem to prevail more every day when its greatest rewards are won by brazen faced, stained, yellow-haired padded limbed creatures—while actresses of the old school, well trained, qualified, decent, cannot earn a living.[70]

What provoked Logan's criticisms was the success of the 1866 musical *The Black Crook* and the invasion of Lydia Thompson's *British Blondes* in 1868, both of which featured choruses of women wearing tights. In articles that appeared in *Lippincott's, Packard's Monthly,* and *Oliver's Optics,* Olive Logan attacked "the leg business."[71] As a result, she began to acquire the reputation of a blue stocking, prompting Mark Twain's sarcastic commentary, "Who is Olive Logan? And what has she done?"[72]

Even while crusading against "the nude drama," however, Olive Logan never lost sight of women's issues, and she continued to speak out for equal pay and the theater as a place where men and women had achieved equality.[73] In her book *Apropos of Women and Theatres* (1868) she wrote:

> There are certainly two branches of industry in this world where men and women stand on an absolutely equal plane in the matter of cash reward.
>
> These are literature and drama.
>
> The stuff that critics write being altogether set aside, the proof of quality of a woman's work is exactly that same matter of pay.
>
> When we bring to other avenues of labor and ambition as ardent a zeal, as earnest as that which some of us have brought to the theatre and the study, then will doors open wide for us.
>
> Women pushed these doors open themselves and men have given Us a seat by their side ever since, within these temples.
>
> Mrs. Browning, Mrs. Lewes, Jean Ingelow, Madame Dudevant, Mrs. Stowe, Charlotte Bronte, Mrs. Howe—these all belong to Us.
>
> Mrs. Siddons, Miss Cushman, Mrs. Kemble, Rachel, Ristori, Mrs. Kean, Helen Faucit, Mrs. Lander—these all belong to Us.
>
> And beside these, and others, of every grade—from the poorest writer of poetry to the most graceful magazinist—from the littlest walking lady to the most popular star actress—all belonging to Us.
>
> The reason why is merely that in these two departments women have worked as long as men work—with the same purpose in lifelong occupation that men have. The doors were long pushed open, and today stand wide.[74]

Above all, Olive Logan believed that it was equal pay that guaranteed women independence. She spelled out her credo in the semi-autobiographical and anecdotal social history of the theater, *Before the Footlights and Behind the Scenes:* "A woman should be able to feel when she lies down at night that she is really thanking her maker, and not her husband, for having given her this her daily bread."[75]

Ultimately, this ability to earn her own living, and a good one, resulted in one of the most frequently expressed calumnies against the actress by the general public: when an actress married a non-professional or someone outside the theater, the lure of the theater would destroy the marriage. Logan countered with something that was almost economic determinism. She said it was the fact that the actress might earn more than her husband that soured the marriage. It was, therefore, the penny pinching and resulting hostilities that came from trying to live on one inadequate salary, Logan said, not the "excitement" of the theater, that caused problems.[76] Consequently, Logan proposed that the woman who had been on the stage return to it, turn her income over to her husband, and hire help to take care of the family.[77]

More than just arguing for the theater as a place where women could obtain substantial professional equality, Logan also championed the notion that women should strive for excellence. She wrote:

> Now girls, Be Men! Learn your business thoroughly. Let no employer have it in his power to say your work is slovenly, and that you're only working along until you can catch a man; and that one man can work faster and better than three women.
>
> If he can, of course he deserves three times your wages; but there is no good reason why you should not be as clever as he if you will only try.[78]

Clearly Logan's life in the theater provided her with the experiences for asserting women's equality and independence. It was her example that taught nineteenth century women that the theater was a place where a woman could attain autonomy, and gave women the hope that this equality could be extended into other areas of life.

Perhaps the best example of the importance of women like Olive Logan to the women's rights movement is a poem which was written ostensibly to attack her crusade against "the Nude Drama" but which implicitly acknowledges this significance:

> But Anna Dickinson roasting the press,
> And Stanton calling for fierce redress;
> And Susan Anthony making a mess
> By snubbing each man who rises
> To open his mouth; and Livermore, she of
> the inches many, and fierce array
> Of facts to deafen and quite dismay
> the cavalier of crisis —
>
> These and the chorus all combined
> Less dangerous are to peace of mind
> Than Logan with face so fair and kind
> And words so fierce and cruel
> Slashing fiercely here and there

Allez au diable, Fillez! Querre!
Assailing the angels debonaire
  of burlesque water gruel.[79]

Logan's work was the first explicit American assertion of the idea of the theater as a place where women could achieve equality and independence. Her lectures and writings spread those ideas to a wide audience. Of course, none of this could have taken place without the practical accomplishments of Charlotte Cushman and Anna Cora Mowatt. In addition, the mutually supportive informal network of relationships between writers and actresses like George Sand and Adah Isaacs Menken and Fanny Kemble and Catherine Sedgwick also created precedents for a network of ties that would bind feminists to actresses. Moreover, it was these relationships that served as forerunners of the support that women activists like Laura Calhoun and Elizabeth Cady Stanton gave Abby Sage Richardson, and which finally provided Logan herself with opportunities to extend her message.

Needless to say, by the last third of the nineteenth century women had heard these messages and began to act on them. It was into this chamber, prepared by the likes of Cushman, Mowatt, Logan, Calhoun, Stanton, and others, that Carrie stumbled on the night of her debut.

NOTES

1. Theodore Dreiser, *Sister Carrie* (New York: New American Library, 1961), p. 166.

2. Rosamond Gilder, *Enter the Actress: The First Women in the Theater* (New York: Theatre Arts Books, 1960), pp. 1-45.

3. Ibid., pp. 18-45.

4. Ibid., pp. 46-66.

5. Ibid., pp. 132-143.

6. William W. Sanger, *The History of Prostitution: Its Extent, Causes and Effects Throughout the World* (New York: Harper Brothers Publishers, 1858), p. 299.

7. Richard Findlater, *The Player Queens* (New York: Taplinger Publishing Company, 1977), pp. 91-92.

8. Ibid.

9. Virginia Woolf, *A Room of One's Own* (New York: A Harvest HBJ Book, 1929), pp. 66-69.

10. Gilder, *Enter the Actress*, pp. 258-291.

11. Hugh F. Rankin, *The Theater in Colonial America* (Chapel Hill: The University of North Carolina Press, 1965), p. 11.

12. Ibid., pp. 22-42.

13. Ibid., pp. 43-139.

14. Ibid., pp. 140-201.

15. David Grimstead, *Melodrama Unveiled: American Theater and Culture, 1800–1850* (Chicago: University of Chicago Press), pp. 1-21.

16. Quoted in Russell Blaine Nye, *The Cultural Life of the New Nation, 1776–1830* (New York: Harper Torchbook, 1960), p. 257.

17. Richard Moody, *Edwin Forrest: First Star of the American Stage* (New York: Alfred A. Knopf, 1900).

18. Walt Whitman, "The Gladiator—Mr. Forrest—Acting," *The Brooklyn Eagle*, December 26, 1846 in Montrose Moses and John Mason Brown, eds., *The American Theatre As Seen By Its Critics, 1752–1934* (New York: Cooper Square Publishers, Inc., 1967), pp. 69-70.

19. Richard Moody, *The Astor Place Riot* (Bloomington: Indiana University Press, 1958).

20. Ibid., pp. 27-58.

21. Ibid., pp. 127-199.

22. *Philadelphia Ledger*, May 14, 1848, quoted in Moody, *Astor Place Riot*, pp., 228-229.

23. *Home Journal*, May 12, 1849, quoted in Moody, *Astor Place Riot*, pp. 228-229.

24. Robert Toll, *Blacking Up: The Minstrel Show in Nineteenth Century America* (New York: Oxford University Press, 1974), pp. 25-57.

25. Ibid., pp. 65-103. See also Alexander Saxton, "Blackface Minstrelsy and Jacksonian Ideology," *American Quarterly* XXVII (March, 1975), pp. 3-28.

26. Billy J. Harbin, "Role of Mrs. Hallam in the Hodgkinson-Hallam Controversy, 1694-1797," *Theatre Journal*, XXXII (May, 1980), pp. 213-222.

27. Maud Macdonald Hutcheson, "Mercy Otis Warren, 1728-1814," *William and Mary Quarterly*, (July, 1953), pp. 379-402.

28. Ibid., pp. 379.

29. Edward T. James, Janet Wilson James, Paul S. Boyer, eds., *Notable American Women, 1607-1950* (3 vols. Cambridge, Mass.: Belknap Press of Harvard University Press, 1971), pp. 202-204.

30. Joseph Leach, *Bright Particular Star: The Life and Times of Charlotte Cushman* (New Haven: Yale University Press, 1970).

31. William Winter, "Charlotte Cushman," in Moses and Brown, *American Theatre*, pp. 88-89.

32. Clara Morris, *The Life of a Star* (New York: McClure, Phillips and Co., 1905), pp. 37-54.

33. Mary Anderson (Mme. DeNavarro), *A Few Memories* (New York: Harper and Brothers Publishers, 1896) pp. 39-41.

34. Quoted in Leach, *Bright Particular Star*, p. 377.

35. Eric Wollencott Barnes, *The Lady of Fashion: The Life and the Theatre of Anna Cora Mowatt* (New York: Charles Scribner's Sons, 1954).

36. Barnes, *The Lady of Fashion*, p. 188.

37. Claudia D. Johnson, "That Guilty Third Tier: Prostitution in Nineteenth-Century American Theaters," *American Quarterly,* XXVI (December, 1975), p. 582.

38. Paul Lewis, *Queen of the Plaza: A Biography of Adah Isaacs Menken* (New York: Funk and Wagnalls Company, Inc., 1964), p. 139.

39. Lewis, *Queen of the Plaza*, pp. 187-270.

40. Allen Lesser, *Enchanting Rebel: The Secret of Adah Isaacs Menken* (New York: The Beechurst Press, 1947), pp. 197-198.

41. Margaret Armstrong, *Fanny Kemble: A Passionate Victorian* (New York: The Mac-Millan Company, 1938).

42. Frances Anne Kemble, *Records of Later Life* (3 vols. New York: Henry Holt and Company, 1844), I, p. 74.

43. James, James, Boyer, eds., *Notable American Women,* pp. 256-258.

44. Quoted in Armstrong, *Fanny Kemble*, p. 176.

45. Ibid.

46. Frances Anne Kemble, *Journal of a Residence in America* (Philadelphia: Carey, Lea and Blanchard, 1835).

47. Constance Wright, *Fanny Kemble and the Lovely Land* (New York: Dodd, Mead and Company, 1972), pp. 161-162.

48. Armstrong, *Fanny Kemble*, p. 283.

49. Ibid., pp. 314-333.

50. Frances Anne Kemble, *Journal of a Residence on a Georgia Plantation in 1838–1839* (New York: Harper and Brothers, 1863).

51. Kemble, *Records of Later Life*, III, p. 103.

52. Ibid.

53. Kathryn Kish Sklar, *Catherine Beecher* (New Haven: Yale University Press, 1973). Keith Melder, "The Beginnings of the Women's Rights Movement in the United States, 1800-1840," (unpublished Ph.D. dissertation, Yale University, 1964). Nancy F. Cott, *The Bonds of Womanhood: "Woman's Sphere" in New England, 1780–1835* (New Haven: Yale University Press, 1977). Anne Douglas, *The Feminization of American Culture* (New York: Avon Books, 1977).

54. Eleanor Flexner, *Century of Struggle: The Woman's Rights Movement in the United States* (New York: Atheneum, 1972), pp. 71-101.

55. Ibid.

56. Nelson Manfred Blake, *The Road to Reno: A History of Divorce in the United States* (New York: The MacMillan Company, 1962), pp. 90-100.

57. Flexner, *Century of Struggle*, pp. 151-152.

58. Madelaine B. Stern "Trial by Gotham 1870: The Career of Abby Sage Richardson," *New York History* XXVIII (July, 1947), pp. 271-287. Also cited in Blake, *Road to Reno,* pp. 100-106.

59. Stern, "Trial by Gotham," p. 282.

60. Ibid., p. 283.

61. "Letter to *Revolution* From Elizabeth Cady Stanton," *Revolution*, IV (December 23, 1869), p. 385.

62. "Stanton Address on Richardson Case at Apollo Hall," *Revolution* V (May 19, 1870), p. 307.

63. Blake, *Road to Reno*, p. 103

64. New York State Courts: Court of General Sessions, *The Trial of Daniel McFarland for the Shooting of Albert D. Richardson the Alleged Seducer of His Wife: by a Practical Law Reporter* (New York: W. E. Hilton Publishers, No. 128 Nassau Street, 1870), p. 65.

65. Ibid., pp. 66-68.

66. J. Robert Wills, Jr., "The Riddle of Olive Logan: A Biographical Profile," (unpublished Ph.D. Dissertation, Case Western Reserve University, 1971).

67. Ibid, p. 119.

68. Olive Logan, "Equal Rights Speech," *Revolution* IV (May 20, 1869), pp. 307-308.

69. "Letter to Revolution," *Revolution* IV (July 1, 1869), p. 406.

70. Logan, "Equal Rights Speech," p. 308.

71. Wills, Jr., "Olive Logan," pp. 127-150.

72. Mark Twain, *Mark Twain's Autobiography* (2 vols.; New York: Harper and Brothers, 1924), I, p. 159.

73. Olive Logan, *Apropos of Women and Theatres with a Paper or Two on Parisian Topics* (New York: Carleton, Publisher, 1869).

74. Ibid., pp. 15-16.

75. Olive Logan, *Before the Footlights and Behind the Scenes, A Book about the "Show Business" in all its Branches* (Philadelphia: Parmalee and Company, 1870), p. 286.

76. Logan, *A propos of Women and Theaters,* pp. 17-20.

77. Ibid.

78. Ibid, p. 21.

79. Reprinted in Logan, *Before the Footlights and Behind the Scenes*, pp. 594-597.

Chapter 3

Women and the Growth of Show Business

ister Carrie was just one of many women who joined the ranks of show business in the late nineteenth century. From 1870 to 1880 the United States census showed an increase in the number of actresses from 780 to 4,652, a rise of about 596 percent. In the period from 1890 to 1910 that number grew by almost 332 percent, from 4,652 to 15,436, and then spurted another 29 percent in 1920 to 19,905.[1] This growth is, of course, linked to changes in the American economy and culture in the post-Civil War period, a time of transition that made the United States into a prominent industrial power and swelled the need for recreation and amusements.

Symbolic of that change was the increase in value of American manufactured goods from $1.5 billion in 1869 to $4.5 billion in 1900. A catalyst for that growth was the tremendous expansion in the fields of transportation and communication. In 1844 Samuel F. B. Morse invented the telegraph and in 1876 Alexander Graham Bell followed with the telephone. However, it was the railroads which provided the real impetus for growth. By 1900 there were 250,000 miles of track in this country compared with 60,000 in 1860, leaving hardly a major community outside the system.

Accompanying and feeding this growth of industrial might was a 30 percent increase in non-agricultural employment between 1860 and 1900, with approximately 4,600,000 employed in factories and 3,000,000 in construction and transportation. This expansion was fed by a seemingly inexhaustible stream of migration which saw 5 million people come to the United States between 1880 and 1890, and 13 million arrive between 1890 and 1910. Mixing with the flood of immigrants who came mostly from southern and eastern Europe was a tide of upwards of 15 million native-born Americans who moved from rural to urban areas in the same period. This dual migration created a truly urban society by 1920, with over 46 percent of the population living in cities by that date.[2]

Industrialization and urbanization did not take place in a stable, efficient manner. The frequent ups and downs of the business cycle in the post-Civil War period created sharp economic, social, and cultural cleavage and tensions. By all accounts, America in the early 1890's contained farmers who were angry and resentful over declining prices, rising debts, isolation, and falling social and political status. Labor and industrial relations were marked by widespread industrial and class strife that often broke out into violent class warfare, while American cities were among the most congested, disease-ridden, and politically corrupt in the world.[3]

However, after 1896 there was a general improvement for American workers. Rising prices helped bring an upturn for American farmers, and, although unskilled laborers still earned relatively the same amount as they did in the 1880's, real wages rose as prices remained stable or even decreased. For the semi-skilled and skilled laborers, deflation, coupled with higher wages in advanced industries like iron and steel, permitted living standards to rise, and some workers began slowly edging out of the working class.[4]

The increase in purchasing power also added to a growth in leisure time. In agricultural areas the work week gradually decreased from sixty-six to fifty-six hours after 1880. In non-farm occupations the work week also declined to about 53.7 hours per week (or 9½ hours a day) by 1910. This increase in leisure time obviously contributed heavily to the expansion of recreation and amusements.[5]

Just as the American farmer and worker were gaining the opportunity to enjoy more leisure time, the American middle class was experiencing a steadily rising interest in entertainments. The old Calvinist notion of the importance of moral will as the means for success of the individual entrepreneur was losing out before the huge corporation or trust, and the individual saw himself become more and more a mere cog in the corporate wheel. Some of this Calvinist moral fervor turned into the reforms embodied in progressivism. On the other hand, some of it was displaced onto personal life and the pleasure embodied in recreation and amusement.[6]

In addition, the declining influence of ministerial antagonism (principally Protestant) alleviated one of the primary restraints on amusements. For decades Protestant clergymen had used arguments that dated back to Jeremy Collier's attack on the theater of the Restoration.[7] However, as traditional deference to elite groups broke down after 1840, as contemporary fundamentalism wrought dogmatic and organizational confusion just as much as they advanced puritanical influences, and as social Darwinism gained a foothold in higher education, religious authority weakened. Moreover, dissenting voices within the clergy like Horace Bushnell and preachers of the Social Gospel like Walter Rauschenbush and Washington Gladden supported morally uplifting entertainment.[8]

As religious opposition to the theatrical profession softened, the profession itself took on a more aggressive stance. The *New York Dramatic Mirror*'s columns seemed monthly to inveigh against some prejudiced cleric or to congratulate one who had seen the light.[9] Also, Walter E. Bentley (a former actor turned minister) greatly aided the religious justification of the profession when in 1899 he and others formed the Actors-Church Alliance, a group that fostered church membership, attendance, charitable work, and high moral standards among actors.[10]

This easing of church resistance, plus the economic and social transformation of America, greatly increased the growth and importance of show business. Indicative of this was its enormous economic growth. In his 1910 book *The Businessman in the Amusement World*, vaudeville agent Robert Grau asked: "Is a volume anent the theatrical businessman justified?"[11] His first paragraph neatly summarizes his view:

> The theatrical manager of 1910, as compared with his predecessor of 1870, is indeed a vigorous personage, for in forty years of progress the amusement purveyor has advanced to a position which places him on a level with the great magnates and financiers of the commercial and industrial world.[12]

Many of the major names in "the Show Business" of the first half of the century died in poverty or close to it. Mrs. John Drew, grandmother of Ethel, John and Lionel, and manager of the Arch Street theater in Philadelphia for thirty years, left a total estate valued at two hundred fifty dollars.[13] Tom Maguire, once known as the "Napoleon of Managers" and owner or builder of eleven playhouses in the West, died broke in New York,[14] while Lester Wallack, one of a triumvirate of managers who ruled New York theater in the 1870's and 1880's, ended his career working for a former employee.[15] Saddest of all, Tony Pastor, "Father of Vaudeville," whose ideas others appropriated to make millions, left a total estate of six thousand dollars when he died in 1908.[16]

By the 1880's show business was already beginning to show signs of coming spectacular financial success. In 1883 P. T. Barnum's "Greatest Show on Earth" earned $1,419,498 and paid a dividend of five hundred sixty thousand dollars. Indeed, after 1888 Barnum's circus never earned less than one million dollars a year.[17] In 1855 New York City boasted eight theaters and six minstrel saloons; by 1880 there were already twenty-five theaters with seating capacities of between fifteen hundred and two thousand and over seven thousand saloons, beer gardens, and concert halls, all supplying entertainment.[18] Similarly, though Tony Pastor died a pauper, others who followed his lead in vaudeville made fortunes. B. F. Keith made a prenuptial agreement with his second wife for five hundred thousand dollars and left an estate valued at $10 million in

1914.[19] When Percy Williams sold his vaudeville chain to Keith in 1912, he received between five and six million dollars.[20] Just as colossal was the fortune of Marcus Loew, who parlayed small-time vaudeville into Loew's Theatrical Enterprises, capitalized at five million dollars in 1910.[21] In fact, even a lowly burlesque franchise cost at least one hundred thousand dollars by 1910.[22]

Theater had not only grown financially, but it had come of age organizationally. Following the depression of 1893, a theatrical syndicate was born under the aegis of Abraham Erlanger and Marc Klaw. This combination included the theaters and production companies of Nixon and Zimmerman, and Haymen and Frohman, and by 1896 controlled at least three hundred to five hundred theaters throughout the country.[23] Following suit, vaudeville managers created their own syndicate in 1899, and in 1908 the newly developed film industry tried its hand at organizing a trust. Finally, by 1905 finance capitalists with connections to the Morgan Bank took their places on the Boards of Directors of the Schubert's and Loew's chains.[24]

Increased prosperity, lack of moral censure, and the growth of leisure time gave rise to a popular demand for new forms of entertainment. The theatrical world responded by offering musical comedy, light comic opera, burlesque, and, most importantly, vaudeville. Indeed, vaudeville was America's most popular entertainment form from 1890 to 1915.[25]

Vaudeville has been traced by some scholars back to the chansons of the fifteenth century French minstrel Olivier Basselin. However, by the nineteenth century it had come to mean any form of light entertainment.

In America, vaudeville grew out of the variety entertainment provided in the saloons of the mid-nineteenth century, and, because they were patronized by men, this entertainment was male-oriented.[26] As the *New York Evening Post* described one of the major concert saloons of the day, it was "extensively patronized by the public, especially on Saturday nights, when all parts of the house are crowded by male visitors [who] wear their hats and caps at pleasure, smoke cigars and pipes and conduct themselves generally in accordance with the popular song of 'we'll be free and easy still.' "[27] The casual, bawdy atmosphere of these saloons is also illustrated in an anecdote told in Douglas Gilbert's *American Vaudeville, Its Life and Times:*

> During the course of a bill [at the Vokes Garden on the Bowery], so runs the yarn, the manager announced to his beer-sodden patrons, "And now, gents, Miss Lillian McTwobucks will sing 'Love among the Roses.' " Whereupon a drunk rose and in stentorian tones replied, "She is a whore." The unabashed manager dismissed the interruption. "Nevertheless," he said, "Miss McTwobucks will still sing, 'Love among the Roses.' "[28]

The coarseness and obscenity of the variety acts at the concert saloons made it anathema to middle class respectability and women in particular.

Antonio "Tony" Pastor, former Barnum museum performer, circus artist and minstrel trouper, cleaned up variety. Seeing himself losing out in the competition with the successful ethnic musical comedies of Harrigan and Hart, Pastor tried to increase his audience by sponsoring a ladies' night. When this failed, he tried giveaways such as coal, ham, and even dresses. However, it was the opening of his 14th Street Theater in October of 1881, with its clean-as-a-hounds-tooth variety, that finally caught on with women and insured the success of vaudeville.[29]

Pastor's formula was copied with similar success by B. F. Keith in Boston. By 1887 Keith, a former circus grifter and proprietor of a Barnum-like museum featuring attractions like "Baby Alice: The Midget Wonder," garnered enough capital to buy the one hundred thousand dollar Bijou Theater in Boston. Keith combined Pastor's concept of clean vaudeville with a policy of making his theaters into veritable palatial pleasure domes. He insisted on comfortable rest rooms for ladies and gentlemen, plush seats, and, in one theater, employed ten people to see to the patrons' ease and comfort. This policy was summarized in Keith's slogan of "Cleanliness, Comfort, and Courtesy."[30]

Keith also began the policy of the continuous performance. One day he took an ad in the Boston paper and proclaimed that at his theater one could "Come when you please, stay as long as you like."[31] The idea spread rapidly, and in New York F. F. Proctor advertised continuous performances at his Union Square Theater in 1889 with the slogan, "After breakfast go to Proctor's, after Proctor's go to bed."[32]

Continuous performances were combined with a relatively low price scale. Tickets ranged from one dollar for the best seats to fifty cents for general admission, and twenty-five cents for the galleries, with matinees at half price. The advent of small-time vaudeville combining motion pictures with cheap acts reduced prices even further—to a nickle, a dime, and twenty-five cents.[33]

By 1910 big-time vaudeville had aligned itself in circuits, with theater chains owned by Keith, Williams, Proctor, and Poli spreading through the East, and Kohl and Castle and the Orpheum Circuit dominating the mid-West and the West. Thus by 1915 there were an estimated 1,000 big-time vaudeville theaters with almost innumerable smaller theaters making vaudeville acts, songs, and performers accessible to every class, sex and region in the country.[34] As one writer commented:

> It is very American. It touches our lives at many places. It appeals to the
> businessman, tired and worn, who drops in for a half hour on his way
> home; to the person who has an hour or two before a train, or before a
> business appointment; to the woman who is wearied of shopping. To

the children who love clowns and acrobats, to the man with his sweetheart or sister; to the individual who wants to be diverted but doesn't want to think or feel; to the Americans of all grades and kinds who want a great deal for their money.[35]

In the same article the author estimated that upwards of five million people a year attended the four Keith theaters, and that the chain supported three hundred workers of all sorts and about thirty-five hundred actors with estimated salaries of at least $13,500 a week. Moreover, a conservative estimate of the gross income of the theaters was approximately twenty thousand dollars per week. The profits of vaudeville were such that when Keith amalgamated with Proctor in 1906 the estimated value of the Proctor theaters alone was eight million dollars.[36]

This unprecedented growth provided actors and actresses with great opportunities. Upwards of twenty to thirty thousand actors and actresses earned close to ten million dollars in vaudeville by 1910.[37] While the standard act on the big-time circuits made an estimated two hundred dollars a week by 1911, Robert Grau judged there were at least fifty acts that made in excess of one thousand dollars a week and hundreds of others that drew at least five hundred dollars per week in salary.[38]

Indeed, salaries doubled, then quadrupled and finally increased about tenfold between the 1880's and the first decade of the twentieth century. When Lillian Russell first appeared as an English ballad singer at Pastor's in the 1880's, she received thirty-five dollars per week, while headliners rarely earned more than one hundred fifty dollars per week. When she returned to vaudeville in 1906, she received three thousand dollars weekly. Similarly, May Irwin, who split one hundred fifty dollars per week with her sister Flo at Pastor's in the 1880's, came back to vaudeville in 1907 at twenty-five hundred dollars per week. Likewise, in 1895 Yvette Guilbert, the French chanteuse, was paid four thousand dollars a week for four weeks at Hammerstein's Olympia Theater.[39] As an article in the 1901 *Independent* said:

> Today a first class vaudeville artist receives much more than the average actor or actress. The result has been to attract bright young men and women to the vaudeville stage. The large pecuniary reward has drawn talent from the church choir, the schools of oratory, dramatic colleges, conservatories of music and even the legitimate stage.[40]

Interestingly enough, it was the legitimate stage that had stimulated the enormous rise in salaries. In 1893, J. Austin Fynes, manager of Keith's Union Square Theater in New York, observed F. F. Proctor drawing crowds into his 23rd Street Theater to hear stars of the operatic stage. Fynes countered with legitimate stage stars Charles Dickson and his wife, Lillian Burhardt, in a playlet titled *The Salt Cellar*, for which they were paid three hundred dollars per week. After a while, other legitimate stage stars like Maurice Barrymore and Sarah Bernhardt were joined by others who appeared in vaudeville at two and three times their Broadway salaries.[41]

The lure of the vaudeville stage was particularly attractive to young women. Sophie Tucker wrote that she and her sister Dora spent every spare dime they saved attending their local vaudeville theater.[42] Mae West told of her love for the spotlight at a local vaudeville amateur night.[43] In addition, magazines like *Cosmopolitan* carried stories which included anecdotes like:

> A young girl who had been in the chorus of musical shows for a couple of years without attracting too much attention decided she would give imitations of the kind that made Cissie Loftus and Elsie Janis famous. For weeks she besieged managers for a chance at any salary at all. Finally William Hammerstein, being short an act for a Sunday afternoon concert, gave her an opportunity. Within a week Belle Blanch as she called herself was booked for a whole year at $500 a week.[44]

Stage-struck young women knew that stars like Eva Tanguay ($3,500 per week), Nora Bayes ($3,000 per week), Elsie Janis ($2,500 per week), and Irene Franklin ($2,500 per week) were the highest paid performers in vaudeville.[45]

The enticements of vaudeville were especially noted by reformers. Jane Addams, who was not hostile to the theater and even saw it as having positive moral functions, nevertheless told heartrending stories of the pernicious influence of movies and vaudeville on young women. In *The Spirit of Youth and the City Streets*, she wrote about young girls who stole so that they would be taken to the theater, or young girls who refused to take trips to the country because they might miss an evening at the nickel theater. She also wrote of the desperation of those who took part in amateur nights and of the young people who lined the street at six in the evening in front of Chicago's fifteen booking agencies.[46] It was in the image of the young women on the stage that she saw the desperate need of urbanites for entertainment and the impoverishment of popular culture. She stated:

> In a song which held the stage of a cheap theater in Chicago for weeks, the young singer was helped out by a bit of mirror from which she threw a flash of light into the faces of successive boys whom she selected from the audience as she sang the refrain "You are my affinity." Many popular songs relate the vulgar experience of city men wandering from amusement park to bathing beach in search of flirtation. It may be these stunts

and recitals of city adventure contain the nucleus of coming poesy and romance as songs of the people, but all the more does the effort need help and direction, both in development of its technique and the material of its themes.[47]

Nevertheless, the impact of vaudeville was enormous on women. For instance, Maimie Pinzer, the soul-searching prostitute-turned-social worker, described her feelings and experiences at a theater watching Irene Franklin:

> The show was generally good; and Irene Franklin, who was the headliner, was simply immense. In her last song she had on a shabby suit and worn shoes with a fuzzy tam o'shanter, with her long hair hanging in long braids, she told she was "bringing up the family." She looked winsome albeit she was untidily dressed, and the song was touching. It was about a girl of 14 whose mother has died, and the father was incapable, and this child was bringing up a family of 6 young uns. It made me think of my poor cousins so I went to their house.[48]

On another evening when Maimie met Sarah Bernhardt outside a theater in Boston and the "Divine One" took her hand and said something in unintelligible French, she wrote in her letters, "I feel good tonight."[49]

The power that popular culture, and especially the popular stage, had on women was apparent to any of its investigators. Bertha Van Vorst, who went to live and work in a working-class community, commented on the tremendous impact a performance of *Faust* had on working girls.[50] In a like manner, though Dorothy Richardson deplored low-life culture, she acknowledged the tremendous hold of trash novels and songs on working girls.[51]

More scientific evidence was provided by the recreation surveys of the day. An analysis prepared by the Drama Committee of the 20th Century Club of Boston in 1909 and 1910 reported:

> The vaudeville situation, as represented by the better class houses, such as Keith's and the American Music Hall, are on the whole not unsatisfactory. These theaters cater to audiences composed largely of women and children and their influence is, for the most part, innocuous, the managers having apparently learned that a clean show pays better, as a business proposition, than one that is vicious or suggestive.[52]

Another measurement prepared for the Russell Sage Foundation for New York in 1911 provided information that at vaudeville and motion picture houses (small-time vaudeville), "women form on the average 40 percent of the audience and *at times are in the majority.*"[53] A Reed College survey of Portland, Oregon, also showed that almost 50 percent of the children in the audience were girls.[54] The investigation stated:

> In view of the reports of the investigation concerning the character of vaudeville shows, the most striking fact revealed in the tabulation is that over 70 percent of the children of Portland go to the vaudeville theater and that 623 or 24.1 percent attend vaudeville shows once a week or oftener. It is worthy of note that the number of girls and the frequency of their attendance is about the same as the number of boys.[55]

While many saw vaudeville as innocuous and others like Jane Addams were dubious, still others were less sanguine. Their opinion can best be summarized by a statement from an article in a 1910 issue of the *American Magazine* entitled "The Decay of Vaudeville," which stated that "vaudeville shows, especially in the 'First Class' houses, that do not contain at least one number calculated to make a decent woman deeply ashamed of presence in that theater is about as rare as snow in Panama."[56]

Nevertheless, the growth in the number of women who attended theaters or who adopted the theater as a profession continued apace. By the turn of the century, writers were commenting on the social and artistic phenomena of the "Matinee Girl," "The Stage-Struck Girl," and the "Feminization of the Stage." One of them, Edward Bok (editor of the *Ladies' Home Journal*), was particularly upset at the presence of young girls at "problem plays." In a 1903 editorial he wrote:

> A man or woman with any sense of the fitness of things cannot go to an average matinee performance of what nowadays is called the "problem play" without feeling that there is something radically wrong in either the watchfulness or the point of view of hundreds of American parents. One will see at these matinees seats and boxes full of sweet young girls ranging from twelve to sixteen years of age. They are not there by the few, but literally by the hundreds . . . it is enough to make a man burn with shame and indignation to see hundreds of girls sitting in the theater, and, with open mouths, literally drinking in remarks and conversations to which no young girl in her teens should listen.[57]

Bok admonished parents to be less permissive and more discriminating when permitting their daughters to attend the theater. However, by 1903 it was already a case of barring the barn door. In 1893 the *New York Dramatic Mirror* already carried a weekly column titled "The Matinee Girl," and an article in a 1900 edition of *Munsey's* referred to her as "unquestionably a product of the end of the century."[58] The always socially acute observer Theodore Dreiser included a short but crucial episode in

Sister Carrie wherein Carrie's attendance at a matinee stirs her material longings.[59]

Matinees became a fixture in American theater after the Civil War, and the term "matinee idol" was already used then to describe actor Harry Montague in 1875.[60] The "Matinee Girl" was, on the other hand, the increasing product of the education, economic self-sufficiency, leisure and relaxing moral restraints on young women by the end of the century. By 1900 the total number of women in the work force had increased to 20.6 percent.[61] Although most of them were employed in low-paying, non-skilled or semi-skilled industrial work, there had been an increase in the number of women in the professions and in higher-paid, white-collar jobs such as typists. Also, by 1890 the total number of women in college (although small in comparison to the total eligible population) represented 35.9 percent of the actual student body.[62] In addition, the technological advances that made possible the manufacture of packaged foods and ready-made clothing gave women increased leisure time. Many women devoted this time to the club movement and even suffragism, but others chose recreation and amusements.

The growing number of female patrons was appreciated by managers. Charles Frohman, German-Jewish son of a cigar maker and a former advance man for minstrel shows, built a 10,000 employee entertainment empire salaried at over 35 million dollars a year, based upon his estimation that women were the most important part of his audience.[63] This was a judgment confirmed by his own 1911 survey which offered the fact that 68 percent of his audiences were women.[64] It was an estimate underscored by a comment from a New York manager quoted in a *Woman's Home Companion* article by Walter Prichard Eaton: "Cut out the women from the audiences and four-fifths of the dramas in the country would shut up shop."[65] This phenomenon was nurtured and accelerated by Frohman, who created a star system based on women like Maude Adams, Ethel Barrymore, Clara Bloodgood, Marie Doro, and Billie Burke, while encouraging the talents of women-oriented playwrights like Clyde Fitch and James M. Barrie.[66]

However, the predominance of women in the theater was not seen as an unmixed blessing. Critics were particularly hard on the "Matinee Girl" whom they criticized for her lack of responsiveness toward the play compared with her enthusiasm for the leading man or matinee idol.[67] Attacks reached such a level of intensity that one article, titled "The Brutality of the Matinee Girl," ridiculed her for her general insensitivity.[68] What is more, she was blamed for being the reason for the declining standards of American drama. An article in the *Ladies' Home Journal* purportedly written by an anonymous actor claimed:

If I were asked: "What is the most pernicious tendency of the American playhouse?" I should unhesitatingly say the bad influence of the matinee girl. And by matinee girl I do not necessarily mean the young girls who are allowed too much freedom by devoted but misguided parents, but in that category I place the indolent woman who passes for an intelligent person, but who is in truth an illiterate candy eating woman whose idea of amusement is found in omnivorous theatregoing.[69]

Another anonymous author in *Current Opinion* inveighed:

Who is responsible for the alleged lack of virility of American drama? Is it the grasping manager, the conceited player, or the uninspired dramatist? Each in turn lays the blame on the other. At last a courageous critic comes forward [Ludwig Lewisohn] with a new and striking thesis. Not any of these, it seems deserves our censure. The real cause of the insipidy of the American dramatic art is she whom Christy and Gibson have fashioned the American girl.[70]

This assault on female audiences even assumed political proportions as evinced by the number of "High Hat" bills that sprouted in the 1890's. These resulted from the hostility and rage many men felt as a consequence of their inability to see the stage caused by women wearing large hats at the theater. For instance, the *Mirror* reported that one man was so offended that he left the theater, borrowed a large hat and returned to sit in front of the woman who had blocked his view. She promptly asked the management to have him ejected.[71] Even the kindly Dean of American Letters, William Dean Howells, was moved to write on the subject: "My transport of moral indignation brings me to the subject of the theater hat . . . at least I feel sure that no woman of refinement can be hurt by the most unsparing denunciation of this means of oppression."[72]

Some managers dealt with the matter by placing polite reminders in programs asking women to remove their hats.[73] Less diplomatic moves were made in the state legislatures and city councils of Ohio, New York, Chicago, New Orleans, and Denver, all of which passed High Hat bills.[74] Some managers lobbied against these bills. Debate often became heated, and, in Ohio, the *New York Dramatic Mirror* reported "women in Cincinnati construing it as a snub against their sex, threaten to have introduced in the legislature a bill to prevent men from leaving the theater between acts 'for drinks.' "[75] Similar threats were made in regard to the Chicago ordinance.[76]

Despite these attacks, women's attendance at the theater continued to grow. Indeed, it increased to such an extent that the theater began to be seen as a woman's sphere. One critic concluded that "half the men who do come to see plays would, if left to themselves, either go to their club or drop in on a vaudeville show or musical comedy. They come because their wives or sweethearts want to."[77] Another claimed "the average man is too seriously engaged in earning a fortune to care a great deal for the theater as art."[78]

The matinee especially was seen as a special time and place for women. Here, according to critics, women could indulge their need for display and competitiveness in beauty and dress. Here, too, women could give full sway to their emotional and sympathetic feelings away from the disapproving gaze of the "practical" sex. The theater, in general, was seen as a place of "inestimable value" for women as an "emotional safety valve" where they could gain a moment's surcease from work and personal and domestic drudgeries.[79]

The female domination of the audience was also reflected on the stage, and at the turn of the century, critics remarked on the "feminization of the stage." Archie Bell, in *Theatre Magazine*, declared that "woman had done more for the theater than any other institution, and at present her supremacy is unquestioned."[80] Bell went on to compare the popularity of women on the stage with men and asserted that "the reigning favorites [male] of the day could be counted on the ten fingers if only male actors were to be named. Woman is predominate in influence and far in the majority in number."[81]

Alan Dale, critic of Hearst's *Journal*, went even further. In an issue of *Cosmopolitan*, he observed that female domination of the stage was the result of women's nature. Dale argued that women's greatness in the theater grew out of their need to always "simulate." He wrote:

> Woman has had to "get along" with man for so many centuries, to pursue him, to please him, to "diplomitize" him that the education in the art of acting (if an art) has been complete. She could scarcely avoid being other than she is. She is born an actor, and when she takes the stage as a means of livelihood she comes into her own.[82]

Dale placed such emphasis on the whole notion of women's nature as the source of acting talent that he even excluded childless actresses from the possibility of achieving greatness in tragic parts. According to him, these roles demanded the qualities of motherliness and self-sacrifice that only mothers possessed. This factor notwithstanding, Dale concluded that, despite the fact that men wrote the plays and built the theaters, "the finest actors are, always have been, and always will be women."[83]

This notion was so widely held that in 1916 Anna Steese Richardson could write with authority, "This is the story of a women-made season. A true feminist might go even further and claim that during the 1915-1916 season the theatre was saved from utter failure by the beauty, brains, and technique of its women."[84] The increasing power of women in the theater was noted by the *Nation*. An editorial, "Women and the Theater," stated:

Our feminized stage has long been anathema to the same critics that object to our ladylike literature. The indisputable eminence of women in acting, the preponderance of women audiences of today, are so striking that it requires an effort to realize that not only were women's parts acted by boys in Shakespeare's day, but that no woman appeared on the English stage until after the Restoration, and no lady appeared in the audience without the protection of a mask. Surely the whirligig of time has brought her revenge.[85]

That women were becoming aware of the responsibilities of this power can be seen from comments in journals like the *Woman's Home Companion*, which stated that "perhaps we even have a duty toward the theaters ourselves which we have not admitted. Theaters are going to be built and operated whether we approve of them or not, there is nothing we can do about it; but at least we can encourage the right kinds of drama and discourage the wrong kinds."[86]

Along with these ideas were a number of events that illustrated the growing power and importance of women in the theater. In 1899 Clement Scott, drama critic of England's *Daily Telegraph* and considered England's most influential critic, gave an interview to the journal *Great Thoughts*. In it he expressed the view that "it was nearly impossible for a woman who adopts the stage as a profession to remain pure." He also added that "the freedom of life, speech, and gesture behind the curtain renders it impossible to preserve the simplicity of manner which is her greatest charm." He concluded: "What is infinitely more to be deplored is that woman who endeavors to keep her purity is almost of necessity foredoomed to failure in her career."[87]

Although dismissed by author Harold Frederic (*The Damnation of Theron Ware*) as a tempest in a teapot,[88] Scott's remarks set off a storm of criticism on both sides of the Atlantic. The outburst was so great that he was forced to make a public apology, and he resigned his position on the *Daily Telegraph*.[89] Some of the angriest denunciations came from American actresses. May Irwin called him a "hypocrite, a journalistic vampire — a man so low, so vile, that he can see nothing but vice wherever he may look."[90] Even the usually high-minded *New York Dramatic Mirror* reprinted a magazine story in which an unnamed source made the assertion that Scott's remarks were occasioned by his being jilted by an actress whose career he had aided.[91]

Vaudeville also acknowledged women's growing importance in the theatrical scene. In 1910 and 1911 *Variety* conducted a poll of its readers in which they submitted their ideal vaudeville bill and the name of the manager who would judge them. Of the top five names most often mentioned, three were women: Annette Kellerman, Eva Tanguay, and Alice Lloyd. For the choice of judge, Miss Jennie Jacobs placed third behind Pat Casey and William Morris, in a field which included impressive names like Martin Beck (head of the Orpheum Circuit) and Marcus Loew (founder of Loew's Circuit).[92]

By the turn of the century, newspapers and journals proclaimed that women were "standing on absolute equality with men" on the stage and that they were "ever the chief support of the theater."[93] Or, as actress Mary Shaw put it most emphatically, "The theatre in America is made by and for women."[94] Indeed, the century that had seen the economic and social transformation of America also saw the theater become part of women's widening sphere.

NOTES

1. Janet M. Hooks, *Woman's Occupations Through Seven Decades*, Woman's Bureau Bulletin Number 218 (Washington, D.C.: U.S. Government Printing Office, 1947), p. 168.

2. Edward Chase Kirkland, *Industry Comes of Age: Business, Labor and Public Policy, 1860–1897* (Chicago: Quadrangle Books, 1961) presents the best overview of the economic transformation of America in this period. Also excellent for this period is Edward Chase Kirkland, *Dream and Thought in the Business Community, 1860–1900* (Chicago: Quadrangle Books, 1964). Also Carl Degler, *Out of Our Past: The Forces that Shaped Modern America* (New York: Harper Colophon Books, 1959), pp. 238-337, provides excellent statistics and analysis of this period.

3. A number of works provide information about this period. Harold Faulkner, *Politics, Expansion and Reform* (New York: Harper Brothers, 1959), Samuel P. Hays, *The Response to Industrialism, 1885–1914* (Chicago: University of Chicago Press, 1957). Ray Ginger, *Age of Excess* (London: The MacMillan Company, 1965).

4. Kirkland, *Industry Comes of Age*, pp. 401-402.

5. Ibid., p. 403.

6. For this analysis see, Larry Linden May, "Reforming Leisure: The Birth of Mass Leisure and the Motion Picture Industry, 1896-1920," (unpublished Ph.D. dissertation, University of California, Los Angeles, 1977), pp. 13-102. Also Lewis Allan Erenberg, "Urban Night Life and the Decline of Victorianism: New York City's Restaurants and Cabarets, 1800-1918" (unpublished Ph.D. dissertation, The University of Michigan, 1974).

7. Jeremy Collier, *A Short View of the Immorality and Profaneness of the English Stage Together with the Sense of Antiquity upon this Argument* (London: S. Kebler, 1697-1698).

8. Henry F. May, *Protestant Churches and Industrial America* (New York: Harper Torchbooks, 1967).

9. As examples see "Disgraced His Cloth," *New York Dramatic Mirror*, January 30, 1897, p. 14.

10. Winfield Burggraff, *Walter Edmund Bentley: Actor, Priest, Missionary, 1864-1962*.

11. Robert Grau, *The Businessman in the Amusement World* (New York: Broadway Publishing Company, 1910), p. 1.

12. Ibid.

13. "Mrs. John Drew," *New York Clipper*, September 25, 1897, p. 708.

14. David Dempsey with Raymond P. Baldwin, *The Triumphs and Trials of Lotta Crabtree* (New York: William Morrow and Company, Inc., 1968), p. 232.

15. James Kotsilibas-Davis, *Great Times, Good Times, The Odyssey of Maurice Barrymore* (Garden City, New York: Doubleday and Company, 1977), p. 270.

16. Parker Zellers, *Tony Pastor: Dean of the Vaudeville Stage* (Ypsilanti, Michigan: Eastern Michigan University Press, 1971), p. 111.

17. Neil Harris, *Humbug: The Art of P. T. Barnum* (Boston and Toronto: Little, Brown and Company, 1973), p. 254.

18. Mary C. Henderson, *The City and the Theater: New York Playhouses from Bowling Green to Broadway* (Clifton, New Jersey: James T. White and Co., 1972), pp. 35-88, pp. 125-172.

19. "B. F. Keith's Will," *Variety*, May 1, 1914, p. 7.

20. Albert F. McLean, Jr., *American Vaudeville as Ritual* (Lexington, Kentucky: University of Kentucky Press, 1965), p. 45.

21. Bosley Crowther, *The Lion's Share: The Story of an Entertainment Empire* (New York: E. P. Dutton and Company, 1957), p. 32.

22. Irving Zeidman, *The American Burlesque Shows* (New York: Hawthorn Books, Inc. Publishers, 1967), p. 65.

23. Jack Poggi, *Theater in America: The Impact of Economic Forces, 1870–1967* (Ithaca: Cornell University Press, 1968), pp. 11-13. See also Alfred L. Bernheim and others, *The Business of the Theater* (New York: Actors Equity Association, 1932), pp. 40-66.

24. Poggi, *Theater in America*, p. 21.

25. McLean, Jr., *American Vaudeville as Ritual*, p. 1.

26. Parker Zellers, "The Cradle of Variety: The Concert Saloon," *Educational Theatre Journal*, XX (December, 1968), pp. 578-585.

27. Ibid., p. 580.

28. Douglas Gilbert, *American Vaudeville: Its Life and Times* (New York: Dover Publications, Inc., 1940), pp. 10-11.

29. Parker Zellers, *Tony Pastor*, pp. 41-71.

30. McLean, Jr., *American Vaudeville as Ritual*, p. 204.

31. Ibid., p. 202.

32. William Moulton Marston and John Henry Fuller, *F. F. Proctor: Vaudeville Pioneer* (New York: Richard R. Smith Publisher, 1943), p. 49.

33. Charles R. Sherlock, "Where Vaudeville Holds the Boards," *Cosmopolitan*, XXXII (February, 1902), pp. 327-328.

34. Abel Green and Joe Laurie, Jr., *Show Biz: From Vaude to Video* (Garden City, New York: Permabooks, 1953), p. 26.

35. Edwin Milton Royale, "The Vaudeville Theater," *Scribner's* XXVI (October, 1899), p. 495.

36. Ibid., p. 485.

37. Alfred Bernheim, "The Facts of Vaudeville, *Equity,* VIII (November, 1923), p. 42.

38. Robert Grau, "The Amazing Prosperity of the Vaudeville Entertainer," *Overland Monthly* LVII (June, 1911), p. 608.

39. Hartley Davis, "The Business Side of Vaudeville," *Everybody's* XVII (October, 1907), p. 527.

40. "Trend of Vaudeville," *Independent* LIII (May, 1901), p. 1092.

41. McLean, Jr., *American Vaudeville as Ritual,* p. 54.

42. Sophie Tucker, *Some of These Days: The Autobiography of Sophie Tucker* (Garden City, New York: Doubleday, Doran and Company, 1945), p. 10.

43. Mae West, *Goodness Had Nothing To Do With It* (New York: MacFadden Bartell Books, 1970), pp. 16-17.

44. Sherlock, "Where Vaudeville Holds the Boards," p. 527.

45. Gilbert, *American Vaudeville*, pp. 327-356.

46. Jane Adams, *The Spirit of Youth and the City Streets* (New York: The MacMillan Company, 1910), p. 87.

47. Ibid., p. 88.

48. Ruth Rosen and Sue Davidson, Eds., *The Maimie Papers* (Old Westbury, New York: The Feminist Press, 1977), p. 57.

49. Ibid., p. 58.

50. Bessie Van Vorst, *The Woman Who Toils: Being the Experience of Two Ladies as Factory Girls* (New York: Doubleday, Page and Company, 1902), p. 93.

51. Dorothy Richardson, *The Long Day: The Story of a New York Working Girl as Told by Herself* (New York: Century Company, 1905), pp. 87-89.

52. "The Amusement Situation in the City of Boston," being a *Report of the Drama Committee of the Twentieth Century Club of Boston* (Boston: Twentieth Century Club, 1910), p. 15.

53. Michael M. Davis, Jr., Ph.D., *The Exploitation of Pleasure: A Study of Commercial Recreation in New York City* (New York: Department of Child Hygiene of the Russell Sage Foundation, 1911), p. 32.

54. William Trufort Foster, *Vaudeville and Motion Picture Shows* (Portland, Oregon; Reed College Record No. 16, 1914), p. 13.

55. Ibid.

56. "The Decay of Vaudeville," *American* LXIX (April, 1910), p. 843.

57. Edward Bok, "The Young Girl at the Matinee," *Ladies Home Journal*, 20 (June, 1903), p. 16.

58. "The Matinee Girl," *Munsey's* XVIII (October, 1900), p. 35.

59. Theodore Dreiser, *Sister Carrie* (New York: New American Library, 1961), pp. 288-292.

60. David Carroll, *The Matinee Idols* (New York: Arbor House, 1972), p. 35.

61. Mary P. Ryan, *Womanhood in America: From Colonial Times to the Present* (New York: New Viewpoints, 1975), p. 197.

62. Eleanor Flexner, *Century of Struggle: The Woman's Rights Movement in the United States* (New York: Atheneum, 1972), p. 232.

63. Hartly Davis, "The Business Side of the Theatre," *Everybody's* XXI (November, 1905), p. 667.

64. "Charles Frohman in Error," *Billboard*, March 11, 1911, p. 16.

65. Walter Prichard Eaton, "Women as Theater-Goers," *Woman's Home Companion* XXXVII (October, 1910), p. 13.

66. Marcosson and Frohman, *Charles Frohman,* pp. 276-289.

67. Carroll, *Matinee Idols*, p. 16.

68. Juliet Wilbor Tompkins, "The Brutality of the Matinee Girl," Lippincott's LXXX (November, 1907), pp. 687-688.

69. "As an Actor Sees Women," *Ladies Home Journal*, 25 (November, 1908), p. 26.

70. "The American Girls Damaging Influence on the Drama," *Current Opinion* XLIII (December, 1907), p. 673.

71. "The Hat Question Again," *New York Dramatic Mirror*, March 12, 1898, p. 14.

72. Howell's is quoted in, "The Hat Again," *New York Dramatic Mirror*, February 29, 1896, p. 14.

73. *New York Dramatic Mirror,* March 12, 1898, p. 14.

74. "No High Hats in Ohio Theatres," *New York Times*, March 26, 1896, p. 6, "Ohio Anti-Hat Law," *New York Times*, April 6, 1896, p.9, "Chicago's High Hat Law," *New York Times*, January 7, 1896, p. 1, "Passing of the Theatre Hat," *New York Times*, September 27, 1896, p. 6., "New York High Hat Bill Opposed." *New York Clipper*, February 16, 1895, p. 797, "The Hat Again," *New York Dramatic Mirror*, February 29, 1896, p. 14, "High Hat in Brooklyn Theaters," *New York Times*, April 18, 1896, p. 6.

75. "Ohio Hat Law," *New York Dramatic Mirror,* April 18, 1896, p. 14.

76. "Chicago's High Hat Bill," *New York Times*, January 15, 1897, p. 2.

77. Eaton, "Women as Theater Goers," p. 13.

78. "As an Actor Sees Women," p. 26.

79. Ibid.

80. Archie Bell, "What Woman Has Done for the Stage," *Theatre,* VII (August, 1907), p. 216.

81. Ibid., p. 217.

82. Alan Dale, "Why Women are Greater Actors than Men," *Cosmopolitan* LI (September, 1906), p. 518.

83. Ibid.

84. Anna Steese Richardson, "A Woman-Made Season," *McClures* LVII (April, 1916), p. 22.

85. "Women and the Theatre," *Nation* CVI (January, 1918), p. 665.

86. Katherine Ferguson, "Shall We Go to the Theater?" *Woman's Home Companion* L (January, 1913), p. 29.

87. "Clement Scott Resigns," *New York Times*, December 11, 1898, p. 1.

88. Harold Frederick, "Clement Scott and the Actors," *New York Times*, January 2, 1898, p. 19.

89. "Clement Scott's Apology," *New York Times*, April 18, 1898, p. 7.

90. *Morning Telegraph*, December 26, 1898, n.p. (*Locke*, 297, p. 22).

91. "The Truth About Clement Scott," *New York Dramatic Mirror*, January 22, 1898, p. 15.

92. "Vote for Judge," *Variety*, February 2, 1911, p. 6.

93. "Woman and the Stage," *New York Dramatic Mirror*, August 25, 1897, p. 12.

94. Henry Tyrell, "Mary Shaw - A Woman of Thought and Action," *Theatre*, II (August, 1902), pp. 21-23.

Chapter 4

The Actress: An Economic and Social View

A 1902 *Theatre* magazine article proclaimed, "One must not forget that the matinee girls form an army of neophytes, for whom it would take very little push to find themselves behind the footlights instead of in front of them."[1] The phenomenon of the "stage-struck girl" was noted by the *New York Dramatic Mirror* in 1893, referring to her as "one who had a natural and strongly marked tendency to see the stage through rose-colored spectacles over the dazzling glamour of the footlights."[2] The article added that she "turned a cold shoulder to common sense and similar 'old Fogeyish' notions and rushes headlong upon the boards without the slightest idea that a successful theatrical career means years of studying, training, drudging, and hard work."[3] Despite these comments, the anonymous author argued that it was foolish to oppose these desires if they were sincere, since opposition only intensified them. According to the author, the best course of action was to point out the pitfalls of an acting career to the young girl.

The surge of young girls to the stage was estimated by one leading New York agent to be at a ratio of twenty-five girls to one man,[4] and its magnitude provoked a series of magazine and newspaper articles filled with advice and warnings. David Belasco, prominent writer, director and producer, told young girls bent on the stage, "There is no royal road to stage success. It is embodied in one word—'work.' "[5] He also urged the would-be actresses to "think long and seriously before trying [their] fortune in the dramatic profession."[6]

Belasco's admonitions were underscored by others. Ethel Barrymore noted that perhaps only one out of a thousand aspirants ever succeeded, and that even this success might not yield anything more than a journeyman's living. As far as stardom was concerned, she added, this might prove ephemeral given the fickle nature of the audience.[7]

The actors and actresses who wrote articles about the theater attempted over and over again to define what produced stage greatness for women. In the final analysis, it came down to abstractions like "temperament," "instinct," and "intelligence." David Belasco offered the idea of "temperament" and then evaded defining it.[8] Ethel Barrymore, who had three generations of acting blood in her veins, wrote that whatever it was, it was not hereditary and instead opted for the notion of an instinct "which makes it possible for one woman to feel, and portray the feelings, passions, and personality of another woman."[9] Viola Allen called this quality "intelligence"—"the quick imagination, the keen intuition, which transports the true actress out of herself and makes her for a time, think, feel and one might say be the character assumed."[10]

All of the arguments and attempts at self-definition assume greater significance when seen not merely as cautionary literature, but as attempts to upgrade the profession, especially in the minds of the middle class who were more and more becoming both its audience and aspirants. This effort can best be seen in the debates between those who believed that the most effective theatrical training could be found in on-the-job repertory and stock companies, and those who promoted the newly developed dramatic schools.[11]

Before the 1880's the greatest source of talent for the stage was the profession itself. Like the Dickensian Crummles, acting families like the Davenports, Booths, and Wallacks supplied recruits for the stage. Theater children like Minnie Maddern Fiske, Faye Templeton, and others went on the stage at a very early age.[12]

Another prime source of talent were the poor and newly arrived immigrants. Making a living on the stage (and, as the century progressed, a rather good one) was an attractive lure for working class men and women. The stage offered high wages, mobility, and escape from oppressive slums and poverty. Marie Dressler took to the stage as a chorus girl to flee a drab home life and a tyrannical father.[13] Separated from her husband and needing to support her infant son, Sophie Tucker came to New York and sang in German beer halls,[14] while Trixie Frigenza (Delia Callaghan) ran away from her family and joined a touring company as a chorus girl rather than continue in her dreary salesgirl job in Cincinnati, Ohio.[15]

Running away to the stage was not the only way working-class men and women got started in the profession. Working-class families learned that touring companies needed children as supers, props, or even bit players, and supplying children (especially girls since they were seen as more tractable) to the companies became a way of supplementing the family income. Both Mary Pickford[16] and Lillian Gish got their start in show business in this way. Gish wrote of that period:

> It was, oddly enough, a great period for children in the theater. In most melodramas the heroine had a child or two or perhaps a little sister. Not much was demanded of the children; few of the roles were speaking

parts of any consequence. Not long after I went on the road with my first play, Dorothy [Gish's sister] found her first acting job. Mother wrote me that Dolores Lorne had taken Dorothy to play "Little Willie" in East Lynne.[17]

However, by the 1880s, middle class women began coming into the profession, lured by newspaper and magazine articles talking of the high salaries and independence enjoyed by actresses like Cushman and Mowatt. Trade papers such as the *New York Clipper* reported every prominent socialite to make a debut, and managers used their presence in plays to attract friends to the theater. Companies like Augustin Daly's drew the elite of New York society to its opening nights,[18] for Daly hired socially connected young girls for a group that was nicknamed "Daly's Debutantes." One of them, Dora Knowlton Ranous (later an editor and translator) wrote in her diary: "He [Daly] wished to engage several girls of good family and education, who had some dramatic instruction, although he preferred that they should have had no actual theatrical experience."[19]

The decline of the repertory company made it imperative that some new form of training be developed for the increasing number of men and women, especially from the middle class, hoping to enter the profession. Although there had been private teachers of acting and elocution for a long time, the idea of a "drama school" began to gain favor. In 1877 the great writer, director and theatrical innovator Steele MacKaye wrote an article titled, "A Plea for a Free School of Dramatic Art."[20] MacKaye was quoted by his son and biographer, Percy, as saying: "There are two great requisites to be attained before the drama can commence its true career: First—a great dramatic school of actors; Secondly—a lofty school of playwrighting."[21]

MacKaye dedicated himself to both, but it was his associate Franklin Sargeant, a teacher of elocution and dramatic reading at Harvard, who brought MacKaye's dream to fruition. In 1884, Sargeant opened the Lyceum Theater School on Twenty-third Street in New York with 100 students. (In its third year, the name of the school was changed to the American Academy of Dramatic Arts.) Indicative of its success were the 300 students it had graduated by 1899, an entering class of 300 students chosen from 3,000 applicants, and at least nine other dramatic schools in New York attempting to emulate it with varying degrees of success. The school's tuition fees of $250 for the first year and $150 for the second made it virtually accessible only to the middle class.[22]

Drama schools came to be seen as the basis for improvement of the stage. Charles Belmont Davis, drama editor of the *New York Herald Tribune* wrote, "I recently spent some time in the classrooms of a drama school in New York, and I am convinced that such institutions are at least one of the important if not absolutely necessary sources from which our theater must look for its much needed uplift."[23] Equally affirmative was David Belasco, who taught for Sargeant and who not only saw the dramatic school as a good place for training, but also as the possible seedbed for a future American national theater.[24]

However, drama schools were not universally applauded in the profession as the best source for learning the craft. Traditionalists felt that on-the-job apprenticeship in repertory and stock companies was the best means to acquire the necessary training. Ethel Barrymore, who received her initial schooling in her grandmother's and uncle's companies, wrote, "I think there is no school of acting comparable to a company engaged in producing plays. The instruction of the schools in this country seems to me inferior to that of the company."[25]

Whatever their feelings about training, there was nonetheless general agreement that a theatrical life was a difficult one. Actors and actresses who wrote about it stressed the hard work, the physical and emotional hardships, and the rigors of constant travel which had to be endured by all. Indeed, perhaps one of the most difficult was getting into the profession in the first place.

Excluding those who were hired directly from the dramatic schools and children whose theatrical families had networks of connections which could provide employment, the most frequent means of securing work was direct application through the mail or in person. One article in the *Woman's Home Companion* titled "The Stagestruck Girl"[26] went so far as to recommend boardinghouse locations in New York (West Forty-fifth Street off Broadway), agents one should see (Bijou Fernandez, Isabell Prentiss, Georgia Wolfe, Wales Winter), and ways of approaching managers.[27] However, most aspiring actors and actresses never even got to see the manager and were turned away by office staff. Incidents of office retainers barring the way were legion and even brought an irate letter to *Variety* from an experienced vaudeville artist who complained, "I was amazed at the treatment accorded artists by various office boys—and girls. With one or two exceptions (certainly not more) the agent's employees were extremely haughty and very unobliging."[28]

When admittance was gained, questions then rose about the importance of beauty, dress, and money. Most agreed that beauty was helpful in gaining an initial place on the stage. *Theatre Magazine* wrote: "Of course good looks finally wear out, and later on talent counts for more than beauty, not in starting out in a stage career, the latter counts first with the manager, who never having seen your work, does see and feel your personality, and the young woman who fills his eyes has a greater chance over her plainer and perhaps more competent sister."[29] However, all generally agreed that in the long run looks were meaningless without talent or discipline. Actress Jane Cowl wrote an article, "Why a Reputation for Beauty Is a Handicap," in which she asserted that good looks took away from any appreciation of the actress's skill.[30]

Considered even more important than beauty was dress. In *The Seamy Side*, a memoir of the stage purportedly written by an anonymous actress of twenty years experience and dedicated to "The Stage Struck Girl,"[31] the Bunyanesque Miss Prudence Grey is told by an older actress, "*Dress*, whatever else you do, dress. It is the one thing that counts with managers. Get the money some way, a manager will never ask you nor does he care how; all he wants to know is that you dress and dress well."[32]

These articles also hinted that a bit of palm greasing might secure a place on the stage. The *Theatre Magazine* observed that "there is another way for the amateur to secure her first professional appearance, and that is to buy it from the impecunious manager."[33] However, most writers in the newspapers and magazines continually warned their readers of the swindles that occurred in these circumstances.[34]

Without benefit of money, connections, dramatic schools, great beauty or fine style, the fledgling actor or actress often had to endure the demeaning process of going from manager's office to manager's office seeking an audition, or, in vaudeville, the demoralizing and dehumanizing "amateur night." There, as Jane Addams described it, "if the stunt does not meet with the approval of the audience, the performer is greeted with jeers and a long hook pulls him off the stage."[35] At one of these events, Sophie Tucker was told by a manager that she was "too big, too ugly" to make it in show business.[36]

Most often an engagement was secured with a small-time repertory or stock company that traveled the independent circuits in small towns, or the small-time vaudeville theaters where the performer shared time with films. Salaries on these circuits had not changed much since Olive Logan reported (in 1870) that wages ranged from ten to twenty-five dollars a week for the super or ballet girl, to twenty to twenty-five dollars for a soubrette and featured actor, and up to $150 for the star.[37] Of course, in better companies pay was higher, but even here starting salaries rarely went above twenty-five dollars. Stars could earn as much as $300 to $500 per week, but only Maude Adams was paid (in 1910) a peak of $900 a week with 50 percent of the box office receipts.[38] In vaudeville, the big-time two-shows-a-day circuits paid standard acts between $150 and $200 per week and went up to $1000 or more per week for headliners.[39] On the other hand, small-time vaudeville performers could expect to do five and sometimes six shows a day for as little as $20 per week.[40]

Although salaries were relatively high, actors and actresses could expect long layoffs. Even for the regularly employed actor or actress, the average season ran between thirty and forty weeks a year. Moreover, performers were not paid for rehearsal time.[41] Vaudevillians, in contrast, could work fifty-two weeks a year. However, they had to pay commissions to agents, do extra shows without compensation or risk being blackballed,[42] and bear the expense of travel and producing their own acts. This latter cost was quite high, an example being the $1000 paid in quarterly installments by Fred and Adele Astaire's mother to Ned Wayburn, the creator of their act.[43] In addition, actors and actresses who appeared in vaudeville sketches had to pay royalties to the author which ranged between $25 and $250 per week, depending on the importance of the author.[44]

In the theater, these expenses were matched, especially for actresses, by costuming. Clara Morris headed a chapter of her stage reminiscences, "The Bane of the Young Actress's Life," and designated it in one word—dress.[45] This problem resulted from the nineteenth century tradition that had actresses and actors supply their own costumes, a situation which caused constant anxiety and indebtedness. Ethel Barrymore, for instance, reported in the early part of her career her part called for a certain costume, and she was "mortgaged, so to speak, for the entire season to the dressmaker."[46] Mary Shaw reported that actresses had to spend as much as $300 to $400 per season (while men spent as little as $150), and called this one of the great inequities of the profession.[47] Annie Russell also mentioned the fear actresses felt over a gown tearing.[48]

The importance of costume can not be overstated. Each week the trade papers ran columns titled "The Matinee Girl" and "About Women" devoted to detailed description and commentary on costume. Sophie Tucker became aware of dress from the moment she stepped into a big-time vaudeville theater. She learned that "if ever you get on the stage, think of clothing, look smart; it helps you out."[49] So well did she absorb the lesson that one critic referred to her as "overdressed,"[50] although this did not hurt Eva Tanguay, who even built her career on exaggerated costumes such as a dress completely made out of pennies.[51]

Although most actresses did not wear this kind of eccentric dress, their costuming bills also were extraordinarily high. It was the expensive tastes and gowns of Mrs. Leslie Carter that drove her into bankruptcy while she was still at the height of her career; her 1908 bankruptcy petition listed clothing and jewelry expenses and indebtedness of $31,169.[52] So hazardous could this indebtedness become, there was even a case of a creditor having an actress dragged off the stage in the middle of a performance when she fell into arrears.[53]

Just as important to the stage beginner as dress was learning stage business, etiquette, and tradition. For the youngster without any training in stagecraft, skills like movement, stage presence, elocution, and makeup were hopefully acquired through observation and advice from more experienced performers. Miriam Burt Young explained how her mother, Myrtle MacKinley Young, was taught by veteran chorus girls how to make up when she joined the road company Floradora sextette,[54] while Sophie Tucker had an old pro, George La Maire, show her how to apply burnt cork to her face when she sang "coon songs" in blackface in the early days of her career.[55]

Assistance like this was not exactly rare, even in a profession noted for its jealousy. That envy caused Sophie Tucker to be deprived of a sure hit song in the Follies of 1909, when Eva Tanguay felt it would take the limelight away from her.[56] Also, in a fictional account in the *Ladies Home Journal* titled "How I Became an Actress," the young girl giving the account tells of being lectured by the leading lady of a small-time repertory company for upstaging her with a bit of stage business.[57]

Performers also had to learn stage discipline, a set of controls enforced by fines. Keeping the stage waiting, missing cues and lateness or absence from rehearsals all brought monetary punishment that ranged from one or two dollars up to loss of a week's salary or even dismissal.[58] In addition, in the 1880s and 1890s when companies still had green rooms (places where the actors could relax back stage, learn their parts, find out about the next day's casting, or socialize), fines would be levied on those who breached decorum by swearing, wearing hats, smoking, petitioning the manager, or other discourtesies.[59] Similarly, in vaudeville, an actor or actress could be fined for not being ready before his act was to go on, swearing, talking directly to the audience, using "blue material," not being in costume, etc.[60]

For most actors and actresses, however, the greatest hardship was life on the road, the road being anything outside of Manhattan's theatrical district. In theater, travel expenses for companies were provided by the manager. However, except for important companies and touring groups like Madame Helen Modjeska's, which had its own railway cars, this did not include anything more than the price of a ticket. If the performers wanted a Pullman on a long trip, they had to pay for it themselves.[61] In vaudeville these "jumps" were always paid for by the performer, an expense which could mount if the actor or actress had to play split weeks (appear in more than one theater in the same week), or if "jumps" were not on a direct line or far apart.[62]

The most common complaint heard about the road was not its dangers, which could include train wrecks[63] and calamitous theater fires,[64] but the condition of the theaters themselves, especially dressing rooms. These were reported to be the dirtiest, draftiest, smallest, and most inadequate one could imagine. Even prestigious companies like Augustin Daly's had to suffer their inconveniences, and Dora Knowlton Ranous even mentions seeing a rat in one dressing room.[65] Conditions were so horrific that a *Billboard* editorial of 1909 complained: "While the audience sits in comfort on silk plush chairs in a theatre furnished like a palace and heated to even temperature, the players are forced to dress in rooms that are little better than stalls, where their comfort receives less attention than usually accorded animals with the circus."[66]

Indeed, so serious was the problem that one performer, a victim of tuberculosis, listed dirty, unventilated dressing rooms as one of the prominent factors causing his disease, according to a *Variety* article titled "The Stage and the T.B.'s."[67]

Alongside long travel and the poor quality of dressing rooms, poor accommodations and poorer food were often major sources of grievance for performers on the road. Most hotel owners disliked theatrical people and, as a rule, the best hotels in towns were off limits to them.[68] As a class of patrons, the hotel manager found players unacceptable due to their penchant for keeping pets, late hours, having parties in their rooms which disturbed other guests, sleeping late (making it impossible for chambermaids to do their work), abusing hotel property by doing washing and cooking in their rooms, and being generally too permissive with their children.[69] In addition, the stranded performer who could not afford to pay his or her bill and had to leave the trunk behind as security was a common occurrence. Indeed, a song hit of the 1890s was called, "He Belonged to a Troupe That Was Stranded in Peoria."[70]

None but the headliners who, according to the theater tradition, isolated themselves from the rest of the company, could afford to stay at the local Grand Hotel, even if they did accept actors. Most performers were relegated by income, tradition, and sometimes by choice to the cheaper hotels that charged between one dollar and one dollar and fifty cents per night. In most cases the actor and actress knew well in advance at what hotels in what cities he or she could board. This knowledge was usually acquired through the trade papers, word of mouth, or handbills and posters put up in theaters by hotel managers and boardinghouse keepers. In addition, the advance man, who traveled ahead of the companies advertising their arrival, usually had a good idea where the troupe could put up. All of these were supplemented by an unofficial consumer guide usually written in the form of handbills and posters with comments like "flies in the soup" and "Stop here, she is the manager's aunt. If you don't you get canned."[71]

The boardinghouse was a product of a bygone era, but, before restaurant service and the commercial rooming house, was the home of thousands of American men and women in the early phases of industrialization and urbanization.[72] Indeed, it was so important a part of the economy that in 1900, 58,860 people (mostly women) listed it as their occupation.[73] Boardinghouses generally charged between one and seven dollars per week, an average rate being between three and five dollars if the boarder took meals out. Certain boardinghouses were known to cater to actors and actresses who frequented them whenever they were in town.[74]

Boardinghouses were criticized for inadequate food and lack of sufficient bathing facilities. Moreover, many boardinghouses did not have parlors where gentlemen could be entertained, thereby creating additional problems for actresses who were forced to invite callers into their rooms.[75] Although this was a condition shared by non-actresses, it was just another element in a social life that condemned women in a society governed by Victorian ideals of social relations.

Historically, the performers' almost outlaw status set them apart from the rest of society. This isolation was intensified by the wandering nature of the profession, the intense, even obsessive, involvement in learning its skills, and the hours of employment which limited contact with the rest of society. Additionally, in Victorian society which placed severe limits on feminine physical display, forcing pregnant women into a seclusion called "confinement" and even placed ruffles on piano legs, the female performer who wore tights was certainly an anathema. Nevertheless, despite the fact that some states even tried to pass ordinances forbidding the wearing of tights, some took a more tolerant attitude. An editorial in the *New York Sun* commented:

> She wears tights on the stage because they are in accordance with the conventions of the theatre. Hundreds of other young women wear them there, and the public are accustomed to see them on the stage as they are to observing the flowing draperies of women in everyday life. The usual feminine dress may be worn shamelessly and tights may be worn with entire modesty. What are called tights reveal the legs, but so also the conventional bathing costume makes that exhibition, and yet modest and innocent women are not afraid to appear in it when the necessities of bathing require.
>
> Custom and conventionality determine what is modest and suitable raiment, and they vary in their requirements according to the occasions and are not fixed by any absolute law without regard to difference of circumstances. The full evening costume of a lady would outrage propriety if it were worn on the street in broad daylight.[76]

The actress was also seen as a pariah in Victorian eyes because her mobility and professional equality did not enable her to fit into a world where a woman's sphere was solely the home and family. Moreover, the easy and constant accessibility of actress to actor necessitated by work further broke down the notion of separate sphere. It was this conflict with the conventionally defined notions of male and female relations that offended Victorian sensibilities and gave the impression of sexual license.

Proper Victorians were shocked by stage men and women referring to each other by their Christian names after only short acquaintance, by men and women taking supper with each other unchaperoned, and by men swearing, wearing their hats and even smoking in front of women. Actress Emma V. Sheridan saw this as a necessary outgrowth of the men and women meeting on the basis of "equality and interest," and added that "manners are more likely to adapt themselves to circumstances and necessity, and to find their suggestion in good humour and kindliness than cast iron into the form of etiquette and be dictated by the caprice of Mrs. Grundy."[77] On the other hand, the rather prudish Miss Prudence Grey of *The Seamy Side* wrote in capital letters, "IF SHE [the stagestruck girl] WISHES TO START 'A LITTLE HELL ON HER OWN HOOK,' JUST LET HER GO ON THE STAGE."[78]

The most frequently evoked image of the collapse in morality of the actress was the "bird and bottle" supper with stagedoor "johnnies" and "mashes" that presumably led to all kinds of sexual licentiousness. Undoubtedly this did happen—witness the stories of Lillian Russell's gastronomical exploits,[79] Lilly Langtry's romantic conquests,[80] and Stanford White's chorus girl-filled birthday cakes and red velvet swings.[81] Nevertheless, in partial justification, many an underpaid or unpaid actress used the bird and bottle supper to supplement her income.[82]

In most cases, it was home to bed to get a good night's sleep. May Irwin wrote, "Midnight suppers, birds, bottles and hijinks generally are no more possible to the one who would succeed in it [the theater] than one who would become a successful banker or drive the limited express."[83] Anna Russell told of the wearying rehearsals and train trips that demanded sleep if the actress was to continue.[84] More than likely, the average woman performer was to experience the same feelings as the fictional vaudevillian, Dollie:

> In the four long years no one sent Dollie American Beauty roses with hundred dollar bills enwrapped in the stems, and an invitation to supper, or a diamond sunburst of which the sender humbly said that if it were worn he would expect the privilege of settling her dinner check. Stage door johnnies had never striven to buy her meals. Once an acrobat had carried her bag to the train because his wife asked him to, and a property man left a widower with six children had inquired with tender meaning if she ever contemplated settling down.[85]

If the women of the theater had a constant companion—especially on the road—it was possibly fear and loneliness. Prior to 1885, even in cities as large as New York, only eleven percent of the guests at the four largest hotels were women. Ladies had separate entrances and were not permitted to sign the register or enter the hotel dining room unescorted.[86] An actress travelling alone could invite insult or provoke terrifying incidents.

The most famous example of this hazard occurred to a company led by Maurice Barrymore in Marshall, Texas, in 1879. Jim Currie, the deputy sheriff of Marshall, shot and wounded Maurice Barrymore after the latter had challenged him to a fist fight when he referred to actress Ellen Cummings as a "high tossed whore." Ben Porter, another actor in the company and Cummings' fiancee, was killed when he tried to stop Currie from firing at the wounded and unarmed Barrymore. The theatrical world was thrown into an uproar over the incident, and hundreds attended Porter's funeral at the Little Church Around the Corner,[87] while the *New York Telegram* wrote that the episode would teach actors "to omit Texas in future tours."[88] Compounding the tragedy was the fact that the Texas jury which tried Currie found him not guilty by virtue of insanity.

Tragedies like the Porter-Barrymore incident were, on the whole, rare. A more frequent occurrence to actresses was sexual harassment. At one extreme was the behavior of the johnnies or mashers who crowded outside the stage doors and sent actresses letters. Clara Morris asserted that "any well brought up young woman respecting the proprieties can protect herself from the attentions of this walking impertinence."[89] Some of the strategies she suggested were to return their letters and gifts, and to complain to the manager if they continued to hang around the stage door.[90]

Needless to say, the attentions of every johnnie were not discouraged. There were numerous instances of marriages between actresses and these men. In fact there were so many cases of chorus girls marrying coronets that Sir Arthur Wing Pinero commented that "the musical comedy girls will be the salvation of the aristocracy."[91] In addition, American millionaires were hardly neglected. Beside the notorious example of Evelyn Nesbitt's marriage to Pittsburgh millionaire Harry Thaw, there was Faye Templeton's elopement with millionaire Howell Osborn, and Anna Robson's marriage to August Belmont. Also, some women of the stage did not discourage extramarital attentions; witness the long relations of Lillian Russell with Diamond Jim Brady and mining fortune scion Jesse Lewisohn.

Sexual harassment ranged from voyeurism to sexual blackmail and even to assault. Dora Knowlton reported that, when the Daly company traveled to Milwaukee on tour, some young men watched the women undress through an uncurtained window and then scampered away when discovered.[92] On another occasion Knowlton was almost imprisoned in a room by a well-known poet who wanted to make love to her.[93] In another instance, Mary Shaw reported the case of an actress who was forced to agree to a date or accept the possibility of scandal because the man threatened to tell the hotel manager that he had left a gold pencil in her room.[94]

Of even more torment and danger to the actress was the skirt-chasing manager who demanded sexual favors in return for continued employment. One man commented, "Well suppose a girl working and traveling alone struck town on Monday morning without any money, and after the night show the 'manager' made advances, telling her she would be 'closed' immediately for the engagement if she did not prove agreeable, what do you think might happen in three cases out of five!"[95] *Variety* was so outraged that it offered to combat the problem by publicizing the name of any offending manager if the story could be authenticated.[96]

When and if real romantic and sexual relationships did occur for actresses, they were more than likely to be with other performers or members of companies than with those whom the trade papers succinctly labelled non-professionals in wedding and engagement announcements. Marie Dressler's first love was the leading man of the first troupe she traveled with. The relationship ended when the actor, named Terry, turned his roving eye to someone else.[97] These temporary liaisons between company members were often referred to as "suitcase romances" because they began with the man carrying the woman's suitcase on and off trains, arranging for her tickets and hotel or boarding accommodations, and progressed to quiet suppers for two in the actress's room after the performance.[98]

However, actresses could and did maintain their virtue and independence, albeit at a cost. Sophie Tucker wrote of her early days:

> On every bill I was always alone. None of the others knew whether I was married or single. I had a way of keeping my business to myself. A husky girl, carrying her own suitcases, attending her own railroad tickets, boarding places, looking out for herself, as capable and independent as a man ("look out for that skirt, she can cuss like a man").[99]

Nevertheless, in her heart Sophie longed for a man, and she bemoaned the fact that "the hoofers, comedians, monologuists never asked me out to dinner or to take a walk between shows. None of them ever said, "She's a good scout, let's take her along,' or even, 'She's a good-looking broad; let's make her!' "[100]

It was isolation and separation that made relationships possible, and it was generally separation that provoked divorce. *Billboard* warned:

> Actors who, though married to one another, are compelled to appear in separate plays, either for lack of a suitable vehicle for the exploitation of both of their talents or for some other cause that makes their appearing together impossible.
> A drifting apart is the inevitable result. Their interests cease to be mutual. Their experiences often change their views until agreement, even on the subject of their art, is out of the question. They are daily thrown into close association with other members of the opposite sex, without seeing each other at long intervals.[101]

By all estimates, divorce among actors and actresses was frequent, though these estimates were inflated by publicity. Although census data are unreliable, the divorce rate for actors between 1886 and 1906 was second to surgeons and physicians in those counted as professional service occupations. The 1,598 divorces of actors in that period count as 0.7 percent of the total distribution, while the 3,244 divorces of physicians and surgeons is 1.4 percent of the nationwide total.[102]

A smaller sample gives a better view of divorces among actresses. In 1904 the *World Magazine* did a social survey of the eighty-six chorus girls in the Lady Teazle Company, the musical version of Sheridan's *School for Scandal* starring Lillian Russell. Of these women aged sixteen and up, thirty-nine were single, twenty were married, twenty-one were divorced and six had divorces pending.[103] Adding the categories of divorcees and pending divorcees together gives a divorce rate of over thirty-one percent in the company, a far higher percentage than the national average of 4.5 divorces per thousand in 1910.[104]

However, as the trade papers were quick to point out in editorials and anniversary announcements, long-lived relationships did exist and flourish even in the difficult environment of the stage. Marriages like E. H. Sothern—Julia Marlowe, William Brady—Grace George, the Cohans, and the Keatons did endure. Some couples supplemented their marital relationship with a professional one, and some non-professional spouses traveled with their mates and managed the act.[105]

The children of these relationships often became members of the team, or even had separate acts. George M. Cohan and Buster Keaton were important parts of their parents' acts. Elliot Nugent traveled with his parents and did a child monologuist act, and George M. Cohan played the violin on his parents' bills before becoming part of their act.[106]

If children did not travel with their parents, they were generally boarded with relatives or grandparents. When old enough, the children could be sent to boarding school. Especially favored among actors and actresses, because of their discipline, were religious and military schools. Ethel Barrymore found herself at a convent,[107] while Sophie Tucker's son went to military school.[108]

Clearly the stage was different from the world envisioned by the starry-eyed aspiring actress. Nevertheless, the theater had a major recompense that did not come only in the form of money, independence, and celebrity. As Ethel Barrymore described it:

> No one but a churl—in fact no one at all—can fail to be pleased, flattered, touched to the heart by the spontaneous admiration of the public. To feel that people like one, smile when one smiles, grow teary when one weeps, give one their affection for no more cogent reason than they cannot help it—which is the most cogent reason on earth after all—is a delight. To escape from one's self every night, to thrill with emotions,

think the thoughts, play the games, use the words of another woman—
to be another woman, interesting, plaintive, charming, tragic, witty, or
whatever her creator made her—is the fullness of joy. To feel the electric
current of sympathy play back and forth across the footlights is well, it
is an intoxication of pleasure.[109]

It was this thought that kept many a stage-struck girl in thrall. Elda
Furry, daughter of an Altoona, Pennsylvania butcher, was so thrilled by
the performance of Ethel Barrymore in *Captain Jinks of the Horse Marines*
that she decided then and there to become an actress. Forty years later—
after running away to New York, becoming a chorus girl, touring, marrying
an actor and divorcing him after one child—as Hedda Hopper she was
chronicling the adventures of other stage-struck girls in their new
mecca—Hollywood.[110]

NOTES

1. "The Woman's Page: For 'Stage Struck' Girls," *New York Dramatic Mirror,* July 29, 1893, p. 12.

2. Ibid.

3. Ibid.

4. "To Stage Struck Girl: 'Don't'," *Morning Telegraph*, June 28, 1903, n.p. (*Locke*, 302, pp. 71-72).

5. David Belasco, "Advice to the Girl with Dramatic Ambitions," *Woman's Home Companion*, October, 1904, p. 7.

6. Ibid.

7. Ethel Barrymore, "The Young Girl and the Stage," *Harper's Bazaar* XL (December, 1906, p. 1000.

8. David Belasco, "Dramatic Schools and the Profession of Acting," *Cosmopolitan* XXXV (August, 1903), p. 361.

9. Ethel Barrymore, "The Young Girl and the Stage," p. 1000.

10. Viola Allen, "On the Making of an Actress," *Cosmopolitan* XXXI (August, 1901), p. 413.

11. Two views on the issue of Dramatic Schools may be found in "Mirror Interview: Mrs. John Drew," *New York Dramatic Mirror,* January 5, 1895, p. 2, and the Editorial, "Dramatic Schools," *New York Dramatic Mirror*, January 12, 1895, p. 8.

12. Archie Binns, *Mrs. Fiske and the American Theatre* (New York: Crown Publishers, 1955), p. 14.

13. Marie Dressler as told to Mildred Harrington, *My Own Story* (Boston: Little, Brown and Company, 1934), pp. 22-39.

14. Sophie Tucker, *Some of These Days: The Autobiography of Sophie Tucker* (Garden City, New York: Doubleday, Doran and Company, Inc., 1945), pp. 22-32.

15. "I Like Acting Out Much Better than Being a Cash Girl at $3 per," *Sunday Telegraph,* March 26, 1905, n.p. (*Locke,* 220, p. 19).

16. Mary Pickford, *Sunshine and Shadow* (Garden City, New York: Doubleday and Company, Inc. 1955), pp. 49-64.

17. Lillian Gish with Ann Pinchot, *The Movies, Mr. Griffith and Me* (New York: Avon, 1969), p. 7.

18. Marvin Felheim, *The Theater of Augustin Daly: An Account of the Late Nineteenth Century American Stage* (Cambridge: Harvard University Press, 1956), p. 23.

19. Dora Knowlton Ranous, *Diary of a Daly Debutante* (New York: Duffield and Company, 1910), p. 1.

20. Quoted in Beverly M. Brumm, "A Survey of Professional Acting Schools in New York City, 1870-1970," (unpublished dissertation, New York University, 1973), p. 18.

21. Ibid.

22. Ibid., pp. 34-49.

23. Charles Belmont Davis, "The Young Girl and the Stage," *Colliers*, 44 (October, 1909), p. 22.

24. Belasco, "Dramatic Schools and the Acting Profession," pp. 364-368.

25. Ethel Barrymore, "The Young Girl and the Stage," p. 1001.

26. William A. Page, "The Stage-Struck Girl," *Woman's Home Companion* XLIII (September, 1916), p. 19.

27. Ibid.

28. Letter to *Variety,* April 24, 1909, p. 6.

29. Harry P. Mawson, "The Truth About Going on the Stage," *Theatre*, II (August, 1902), p. 10.

30. Jane Cowl, "Why a Reputation for Beauty is a Handicap," *American* LXXXIV (August, 1917), pp. 50-51.

31. *The Seamy Side: A Story of the True Conditions of Things Theatrical by One Who Has Spent Twenty Years Among Them* (Boston: Percy Ives Publishing Company, 1906).

32. Ibid., p. 139.

33. Mawson, "The Truth About Going on the Stage," pp. 10-11.

34. "White Rats After Irresponsible Agents," *Variety*, July 13, 1907, p. 12.

35. Jane Addams, *The Spirit of Youth and the City Streets*, (New York: MacMillan Company, 1910), p. 87.

36. Tucker, *Some of These Days*, p. 34.

37. Olive Logan, *Before the Footlights and Behind the Scenes: A Book about "The Show Business" in all its Branches* (Philadelphia: Parmalee and Company, 1870), p. 93.

38. Hartley Davis, "The Business Side of the Theatre," *Everybody's*, XXI (November, 1909, p. 672-673.

39. Charles R. Sherlock, "Where Vaudeville Holds the Boards," *Cosmopolitan* XXXLI (February, 1902), p. 427.

40. Douglas Gilbert, *American Vaudeville: Its Life and Times* (New York: Dover Publications, Inc. 1963), pp. 20-21.

41. Rennold Wolf, "The Salary of Actors—When They Get It," *American* LXII (September, 1916), p. 76.

42. Alfred Bernheim, "The Facts of Vaudeville," *Equity Magazine* IX (January, 1924), p. 45.

43. Fred Astaire, *Steps in Time* (New York: Harper and Brothers, Publishers, 1959), p. 32.

44. *Variety*, July 18, 1913, p. 5.

45. Clara Morris, *Stage Confidences: Talks About Players and Play Acting* (Boston: Lothrop Publishing Company, 1902), p. 147.

46. Ethel Barrymore, "The Young Girl and the Stage," p. 999.

47. "Injustices to Actresses," *Theatre Magazine* VIII (May-June, 1892), pp. 167-168.

48. Annie Russell, "What It Really Means to be an Actress," *Ladies Home Journal*, 26 (January, 1909), p. 17.

49. Tucker, *Some of These Days*, p. 28.

50. *Variety*, November 21, 1913, p. 13.

51. *Variety*, February 6, 1909, p. 14.

52. Charles Harold Harper, "Mrs. Leslie Carter: Her Life and Acting Career," (unpublished Ph.D. dissertation, University of Nebraska, 1978), pp. 163-164.

53. "Julius Boasberg Has Woman Dragged from Palace Stage," *Variety*, January 1, 1915, pp. 3, 6.

54. Miriam Young, *Mother Wore Tights* (New York: McGraw-Hill, 1944), p. 10.

55. Tucker, *Some of These Days*, p. 40.

56. Ibid., pp. 77-78.

57. "How I Became an Actress: A Girl's Actual Experiences on the Stage and What Happened After She Got On," *Ladies Home Journal*, 28, (May, 1911), p. 14.

58. Logan, *Before the Footlights*, pp. 64-66.

59. Ibid.

60. Douglas, *American Vaudeville*, p. 202.

61. Charles Belmont Davis, "On the Road with the Players," *Outing*, LII (August, 1908), p. 534.

62. "The Seamy Side of Vaudeville," *Variety*, June 6, 1913, p. 6.

63. There are no accurate statistics available on how many artists lost their lives in train wrecks. Nevertheless by many accounts it was not an infrequent occurrence. One of the most famous of theater people to lose his life in a train wreck was Sam S. Shubert, one of

the founders of the Shubert theater chain. His death is recounted in Jerry Stagg, *The Brothers Shubert* (New York: Ballantine Books, 1969), pp. 72-74. Also an account of a train wreck in *New York Clipper,* January 23, 1892, p. 760.

64. There are no exact statistics on theater fires in the nineteenth and early twentieth century. However, there were three major catastrophes in the nineteenth century and early twentieth century. They were the Richmond Theatre fire of 1811 in which 70 died, Mrs. Conway's Theatre fire in Brooklyn in 1876 in which 285 died, and the most disastrous of all, the Iroquois Theatre fire in 1903 in which 602 died. For an account of the latter see Eddie Foy and Alvin F. Marlow, *Clowning Through Life* (New York: E.P. Dutton and Company, 1928).

65. Ranous, Dora Knowlton, *Diary of a Daly Debutante* (New York: Duffield and Company, 1910).

66. "Give the Actor Quarters more Comfortable," *Billboard*, October 30, 1909, p. 12.

67. "The Stage and the T.B.'s," *Variety,* December 23, 1911, p. 32.

68. Jefferson Williamson, *The American Hotel: An Anecdotal History* (New York: Alfred A. Knopf, 1930), p. 126.

69. Ibid.

70. Ibid.

71. Van Hoven, "Boarding Houses And —," *Variety,* December 25, 1914, p. 25.

72. Albert Benedict Wolfe, *The Lodging House Problem in Boston* (Boston and New York: Houghton, Mifflin and Company, 1906).

73. U.S. Department of Commerce and Labor Bureau of the Census, *Special Report: Occupations at the Twelfth Census* (Washington, D.C.: Government Printing Office, 1901), p. 7.

74. Joe Laurie, Jr., *Vaudeville From the Honky Tonk to the Palace* (New York: Henry Holt and Company, 1933), pp. 276-286.

75. Wolfe, *The Lodging House Problem,* p. 46.

76. *New York Sun* Editorial quoted in "Tights and the Stage," *Theatre*, VIII (May-June, 1892), p. 176.

77. E.V. Sheridan "Manners Among Stage People," *Theatre,* VII (August, 1890), pp. 28-29.

78. *The Seamy Side,* p. 290.

79. John Burke, *Duet in Diamonds: The Flamboyant Saga of Lillian Russell and Diamond Jim Brady in America's Gilded Age* (New York: G.P. Putnam's Sons, 1972).

80. Noel Gerson, *Lilly Langtry* (London: Robert Hale and Company, 1971).

81. Michael MacDonald Mooney, *Evelyn Nesbit and Stanford White: Love and Death in the Gilded Age* (New York: William Morrow and Company, Inc., 1976).

82. "How I Became an Actress," p. 14.

83. May Irwin, "The Business of the Stage as a Career," *Cosmopolitan,* XXVIII (April, 1900), p. 656.

84. Annie Russell, "What It Really Means to be an Actress," p. 17.

85. Helen Green, "One Day in Vaudeville," *McClures,* XXXIX (October, 1912), p. 644.

86. Norman S. Hayner, *Hotel Life* (Chapel Hill: University of North Carolina Press, 1936), pp. 98-99.

87. James Kotsilibas-Davis, *Great Times, Good Times: The Odyssey of Maurice Barrymore* (Garden City, New York: Doubleday and Company, 1977), pp. 127-149.

88. Ibid., p. 134.

89. Morris, *Stage Confidences,* p. 168.

90. Ibid.

91. Horace Wyndham, *Chorus to Coronet* (London: British Technical and General Press, 1951), p. 13.

92. Ranous, *Diary*, p. 231.

93. Ranous, *Diary*, p. 225.

94. Mary Shaw, "The Actress on the Road, *McClures*, XXXVII (July, 1911), p. 265.

95. "The Skirt," Women on 'Small Time' and the 'Chasing' Manager," *Variety*, March 5, 1910, p. 5.

96. Ibid.

97. Dressler, *My Own Story*, pp. 42-46.

98. *The Seamy Side*, p. 82.

99. Tucker, *Some of These Days*, p. 36.

100. Ibid.

101. "Domesticity and the Stage," *Billboard*, August 1, 1908, p. 16.

102. U.S. Department of Commerce and Labor, Bureau of the Census, *Marriage and Divorce 1887–1906* (Washington, D.C.: Government Printing Office, 1908), p. 25.

103. "The Chorus Girl—Before and After," *World,* December 18, 1904, n.p. (*Locke,* 412, pp. 9-11).

104. William O'Neill, *Divorce in the Progressive Era* (New Haven: Yale University Press, 1976).

105. "Happy Marriages Among People of the Stage" *Billboard,* October 30, 1909, p. 12. Also "The Hacketts Golden Wedding," *New York Clipper,* August 17, 1907, p. 686.

106. Ward Morehouse, *George M. Cohan: Prince of the American Theatre* (Philadelphia: J.B. Lippincott, Company, 1943), Tom Dardis, *Keaton: The Man Who Wouldn't Lie Down* (New York: Charles Scribner's Sons, 1979).

107. Ethel Barrymore, *Memories: An Autobiography* (New York: Harper and Brothers, 1955), p. 22.

108. Tucker, *Some of These Days*, p. 120.

109. Ethel Barrymore, "The Young Girl and the Stage," p. 1000.

110. Hedda Hopper, *From Under My Hat* (Garden City, New York: Doubleday and Company, Inc., 1952), pp. 29-30.

(left) A scene from Shaw's *Mrs. Warren's Profession* with Mary Shaw seated as Mrs. Warren and Catherine Countess as Vivie Warren.

(above) A caricature of Mary Shaw as Vida Levering in *Votes for Women.*

(left) The opening night program of *Votes for Women.*

(left)   Lillian Russell as she appeared shortly after her debut at Tony Pastor's.

(bottom)   Lillian Russell (second from left) with her co-stars of the Weber & Fields Company. (left to right) DeWolf Hopper, Lew Fields, John G. Kelley, Fritz Williams, Fay Templeton, Sam Barnard, Lee Harrison, Bessie Clayton, Joe Weber.

Lillian Russell in a portrait shot around 1901.

(above)   Lillian Russell appointed an honorary sergeant of the U.S. Marine Corps leads them in a parade in 1918.

(below)   Lillian Russell with her fourth husband, Pittsburgh newspaper publisher, Alexander P. Moore.

Ethel Barrymore as Lady
Frederick in 1908.

Ethel Barrymore as Mme. Tretoni
in her first starring role in
*Captain Jinks of the Horse
Marines.*

(left) Ethel Barrymore with two of her children, Samuel Colt and Ethel Barrymore Colt.

(below) Ethel Barrymore as Kate, with Charles Dalton as Sir Harry Sims and Mrs. Sam Sothern as Lady Sims in *The Twelve Pound Look*.

Chapter 5

Mary Shaw: The Actress as Clubwoman and Suffragist

ooking back on twenty-five years in the theater, May Irwin wrote in 1900: "I can see a vast change in the whole machinery of the stage. It is no longer the haphazard, wildcat affair that recruited its bright lights from vagabondia."[1] At the dawn of the twentieth century, this was undoubtedly so. The expanding economic opportunities in the field, the influx of the middle class into both the profession and the audience, the enormous publicity given actors and actresses in the press, and the lessening of clerical hostility to an occasional fundamentalist jab raised the prestige and importance of the theater. To no small degree this increasing significance was also due to the actions of actors and actresses themselves through their social and professional clubs.

The organization of these clubs fits neatly into Alexis De Tocqueville's description of Americans' need to "constantly form associations religious, moral, serious, futile, general, or restricted, enormous, or diminutive."[2] Historians contemplating this phenomenon, particularly the increasing number of associations at the end of the nineteenth century, have ascribed it to the need for stability in the midst of frightening and complex social and economic change.[3] This was true for actors no less than farmers, workers, and professionals, though actors' clubs additionally provided a means for gaining wider cultural and social acceptance of the profession. Actresses formed separate clubs for similar purposes, though the clubs also helped women to develop the organizational and public speaking skills that Mary Shaw, for one, later used to such excellent effect in the women's suffrage movement.

The most important of the men's organizations, The Actors' Fund, was created as a professional response to the problems of the penniless actor and actress. Institutional solutions such as the insurance policies issued by the Actors Order of Friendship and bequests from successful actors like Edwin Forrest for the establishment of a home for aged actors were insufficient. In addition, the traditional means of meeting crises — the benefit — became more and more inadequate to meet the needs of indigent actors and actresses, especially during the recurring period of recessions and depressions in the 1880s and 1890s.[4]

Highlighting the insufficiency of this system were the benefits that the profession held for the relief of others. In 1880, the *New York Herald* called on New York City to raise $100,000 to aid starving people in Ireland and advocated installing contribution boxes in all theaters to aid in the collection.[5] This demand outraged the young and crusading editor of the newly founded *New York Dramatic Mirror*, Harrison Grey Fiske. The *Mirror* argued:

> Since the newspapers have taken up the task of supplying Ireland with funds, let them carry it out and let all of us help them to the fullest extent of our means, reserving the theatrical channel for another occasion. One of the good works which has been too long neglected in the theatres is the establishment of a Sinking Fund to be managed by an executive here in New York for which the prompt relief of actors in distress and for the prompt remedy of any wrongs from which professionals may suffer.[6]

The *Mirror*'s campaign for an actor's fund continued for the next two years. In 1882, Fiske's and the *Mirror*'s resolve was strengthened by the death of actress Eliza Newton, who seemed destined for a pauper's grave due to lack of funds. The case was brought to the attention of the *Mirror* by Lucille Adams, Mrs. Newton's friend. In an editorial titled, "A Greek Unburied," the *Mirror* took the profession to task for not taking care of its own.[7] A week later a similar case involving comedian William Norton intensified the *Mirror*'s appeal. Finally on March 12, 1882, after calls from a number of managers, a meeting was set up to discuss the organization of just such a fund. A number of benefits were arranged, some individual contributions were received, and the Actors' Fund was formally incorporated on June 8, 1882. At its first meeting on July 15, 1882, Fund organizers chose Lester Wallack as president and A. M. Palmer as vice president.[8]

Under the leadership of Palmer, who became its third president in 1885 and served for the next twelve years, the Fund achieved its greatest economic stability and professional prominence. Palmer had come to theatrical management from a career in law and after a stint as a Republican party patronage appointee to the Internal Revenue Service. There he met and served under Sheridan Shook, another Republican politician, wealthy brewery owner, and chief of the Internal Revenue Service in New York's thirty-fifth district from 1861 to 1869. Shook owned the Union Square Hotel and, in 1870, converted part of it into a theater. After a scandal forced both Shook and Palmer to resign from the Internal Revenue Service, Palmer took over management of the theater. Palmer's astuteness soon became evident, and he produced a number of theatrical hits, culminating in the fabulously successful *Two Orphans* in 1874. Palmer's success as a manager, coupled with his political connections, made him an ideal choice for Fund president. He used his ties to gain wide acceptance for the Fund and to advance the cause of the stage. Palmer saw to it that leading politicians like ex-Mayor Grace of New York and others were added to the Fund's Board of Trustees, and he also used his political connections to lobby successfully in the state legislature for laws that garnered additional income for the organization.[9]

Sharing Palmer's ambition to see the profession advance in stature and significance was America's leading tragedian, Edwin Booth. Booth had long wanted to create a suitable memorial to his father, the brilliant, but eccentric Shakespearean actor Junius Brutus Booth. He also wanted to increase and enhance the links between the theater and other professions.[10]

In 1887 the idea for a club was raised on banker E. C. Benedict's yacht *Oneida* by a group which included Booth, Lawrence Barrett, Lawrence Hutton, and Thomas Bailey Aldrich. A larger meeting was held that winter which added to the group Mark Twain, General William T. Sherman, and a number of other actors and managers. Shortly thereafter, on January 1, 1888, in a house donated by Booth on Gramercy Park and designed by architect Stanford White, the club designated "The Players" came into existence.[11]

The Players was not the oldest actors' club in America, that distinction belonging to the Lambs' Club, founded in 1874. The Players' charter required that the club include men engaged in "literature, poetry, sculpture, architecture, or music, or who is a patron or connoisseur of the arts."[12] This latter phrase opened membership to those in professions other than the theater. Indeed, as Booth said in his Founders Night speech, the purpose of the club was to bring:

> them [actors], regardless of their theatrical rank, in communion with those, who, ignorant of their personal qualities hidden behind the mask and motley, know them as actors only. Frequent intercourse with gentlemen of other arts and professions, who love the stage and appreciate the value of the drama as an aid to intellectual culture, must inspire the humblest player with a reverence for his vocation as one among the first of "fine arts"—which too many regard as merely a means to the gratification of vanity and selfishness.[13]

The Players, however, was not to everyone's liking. One letter to the *Dramatic Mirror* complained of its inhospitable atmosphere and said that it was increasingly becoming the dictatorship of a tightly knit clique under the "despotic control"[14] of manager Augustin Daly and his brother, Judge

Joseph Daly. The letter even went so far as to say that "the Players can be neither an agreeable resort for persons of social and artistic tastes, nor a players club in the true sense of the term."[15]

No matter how inhospitable it might seem to some, the Players soon found an imitator in the Twelfth Night Club, the club for actresses, founded by the young actress Alice Fischer. When challenged by her fiancee to create a similar institution after expressing envy of the Players, Fischer responded with an invitation to a number of other actresses to start their own social club. Initially called the F.A.D. Club (for Fencing, Art, and Dancing), the members subsequently changed the name to the Twelfth Night Club and, in contrast to the luxurious surroundings of the Players, frequently met in Alice Fischer's boardinghouse bedroom.[16]

Within a year of its founding, the club had two hundred members. Although it was essentially a social club, the organization did mount impressive benefits for actresses like Clara Morris and Fanny Janauschek. More significantly, one of the club's founding members and its first treasurer was Vida Croly, the actress-daughter of Jennie "June" Croly.[17]

Jennie "June" Croly was a journalist and writer whose husband David was also a journalist and editor. When she and other women were barred from attending the New York Press Club's 1868 dinner honoring Charles Dickens, they decided to set up their own club. Histories of the women's club movement in America began with the establishment of Sorosis, as the club was called, and with the New England Women's Club, founded in the same year. In 1890, the year that saw the National Women's Suffrage Association and the American Woman Suffrage Association finally combined, women's clubs around the country united to form the General Federation of Woman's Clubs (GFWC), with a membership of 20,000.[18]

Although the women's club movement membership was a heterogeneous and ideologically diverse group ranging from women who were suffragists to those primarily concerned with social, philanthropic, and literary endeavors, it was an important institutional step in the growth of American feminism. As early as the 1840s, Harriet Martineau commented on the pedantry she observed among American women, but still saw this as a step toward greater awareness and intellectual clarity and "a hopeful symptom."[19] Thus, the experience of creating socially and psychologically supportive club networks with other women was, for women socialized by a Victorian culture demanding passivity, a positive and, in some cases, progressive experience. Whether this resulted in some form of "Domestic Feminism"[20] which sought and gained greater control for women within the traditional sphere of the family, or culminated in "Social Feminism"[21] which attempted to expand woman's role outside the family by reforming society, the clubs still had a profound impact on women's consciousness.

Sharing the club experience were a number of actresses and wives of theatrical managers, who ultimately helped found the most important actresses' club in America, the Professional Woman's League. Nonetheless, the actual inspiration for the League's founding was not Sorosis but the Actor's Fund.

In 1892 the Fund sponsored a fund-raising fair, whose success was in no small part due to the women who helped in its planning and organization. Following the fair, a number of women (some of whom were also members of Sorosis) suggested organizing a permanent women's auxiliary to the Fund; however, their proposal was rebuffed in favor of one which called for a club specifically designed to help actresses.[22] The club was named the Professional Woman's League, but the title is something of a misnomer. Although the charter designated membership as open to those women "engaged in dramatic, musical, and literary pursuits with the purpose of rendering them helpful to each other,"[23] membership was predominantly comprised of actresses. Moreover, members from professions other than the theater were eligible only for the club's social, rather than philanthropic, aspects. The League's philanthropy, however, did not take the form of direct charity, but was instead geared to self-help programs. Their most important offering was a dressmaking class where young actresses could learn how to make their own costumes. In addition, older, more successful actresses were encouraged to donate parts of their unneeded wardrobes to the club's collection. For all members there were classes in languages, art, music, business law, and debates and discussions.[24]

From the very first, the club was marked by a degree of contentiousness. One of its first squabbles concerned the election of Mrs. A. M. Palmer as president. Mrs. Palmer, one of the original foursome who inspired the formation of the club, was a non-actress who was considered by some a "climber." However, she was elected, and the growth of the club was phenomenal, membership climbing to two hundred in the first year of its existence.[25]

A more serious conflict occurred between the League and its mother club, Sorosis. Ironically, the sudden success of the League did not endear it to the founding club. In May, 1893, shortly before the League's formal inaugural, Lotta Crabtree, an actress who had been sponsored for membership in Sorosis, was blackballed.[26]

Actually to merely refer to Lotta Crabtree as an actress is somewhat inaccurate. Lotta Crabtree (Charlotte Mignon Crabtree) was a nineteenth century American popular cultural phenomenon, her career spanning the days from the California gold fields to the nineties. Initially taken under the wing of Lola Montez and manager Tom MacGuire, she then came East where her singing and dancing captured the hearts of America, with men and women dancing the "Lotta Polka" and the "Lotta Gallop." Her appearances in melodramas like *Little Nell* and *Heart's Ease* played to turn-away crowds. Appearing in Europe in the eighties, she managed to enthrall the French and English as well. By 1892 she was in retirement and was undoubtedly the most well-known, beloved, and, by most estimates, one of the richest women in America.[27]

Sorosis' rejection of Lotta created a field day for the newspapers. The *New York Times* made it front page news and even carried an editorial mentioning the "Lotta case," while decrying the whole practice of blackballing.[28] As for the membership of Sorosis, particularly those connected with the theater, their attitudes ranged from shock, to disbelief, to rage. Mrs. A. M. Palmer, hearing the outcome of the vote, was reported to have threatened to resign. Some, including Lotta, attributed her rejection to the fact that she was an actress. However, since Sorosis already had actress members this seemed hardly likely.[29]

Another explanation was advanced by actress Isabelle Evesson. She suggested that the reason for the rejection was the sudden success of the PWL. Evesson said:

> A few months ago there was formed the Professional Woman's League composed of women of the stage and women who were prominent in the literary field. Today it has about 300 members, many of whom are members of Sorosis. The scope of the League is broader and more liberal than that of Sorosis, and I suppose that fact has caused a few disgruntled members of Sorosis to blackball any member of the stage whose name is proposed.[30]

Tempers finally cooled and good relations were eventually restored between the sister clubs, but not before Minnie Maddern Fiske indirectly referred to the incident by paying special tribute to Lotta in her speech at the club's inaugural.[31] Unfortunately, within a year of the Lotta incident the League was guilty of the same sin. The League blackballed the young actress Victory Bateman because she had been named as a co-respondent in a divorce case. Miss Bateman, however, was innocent, and, unlike Lotta, who merely shrugged off the incident, she sued for damages.[32]

Despite these occurrences the League grew and prospered. Its annual bazaars were usually financial successes, especially among men and women who enjoyed the idea of being served and catered to by famous and lovely actresses. Also, its all-female minstrel shows and performances of Shakespearean plays were big hits. As a result, by 1910, the League's membership had climbed to about six hundred.[33]

On another level, the League's practical achievements such as its sewing, language, dancing, music, and law classes gave members a sense of what women could accomplish. The League put women, especially actresses, in touch with one another, resulting in mutual intellectual, social, and psychological sustenance. As one of its founding members, Miss Bertha Welby, said: "I never knew that there was so much talent and so many charming personalities among the women of the stage until I met them here in the League gatherings."[34]

Along with its self-help ideas, another central motif of the League was its emphasis on women's achievement in society. At the League inaugural, both President Palmer and Mrs. Rachel MacAuley, the chairman of the Executive Committee, stressed early accomplishments like the dressmaking classes and bazaars, but they also boasted of the League's discussion of "Olive Schreiner's Place in the History of Women," led by Margaret Ingersoll.[35]

The club developed and continued to sponsor feminist lectures, not always to the satisfaction of some of the League's supporters. In the second year of its existence Miss Maud Banks gave an address on women's rights which the *Dramatic Mirror* dismissed as "sophomoric."[36] Nonetheless, in her third-year inaugural address, Mrs. A. M. Palmer gave a speech that celebrated the contributions of Elizabeth Blackwell, Lucy Stone, Lucretia Mott, Susan B. Anthony, and others. She also applauded the fact that women had stepped outside "the stoutly braced walls of tradition and custom that fenced in the limited space known as 'woman's sphere,' " and she looked forward to the day "when the subordinate should become the equal; when shoulder to shoulder, eye to eye, the man and the woman should stand as God created them — workers together."[37]

This emphasis on women's achievement and abilities reached its apogee at the club's tenth anniversary all-women exhibition at Madison Square Garden. The exhibition aroused great interest and garnered large profits. Its booths, crafts, and entertainment were all created, staffed, and provided for by actresses, all-women bands, vaudeville troupes, and athletes.[38] One newspaper called the exhibition an "Adamless Eden,"[39] and another stated that "femininity is the star, in fact, everything masculine has been dropped from the programme."[40]

Not only was the exhibition staffed and run by women; its major theme was the contribution of women throughout history and in all nations. In addition, the exhibition also paid attention to the great part played by women in fields that men thought they monopolized.

The League's feminism, however, stopped short of embracing suffrage, which the General Confederation of Woman's Clubs did not endorse until 1914.[41] Although the League had members like Mary Shaw and Lillian Russell who were staunchly in favor of suffrage, it also had others who were cool to the idea. The club's fifth president (1909-1914), Amelia Bingham, was one of these. An acknowledged star of the day, Bingham had been outspoken in her support of suffrage until, while on a trip to England in 1910, an encounter with the militant tactics of the British suffragists convinced her otherwise. When she returned to the United States she said:

> I do not believe that women of this country will ever have the ballot, that is the unlimited ballot. I do not believe the majority want it. I know I don't. I have quite enough responsibility as it is. The men are perfectly welcome to all that goes with voting. I do think women make good members of school boards and I think they can do a great deal of good work and all that. But I think if the average woman does the work that she should do, she is too busy to study conditions as she should in order to vote.
>
> The women of my profession certainly are too busy. There are a few of us who are suffragists and they are usually the young women who are out of positions and want something for excitement.[42]

Bingham's disclaimers to the contrary, there was considerable support for suffragist opinion in her profession and in the League. In fact, Bingham's description would have appalled Mary Shaw, who was not young at the time (56), out of work (she was starring in a Broadway play), or wanting for excitement (her first New York performance of Shaw's *Mrs. Warren's Profession* nearly caused a riot). In the words of her biographer, Mary Shaw was "one of the many women and men who dedicated their lives to the proposition that women and men are equal, but also have to assume their respective responsibilities, shared or individual, in the ordering of their society so that we all might be free."[43]

Supported by many actresses, less because of her firm stance on suffrage than her advocacy of a more leisurely social role for the League, Shaw launched an unsuccessful bid (1913) for its presidency. She lost by three votes in the bitterly contested election. Lillian Russell, who supported Shaw and had herself been elected the club's fourth vice president that year, stated her intention not to serve and vowed never to set foot in the club again. Her sister Suzanne Leonard Westford, a former club president (1906-1910), even predicted a split in the League. She was proven correct in less than a month when she, Shaw, Russell, and others formed the Gamut Club, whose relaxed atmosphere appealed to women in all professions. Membership quickly reached two hundred.[44]

Despite her failure to gain its presidency, the League served as a supportive and nurturing environment for Shaw's early activism. It was a letter from her written to the *Dramatic Mirror* after the Fund fair in 1892 that had helped spur creation of the organization.[45] A charter and life member of the League, former chairman of its executive committee, and frequently one of its vice presidents, Shaw's leadership in debates, discussion, and theatricals, as well as her executive ability, had been singled out for praise by the press and by members themselves.[46] Indeed the League served as an excellent place to develop these skills, and, as Henry Tyrell said: "To hear her speak from the platform, as she does upon occasion — at a Professional Woman's League meeting or the Actors Church Alliance, for example — is to confirm the impression of an extraordinary intellectual force, mixed in some strange way with frankly feminine charm."[47]

The League helped Mary Shaw develop not only as a public speaker and as an executive, but gave her the impetus to define a role for herself that went beyond the confines of the stage. These early experiences blossomed into a career that included militant advocacy of women's suffrage, the championing of the cause of realism on the stage, and an attempt to create a Woman's National Theater. Shaw's experiences led her to say, "There is but one kind of success, and that is to live your life out fully and sincerely. I can only say that the League, the Dorothea Dix Home, and the Church Alliance, and all that sort of thing, appealed to me with the same convictions that playing Lady Macbeth does."[48]

Jestingly, Shaw ascribed this duality to a temperament that was half Irish and half New England Puritan. The daughter of a socially prominent Boston municipal official, Mary Shaw started her career as a teacher. Unhappy with schoolteaching, she turned to the stage, and in 1879, the same year she married, she made her debut with the Boston Museum Company. Shortly thereafter her husband died, leaving her with a two-and-a-half-year-old son. Subsequently, she joined the Augustin Daly Company in New York and then became a supporting actress in Helena Modjeska's Company.[49]

In Modjeska's company, along with being exposed to the craft of a great actress, Shaw also had a chance to observe at first hand a woman of great charm and intelligence, for Modjeska had before emigrating conducted literary salons in her native Poland with writers like Henry Sienkiewiecz (*Quo Vadis*).[50] In her memoirs Modjeska remembered Mary Shaw as a "studious intellectual young woman with a great deal of talent. She never slighted even the smallest details in her parts, but always worked for improvement."[51] Mary Shaw, for her part, recalled the years with Modjeska as "one of the most enjoyable periods of my theatrical life. Her company was one of the finest and best balanced I have ever seen, and we were all congenial to each other."[52]

Mary Shaw also could not have helped but be impressed with Modjeska's political convictions. Both Modjeska and her husband, the Count Bozenta, were fierce Polish nationalists. Born in Cracow in 1840, by 1868 Modjeska was the leading lady of the Warsaw Imperial Theater. Ill health and her anti-Russian sympathies forced her and a group of other Poles to emigrate to America. Arriving in California in 1876, they tried to set up a utopian colony along the lines of "Brook Farm." When these efforts collapsed, Modjeska decided to return to the stage. Learning English in six months, she made her American debut in San Francisco in 1877. Although she never lost her accent, she continually toured in this country and abroad from 1877 until her death in 1909.[53]

In 1893 Modjeska was invited to deliver an address on "Women and the Stage" at the Chicago World's Fair Auxiliary Woman's Congress.[54] This led to Mary Shaw's own invitation to address the International Woman's Congress in London in 1899, where she spoke on "The Stage as a Field for Women." Tracing the history of the stage and its players from their outcast days to their current status, she pleaded with her audience for sympathy for actresses and a special sense of responsibility for what was done on the stage. She said:

> There is an axiom in my profession that the most successful plays and players are the ones that please women. When you are inclined to criticize the stage ponder over this thought a little. It is a truth pregnant with meaning for women, and if you take this seed thought with you to your several homes and keep it in your minds during all your relation with the stage and its people, it will finally rouse, perhaps some new and strange convictions as to women's influence and responsibility toward the stage.[55]

That Mary Shaw took this responsibility seriously herself can be seen first and foremost in her championing of the plays of Ibsen and Shaw.

Realism was a reaction to the historical dramas filled with cape and sword romance, and the melodramas of "fallen women" that flourished on the early nineteenth-century stage. By mid-century the first departure from this convention on the English-speaking stage came with the so-called "cup and saucer" plays of Tom Robertson. Dramas such as *Society, Caste, Home, Progress, Birth,* and *War* took place in aristocratic drawing rooms, but nevertheless called for realistic set detail and a naturalistic style of acting.[56]

Aiding the development of realism was the formation of a theater that eliminated the restraints imposed by the commercial theater and provided an environment that could support new plays by young authors. This kind of atmosphere was first introduced by Andre Antoine at his Parisian Theatre Libre, which sponsored new plays by previously unproduced playwrights in a non-commercial setting. Although a financial failure, the Theatre Libre idea inspired the creation of Otto Brahm's Freie Volksbuhne in Berlin and J. T. Grein's Independent Theater in London. The experimental nature of these theaters made it almost inevitable that they become showcases for the realistic drama pioneered by Ibsen, Shaw, Strindberg, and Hauptmann.[57]

In contrast, without either the institutional framework of a Theatre Libre or a Freie Volksbuhne or a tradition of quality writing for the stage,

American attempts at realism languished. Significantly, whatever early attempts there were occurred in plays dealing with contemporary problems like temperance and divorce, which were of special interest to women. T. S. Arthur's *Ten Nights in a Barroom* was a great hit and became an organizing tract for the Women's Christian Temperance Union. Similarly, Augustin Daly's production of *Divorce* in 1871 started a trend that resulted in the production of eleven plays (before 1914) with divorce as their central theme. Although none gave the slightest hint that divorce might be an acceptable solution to a marriage where there was neither love nor happiness, they did focus attention on a social problem of increasing concern.[58]

More important was the work of James A. Herne, referred to by his biographer as the "American Ibsen." Although Herne's plays were not as artistically successful as the Norwegian's, *Shore Acres* and *Margaret Fleming* had both realistic settings and dialogue. In particular, *Margaret Fleming*'s attack on the double standard and the wife's refusal to reconcile with her husband despite his pleas for forgiveness were a great departure from the conventional stage image of women.[59]

Nevertheless, it remained for the plays of Ibsen to awaken the first stirrings of realism on the American stage. Ibsen began writing the historical-poetic drama *Catiline* in 1844. By 1875 he had turned to more realistic themes and forms in *Pillars of Society*. In 1879 he wrote what, for many women, was to become a manifesto, *A Doll's House*.[60]

The early history of *A Doll's House* in America is a rather curious one. First performed in English in Milwaukee, Wisconsin, on June 2, 1883, it was called *A Child Wife*, and adhered to the European practice of changing the ending; in the altered version Nora returns to Torvald. With that ending and another title change (*Thora*), the play was still very strong medicine for an American audience, and Madame Helena Modjeska's company, which gave it its first professional performance at Lexington, Kentucky on December 7, 1883, immediately withdrew it. Two English actresses, Beatrice Cameron (Mrs. Richard Mansfield) and Janet Upchurch, subsequently toured it in the United States in 1889 and 1890.[61] These tours prompted the *Dramatic Mirror* to comment:

> The *Doll's House* might be a mildly interesting performance if it possessed what it hasn't yet had in America — a suitable Norah. The acceptability of the piece depends entirely upon the skill and fitness of the actress to whom the character is assigned. But it may be said safely that under the most favorable conditions The *Doll's House* would not give sustained pleasure to any class of theatre goers in this community.[62]

Ultimately the right actress was found when Minnie Maddern Fiske appeared in the play on Broadway in 1896, and then went on tour with it.

In the Modjeska production, the role of Mrs. Linde was played by Mary Shaw.[63] It was to be the start of a lifelong dedication to the plays of Ibsen, whom Mary Shaw considered a genius. However, it was in Ibsen's *Ghosts*, rather than *A Doll's House*, in which Mary Shaw made her mark.

In many ways *Ghosts* was a more controversial play than *A Doll's House*. Indeed, if *A Doll's House* provoked, *Ghosts* outraged audiences. *Ghosts'* major theme was the hereditary consequences of syphilis, and it even featured a young man dying of paresis. Such was its power that the venerable and influential critic of the *New York Herald*, William Winter, who disliked Ibsen and had merely quibbled at *A Doll's House* with the comment that "any considerable number of husbands and wives are able to live for years without in the least comprehending each other's character,"[64] protested that *Ghosts* gave off the "curious perfume" of "a dead rat in a dark cellar."[65] In fact so fierce was his and other critics' indignation that the plays of Ibsen and other realists were promptly dubbed "sewer drama."[66]

Before Mary Shaw performed *Ghosts*, it had seen only a limited number of American performances. It was first produced in Chicago in 1882 before a German-speaking audience, where it was advertised as the play banned by the German censor. Its first English performances in America were played in Boston and New York in 1894. In 1899, Mary Shaw played the role of Mrs. Alving for the first time at a special New York performance which was directed by Herr Emmanual Reicher of the Freie Volksbühne and given before an American audience that included such notables as William Dean Howells, David Belasco, and Franklin Sargeant. The reviews from this limited performance were generally good and specifically singled out Mary Shaw for praise. This success encouraged her to open the play on Broadway in 1903 and take it on tour in that year and 1904.[67]

The 1903 Broadway production prompted Winter's diatribe. Despite this and other adverse criticism, Mary Shaw continued her tour and gave the country its first sustained exposure to *Ghosts*. In each city the play generated interest, excitement, and controversy. A Denver critic quoted an audience member as saying: "[The play] is utterly intolerable and impossible."[68] Even some of Mary Shaw's warmest supporters were uneasy about it, and Jane Addams, who had invited her to perform a matinee at Hull House, asked her to cancel the production.[69]

On the other hand, W. L. Hubbard of the *Chicago Sunday Tribune* wrote that the play had "food for thought in it,"[70] and that "the person who sits through a performance of *Ghosts* carries away with him a moral lesson which is only more potent and convincing because it has been shown to him and not preached at him."[71] Seconding Hubbard's opinion was a miner who saw the play in Cripple Creek and, according to Mary Shaw, said to his companion, "Say, Bill, that play made a feller use his cocoanut."[72] In addition to its intellectual power, the play generated emotional power and could, and did, overwhelm people. For instance, Fola La Follette, the actress-daughter of Senator Robert La Follette, recalled that she cried the night she saw Mary Shaw in *Ghosts*.[73]

Despite some of the critical disapproval, the furor caused by *Ghosts* was mild in comparison with the controversy that surrounded Mary Shaw when she played in George Bernard Shaw's *Mrs. Warren's Profession*. Like Mary Shaw, George Bernard Shaw was also an early convert to Ibsen and, in his book *The Quintessence of Ibsenism*,[74] defended the playwright against those who considered his work "an open drain" and a "loathsome sore unbandaged."[75]

In 1892, after a still unheralded career as a music-drama critic and a novelist, G. B. Shaw decided to try his hand at the drama and wrote the realistic *The Widower's House*. By 1905 a number of Shaw's plays, including *Candida*, *The Man of Destiny*, *You Can Never Tell*, and *How He Lied to Her Husband*, had been successfully produced in America.[76]

The leading Shavian exponent in America, often called his "high priest," was Arnold Daly. Unfortunately Daly started off his 1905 season with *John Bull's Other Island*, which proved a dismal failure with American audiences. Searching around for another hit, Daly decided to produce Shaw's *Mrs. Warren's Profession*. This play had already stirred up quite a bit of controversy in England. Its theme of a woman who prefers prostitution to a life of poverty had not gone down well with the English authorities, and it was denied a Lord Chamberlain's license for public performances. Fearing similar consequences in America, Shaw was against its production and even wired Daly, requesting him not to produce the play.[77]

How right Shaw was, was evident from the play's first night in New Haven. A combination of Yale undergraduates' rowdyness and the town fathers' blue-stocking morality forced its cancellation after only one performance. Undaunted, Daly decided to try the play in New York. If anything, opposition in New York was stiffer. Anthony Comstock, America's foremost guardian against the evils of pornography, wrote a letter to the *New York Times* demanding that Daly cancel the production, and Mayor George McClellan instructed his police commissioner to close it if it did open. Nevertheless, on October 30, 1905, Daly opened the play with Mary Shaw in the title role of Mrs. Warren, the brothel keeper. Outside the theater a circus atmosphere prevailed as people bid as much as thirty dollars for a ticket, and reporters from the *New York Sun* passed out ballots to the audience asking them to vote on whether or not the play was fit to be seen.[78]

Although the vote of the 953 who attended was 304 in favor to 272 against,[79] the play was closed by Police Commissioner MacAdoo, and all those connected with the performance were arrested. The next day the *New York Herald* called the play "the limit of indecency,"[80] and its critic, William Winter, referred to it as a "blot on the theater."[81] Others were just as vehement, calling it "illuminated gangrene" and "revolting in theme and inhuman in character."[82]

So outraged at the closing of the play, Mary Shaw later charged that Mayor McClellan had used the incident as a "political ruse." According to her, the whole affair was used by the Tammany backed McClellan administration to deflect criticism from its opponents who charged that the play was Tammany's way of "invading the theater and demoralizing the young men and women of the city."[83]

Later the next year some sanity was restored, and all charges were dropped against Daly and his company. The manager of the theater, Samuel Gumpertz, was the only one who stood trial, and he was acquitted of all charges. Despite the clean bill of health, Daly decided to drop production of the play. This permitted Mary Shaw to obtain the rights from George Bernard Shaw and take it on tour in 1907 and 1908.[84]

In many ways her tour in *Mrs. Warren's Profession* was almost a reprise of her tour in *Ghosts*. Some critics attacked Shaw's "notorious"[85] play as an outrage, while others commented on its strength and reported that audiences considered it "high art."[86] Some critics also used the tour as an opportunity for belated recognition of Mary Shaw's service to the theater in her earlier tours of *Ghosts*. Colgate Baker in the *San Francisco Chronicle* wrote:

> The American theatre-going public has long owed a debt of gratitude to Mary Shaw which it is chary of paying. It is not merely that she had the courage to produce Ibsen's plays, in spite of many discouragements, but because she has given us insights into how they should be acted, a standard for the interpretation of modern psychological drama which is of considerable value to the public and the theatrical profession.[87]

Besides the critical response to *Mrs. Warren's Profession* and *Ghosts*, Mary Shaw welcomed the opportunity it gave her to speak to women's audiences around the country and to stress their collective power in the theatrical world.

Wherever she appeared in both plays she made it a practice to speak before the local women's club. There, while extolling the virtues of the play, she would also urge women to decide for themselves how they felt about the dramas. Invariably she found their reactions were positive. Writing about this experience, she said, "In all the hubbub not a woman's voice has been heard, it was simply men and their opinions."[88] The response convinced her that men did not have the "souls" to understand the "woman's plays" of Ibsen and Shaw. This belief combined with her opinion that these were the most important plays of the day, and her often stated view that women were already the economic backbone of the theater prompted her to urge her audiences to exercise that power. In a speech before the Friday Morning Club of Los Angeles, while on tour in *Mrs. Warren's Profession,* she said, "The stage has become feminized . . . and if a play displeases women it is in their hands to change it."[89] Moreover, as she told her audiences and newspaper interviewers, that power was not solely confined to the stage. Using Ibsen's heroines as models, she quoted Olive Schreiner's remark that " 'God did not ask man whether woman should have power. He gave it to her,' and this dramatist [Ibsen] realized that this power she should use in one way or another, if not legitimately then to make mischief."[90]

Ultimately harnessing that power over the theater and using it for the benefit of all women became one of her highest priorities. In 1913 she and a number of other women attempted to set up a Woman's National Theater. As Mary Shaw saw it:

> The theater is an institution supported almost entirely by women and more than half interpreted by women. Yet it entirely lacks the women note, as far as management and production are concerned. We are planning to put that note into American drama. So far we haven't been able to do more than talk about it, but if we keep on doing that — and I intend to — it is reasonable to expect to get action some time.[91]

Needless to say, talk about it she did. And, as one reporter said after hearing her on the subject of the Woman's National Theater, "The world of the rostrum inclusive of the pulpit should take off its collective hat to her. The knotted and combined curtain speakers of Broadway should go to her for lessons."[92] Despite her eloquence, the project floundered for lack of funds. However, it reflected the growing ferment in the theater prior to 1917, a ferment which included George Pierce Baker's Harvard playwrighting workshop, the Provincetown Players, and others that were working toward the transformation of the American stage.[93]

Undeterred by the failure of the Woman's National Theater, Mary Shaw still attempted to use the stage for the betterment of women. In particular she sought to employ theater as a weapon in the struggle for women's suffrage. Her work in the fight for the vote was part of the intensifying campaign mapped out by new leaders like Harriet Stanton Blatch, Alice Paul, and Carrie Chapman Catt, which was moving the suffrage movement into high gear after a period of relative stagnation. In the renewed struggle the theater, like marches and lobbying in Congress for a federal amendment, played an important role.[94]

Prior to 1900 the treatment of women's suffrage and the "New Woman" on the stage had been hardly sympathetic. Symptomatic of its handling were plays like Charles Hoyt's *A Contented Wife* (1897) and Sydney Grundy's *The New Woman* (1895).[95] In the Hoyt play a wife in a progressive western state decides, in a fit of pique, to run against her husband for mayor after he criticizes her for sewing a button on wrong. In a more serious vein the Grundy play tells of a young man who tires of his wife and chases after a more emancipated woman. However, this drama is hardly less harsh in its condemnation of the feminist. Grundy's attitude towards her is best expressed by a lady's maid who says:

> You call yourselves "New Woman"—you're not new at all. You're just as old as Eve, and just as hungry for the fruit she plucked. You only want one thing—the same thing every woman wants—the one thing no woman's life is worth living without! A true man's love! Ah! if we all had that, there'd be no problem of the sexes then.[96]

By 1910 a number of plays inspired by the British suffrage movement's activities began to appear. One of these pro-suffragist plays was written by an American-born actress, Elizabeth Robins, who lived in England. Robins' play, *Votes for Women*, was a compound of "fallen women" melodrama and suffragist propaganda. Its heroine Vida Lovering is a woman with a past who becomes a suffragist. Years after her betrayal, in the midst of the campaign for women's rights, her former lover's fiancée joins the crusade. When she finds out what her future husband, now turned politician, did to Vida, she vows to reject him. Vida, however, dissuades her, forgives her ex-lover, and even converts him to the cause.[97]

With active encouragement and criticism from Robins' friend Henry James, *Votes for Women* was accepted for production by Grenville-Baker's company and was first performed in London in April 1907.[98] Following the play's debut, the play bureau of the Actors' Alliance of America (of which Mary Shaw was a member) decided to stage the play. Under the auspices of that group, *Votes for Women* opened in New York on March 5, 1909, with Mary Shaw in the title role of Vida Lovering.[99]

Although Mary Shaw denied any propagandistic intent, saying "My interest in *Votes for Women* is purely that of an artist. I believe the psychological moment for the production of a play about woman's suffrage has arrived,"[100] the critics did not accept her disclaimers. Louis V. DeFoe wrote in the *New York World*: "It is possible that the Suffragette cause in New York will suffer rather than profit by the propagandist drama *Votes for Women*.."[101] To some, the play was guilty of a greater sin—dullness. The anonymous critic of the *New York Clipper* wrote that *Votes for Women* "doesn't gain the hearers' sympathy—it only bores insufferably."[102]

For Mary Shaw, though, the play was a stunning personal triumph; Adolph Klauber, the critic of the *New York Times*, referred to her performance as "superb."[103] Moreover, even some of the play's harshest critics were moved to point out that the second act Trafalgar Square demonstration was "tremendously interesting and effective."[104] In this scene Robins used a mass suffragist meeting at the Nelson monument as a device for portraying the various social types in the movement. For instance, a working-class suffragist announces to the listening crowd and passersby that "politics is only housekeeping on a larger scale,"[105] while a Christabel Pankhurst character named Ernestine Blunt tells them "women have had quite enough of men's chivalry and would be willing to put up with a little power instead."[106]

Despite the publicity it received and a glittering first night audience made up of many from New York's 400, *Votes for Women* closed after six performances.[107] Nevertheless, for Mary Shaw this was just one part of her attempt to use the theater to further the cause of women's rights. In fact, it marked the beginning of her own playwrighting efforts for the movement.

Actually, Mary Shaw had been writing and performing in satirical political sketches ever since the early days of the Professional Woman's League. The first sketch she wrote for the suffrage movement, "An Impressionistic Sketch of the Anti-Suffragist's," was performed at an Equal Suffrage meeting held in the Hotel Astor in January, 1912.[108] The piece concerned a group of "anti's" who meet to rehearse some of the arguments that they would give to a legislative committee, only to find themselves converting to suffrage.

A highlight of the play was the opening recitation of the "anti's pledge": "I pledge myself to remember each day, at every hour, that there are only two great moments in a woman's life, when she gives her first kiss to her lover, the second when she kisses her own little baby."[109] The play, which one critic said bristled with "bright sayings and clever arguments,"[110] also contained lines like: "A true woman cannot love unworthy women; she can only love unworthy men";[111] and "The more inferior to women men are, the greater their chivalry."[112]

Performing in the first production of the sketch was a group called the "Twenty-Fifth District Players." This group, organized by Reverend Marie Jenney Howe, leader of the Twenty-Fifth District New York Woman's Suffrage Party, consisted of both professionals and non-professionals who toured the state performing in suffrage plays.[113]

This group also performed Mary Shaw's second feminist sketch, *The Parrot Cage*. This playlet, which one critic called a "biting little satire," featured a group of parrots, each of whom espoused one of the conventional arguments against suffrage. Eventually all are converted by a suffragist parrot.[114]

These writing chores were not the only activities Mary Shaw pursued on behalf of the suffrage movement, for she also traveled around the country and spoke to women on its behalf. From her statements to groups of women and to newspapers and magazines, it becomes clear that she was a suffragist who did not see the vote as the final goal in the liberation of women. Addressing a New Orleans group she said, "I am not only a suffragist. I am a feminist, and have made up my mind that some inherent force is pushing women to a higher civilization."[115] These ideas place Shaw within that broadly defined group of suffragists whom William O'Neill has called "hard core feminists." According to O'Neill, these women placed women's rights ahead of everything else. In contrast, again using O'Neill's definition, were the "social feminist" supporters of suffrage who put social reform ahead of women's rights.[116]

Though she was no systematic political thinker, Shaw's rationale for suffrage went against the then dominant movement sentiment. As Aileen Kraditor has pointed out, from the 1890s onward the suffrage movement became more conservative, and the major arguments for the right to vote were based on "expediency" rather than the original rationale of "natural rights."[117] The "expediency" position contended that women needed the ballot in order to protect themselves and to further the cause of social reform. This argument departed from the beliefs of pioneer suffragists like Elizabeth Cady Stanton and Susan B. Anthony, who based their campaign for the vote on the "natural rights" philosophy embodied in the Declaration of Independence and the ideal of justice that they saw as inherent in a democratic society. Echoing their sentiments, Mary Shaw rejected "expediency" and based her belief in suffrage on the position that our society would never truly be just or democratic until it fulfilled principles of the Declaration of Independence:

> We argue from expediency when we ought to be brave enough to face principles, ideals. We ask if women suffrage will improve the home, the women of the world. Far reaching claims are made that it will. Raised accusations are made to show that it won't. That's all beside the point. When I hear people say that Woman's suffrage will or will not improve women, I feel the answer to both is the principle of democracy at stake must and will override expediency whatever the hazard. Woman suffrage is a part of the democratic movement, one step further toward the goal of self-government. Quite apart from expediency, its promise lies in its essential democracy.[118]

By rooting her belief in suffrage on the *a priori* grounds of natural rights, Mary Shaw saw its significance for women more in individual, psychological and moral terms than as a means for social change. As she told the *New York Sun*:

> To me the first fruits of suffrage seem to be the sustaining thought—the equality of women's value as compared with man's. We must foster the belief that what we are and stand for is of as much importance. It is

along that line that we must develop ourselves and not allow our habits of thought, our inheritance, to retard our best expression. We must search for things within ourselves, not in our environment, and not drug ourselves with formulas and compromises. Suffrage is valuable as one means of the realization of this importance. The conception of political equality is an enlightenment to many women. It is a new thought that will lead us on a great distance. With men the ballot has done wonders in increasing social and spiritual value. There is nothing like enfranchisement to bring home responsibility and the importance of the individual.[119]

Nevertheless, though these remarks are filled with a high degree of idealism, they fall short in programmatic content. When it came down to this, Mary Shaw could offer very little future prospects to women except the ideas of women as guardians of the race and of the need for solidarity. She told the New Orleans audience: "We women are the race! Men have their function, but to women is given conservation of the race. Therefore, it is time we began to take a little notice of each other."[120]

Although she came up with little specific long-term plans for women, Mary Shaw did see some very practical things women could accomplish. As she had spoken of time and time again, women had power over the theater, and she also believed that women should enter the professions in greater numbers. This prompted her and other actresses to form the Gamut Club as a haven for women of different professions.[121]

Regardless of her emphasis on women, Mary Shaw was not a man-hater; obviously, for an actress trying to gain as wide an audience as possible, such a reputation would be self-defeating. Though she criticized men particularly for their lack of appreciation of Ibsen and Shaw, she was quick to praise when the occasion warranted. On her tour in *Mrs. Warren's Profession* she recalled with pleasure her conversation with some Jesuits who called on her to discuss the play. She was also delighted by the reception she received in Los Angeles at the all-male Gamut Club: the members of the club serenaded her and made her an honorary member. So impressed was she by their treatment that she adopted the name for her own club in New York and referred to her experience with the Los Angeles club as one of "the most memorable experiences of my life."[122]

Nor was Mary Shaw alone in her profession in advocating suffrage or working strenuously on its behalf. So widespread had pro-suffrage sentiment spread in the profession that, in 1909, *Billboard* carried the headline: "Women of the Stage All Desire to Vote," and the article went on to say: "It may be only a passing fad, but woman's suffrage is just now the subject of general discussion among people of the stage. Some of them have really become worked up about it, to such an extent that at teas and after theatrical performances, it is the sole topic of conversation."[123]

More than just a tempest in a teacup and the subject of polite conversation, there was actually widespread action and public commentary on the part of actresses. Alice Fischer Harcourt, founder of the Twelfth Night Club, vowed publicly to go to Wyoming in order to vote.[124] Henrietta Crosman, one of the biggest names in the theater of the day, announced to a meeting of the William Lloyd Garrison Equal Suffrage League that she was a "militant suffragist." She also said that women should "get together an army of working women — women who work with their hands in factories and mines and sweatshops — and send them to Washington, let them storm the doors of the Capitol and demand their rights."[125]

As if heeding Crosman's call, a number of women did organize an Equal Rights Parade, but in New York instead of Washington. Marching in that parade was an actresses' division led by Fola La Follette, whose barnstorming readings of the play *How the Vote Was Won* for sixty-five straight nights was something of a suffragist and Chautauqua record.[126]

Joining their sisters on the legitimate stage were vaudeville headliners like Emma Carus and Trixie Friganza, who declared themselves to suffragists and spoke out publicly on the issue.[127] Not merely content to take these issues into the streets, newspapers, Chautauquas, and legitimate theaters, the actresses took their activities to the vaudeville theaters as well. In 1909 Hammerstein's Victoria Theater, which was the most popular and famous theater in vaudeville before the coming of the Palace, featured a "Suffragette Week."[128] Although pilloried in *Variety* as a "freak act," the actresses led by Fola La Follette spoke to audiences which even *Variety* estimated might reach 150,000.[129]

Despite the negative reviews of the suffragette shows, the idea caught hold. Percy Williams did an all-women suffragette show of his own at the Colonial Theater under the direction of Emma Carus, and Keith and Proctor followed suit with a similar attraction at their Fifth Avenue Theater.[130] In short, the arguments of the suffragists began to be heard in yet another important institution of American society.

However, before that took place, actresses had to become suffragists. Part of that process, of course, lies within the realm of the individual psyche. However, other parts were tempered by a profession that treated women as equals, and after 1890, provided them with a network of clubs and other institutions that helped to nurture these ambitions and goals.

Ultimately, these experiences encouraged Mary Shaw and other actresses to begin using their craft in the struggle for women's rights. In the long run this identification with and access to the stage gave suffragism a big boost into the mainstream of the American mind. Indeed, because of their work, by 1909 Israel Zangwill could write: "As far as feminine fascination is concerned she [the suffragist] is becoming indistinguishable from the typical actress."[131]

NOTES

1. May Irwin, "The Business of the Stage as a Career," *Cosmopolitan*, 28 (April, 1900), p. 655.

2. Alexis de Tocqueville, *Democracy in America*, edited by J. P. Mayer (Garden City, New York: Anchor Books, 1969), p. 513.

3. Robert Wiebe, *The Search for Order, 1877–1920* (New York: Hill and Wang, 1967). See also Neil Harris, ed., *Land of Contrasts, 1880–1901* (New York: George Braziller, 1970).

4. Louis M. Simon, *A History of the Actor's Fund of America* (New York: Theatre Arts Books, 1972), p. 15.

5. Ibid.

6. Ibid., pp. 16-17.

7. Ibid., p. 32.

8. Ibid., p. 44.

9. Pat Ryan, "A. M. Palmer, Producer: A Study of Management, Dramaturgy, and Stagecraft in the American Theater 1872-1896," (unpublished Ph.D. dissertation, Yale University, 1959), Chapter 1.

10. Eleanor Ruggles, *Prince of Players, Edwin Booth* (New York: W. W. Norton and Company, Inc., 1953), p. 334.

11. Gustave Kobbe, *Famous Actors and Actresses and Their Homes* (Boston: Little, Brown and Company, 1903), pp. 342-345.

12. Ibid.

13. Richard Lockridge, *Darling of Misfortune, Edwin Booth 1833–1893* (New York: Century Company, 1932), p. 231.

14. "Not a Players' Club," *New York Dramatic Mirror*, November 15, 1890, p. 3.

15. Ibid.

16. "The Twelfth Night Club," *New York Herald Tribune*, January 6, 1929, pp. 10-11, 18.

17. Ibid.

18. Karen J. Blair, "The Clubwoman as Feminist: The Woman's Culture Movement in the United States, 1868-1914, (unpublished Ph.D. dissertation, State University of New York at Buffalo, 1976), pp. 33-85. See also William L. O'Neill, *Everyone Was Brave* (New York: Quadrangle/New York Times Book Company, 1971), pp. 84-90.

19. Harriet Martineau, *Society in America* (2 vols. Paris: Baudry's European Library, 1842), II, p. 157.

20. Daniel Scott Smith coined the term "Domestic Feminism" in "Family Limitation, Sexual Control, and Domestic Feminism in Victorian America," in *Clio's Consciousness Raised*, Mary Hartman and Lois Banner, eds. (New York: Harper and Row, 1974), pp. 119-136.

21. William O'Neill coined the term "Social Feminism" in *Everyone Was Brave*, P.X.

22. "Professional Woman's League Organized," *The New York Clipper*, December 31, 1892, p. 689.

23. "Most Unique Club in the World, The Professional Woman's League, What It Does for Actresses," *Billboard*, November 11, 1909, p. 12.

24. Ibid.

25. "The Woman's Association," *New York Dramatic Mirror*, December 17, 1892, p. 5.

26. "Sorosis Was Anger-Swept," *New York Times*, May 19, 1893, p. 1. Also "Miss Crabtree's Rejection," *New York Times*, May 20, 1893, p. 1.

27. David Dempsey with Raymond P. Baldwin, *The Triumphs and Trials of Lotta Crabtree* (New York: William Morrow and Company, 1968).

28. "Club Ethics," *New York Times*, May 30, 1893, p. 4.

29. *New York Times*, May 19, 1893, p. 1.

30. *New York Times*, May 20, 1893, p. 1.

31. "Official Inaugural of the Professional Woman's League," May 29, 1893, *New York Public Library*, p. 16.

32. "Victory Bateman announces that she will bring suit against the Professional Woman's League," *New York Clipper*, December 30, 1893, p. 689.

33. *Billboard*, November 11, 1909, p. 12.

34. "An Active Organization," *New York Dramatic Mirror*, August 12, 1893, p. 12.

35. "Official Inaugural," May 29, 1893, p. 13.

36. "Miss Banks Sophomoric Plea for Woman's Rights," *New York Dramatic Mirror*, April 14, 1894, p. 13.

37. "President's Address," *Professional Woman's League, New York Annual Report*, May, 1894, pp. 12-13.

38. "Souvenir Book, Woman's Exhibition Given Under Auspices of the Professional Woman's League," October, 1902, *New York Public Library*, pp. 43-85.

39. Kate Stockton, "Woman's League Exhibition at the Garden is a Real Adamless Eden," *New York Evening Journal*, October 7, 1902, p. 12.

40. "Woman's Exhibition Opens at the Garden," *New York Times*, October 7, 1902, p. 8.

41. O'Neill, *Everyone Was Brave*, p. 167.

42. " 'Suffragettes Terribly Funny,' Says Amelia Bingham," *Cleveland Leader*, July 20, 1910, n.p. (*Locke*, 71, n.p.).

43. John D. Irving, "Mary Shaw, Actress, Suffragist, Activist (1854-1929)" (unpublished Ph.D. dissertation, Columbia University, 1978), p. VII.

44. "Gamut Club Officers Elected," *New York Times*, May 16, 1913, p. 7.

45. "For a Woman's Auxiliary," Mary Shaw letter to the *New York Dramatic Mirrror*, August 6, 1893, p. 3.

46. "The Work of the League," *New York Dramatic Mirror*, July 22, 1893, p. 2.

47. Henry Tyrell, "Mary Shaw—A Woman of Thought and Action," *Theatre* II (August, 1902), p. 21.

48. Ibid.

49. Irving, "Mary Shaw," pp. 1-35.

50. Helena Modjeska, *Memories and Impressions of Helena Modjeska: An Autobiography* (New York: The MacMillan Company, 1910).

51. Ibid., p. 463.

52. "Mirror Interviews. Mary Shaw," *New York Dramatic Mirror*, June 26, 1897, p. 2.

53. Modjeska, *Memories and Impressions*, pp. 259-559.

54. Ibid., p. 512.

55. Mary Shaw, "The Stage as a Field for Women," *New York Dramatic Mirror*, July 15, 1899, p. 15.

56. George Rowell, *The Victorian Theater: A Survey* (London: Oxford University Press, 1956), pp. 75-78.

57. Samuel M. Waxman, *Antoine and the Theatre-Libre* (New York: Benjamin Bloom, 1922). See also Cecil W. Davies, *Theatre for the People: The Story of the Volksbuhne*, (Austin: University of Texas Press, 1977).

58. Donald Nelson Koster, *The Theme of Divorce in American Drama, 1871–1939* (Philadelphia: University of Pennsylvania Press, 1942).

59. John Perry, *James A. Herne, The American Ibsen* (Chicago: Nelson-Hall, Inc., Publishers, 1978).

60. The two best biographies of Ibsen are Holvdan Koht, *Life of Ibsen* (New York: Benjamin Bloom, Inc., 1971) and Michael Meyer, *Ibsen* (New York: Doubleday and Company, 1971).

61. Koht, *Life of Ibsen*, p. 337.

62. "In Re Ibsenism," *New York Dramatic Mirror*, January 31, 1891, p. 4.

63. Irving, "Mary Shaw," p. 37.

64. William Winter, *The Wallet of Time* (2 vols. New York: Moffat, Yard and Company, 1913), II, p. 567.

65. Ibid.

66. Rowell, *The Victorian Theatre*, p. 129.

67. Irving, "Mary Shaw," pp. 36-41.

68. "Review of Ghosts," with Mary Shaw, *Denver Post*, May 12, 1903, p. 5.

69. Irving, "Mary Shaw," p. 83.

70. W. L. Hubbard, "News of the Theaters," *Review of Ghosts, Chicago Daily Tribune*, May 8, 1903, p. 5.

71. Ibid.

72. Walter Prichard Eaton, *Plays and Players: Leaves from Critic's Scrapbook* (Cincinnati: Stewart and Kidd Company, 1916), p. 306.

73. Theodora Bean, "Catching up with Mary Shaw," *Morning Telegraph*, March 25, 1917 n.p. (*Locke*, 431, p. 119-121).

74. Bernard Shaw, *The Quintessence of Ibsenism* (New York: Hill and Wang, 1962).

75. Rowell, *The Victorian Theatre*, p. 129.

76. St. John Ervine, *Bernard Shaw, His Life, Work and Friends* (London: Constable and Company, 1956). See also Archibald Henderson, *George Bernard Shaw: Man of the Century* (New York: Appleton-Century Crofts, 1956).

77. Henderson, *George Bernard Shaw*, p. 510.

78. Mary Shaw, "My 'Immoral' Play: The Story of the First American Production of 'Mrs. Warren's Profession'," *McClures*, 28 (April, 1912).

79. St. John Ervine, *Bernard Shaw*, p. 347.

80. Ibid.

81. William Winter, review of *Mrs. Warren's Profession* with Mary Shaw, New York Tribune, March 31, 1907, n.p. (*Locke*, 431, p. 39).

82. St. John Ervine, *Bernard Shaw*, p. 347.

83. Mary Shaw, "My 'Immoral' Play," p. 689.

84. Irving, "Mary Shaw," pp. 111-112.

85. Review of *Mrs. Warren's Profession*, *St. Louis Post Dispatch*, April 23, 1907, p. 12.

86. Review of *Mrs. Warren's Profession*, *Buffalo Times*, April 5, 1907, n.p. (*Locke*, 431, p. 40).

87. Colgate Baker, review of *Ghosts*, with Mary Shaw, *San Francisco Chronicle*, March 6, 1908, p. 7.

88. Mary Shaw, "My 'Immoral' Play," p. 692.

89. *Los Angeles Examiner*, March 28, 1908, n.p. (*Locke*, 431, p. 40).

90. "Mary Shaw on Ibsen's Plays," *Washington Post*, June 28, 1903.

91. *Morning Telegraph,* November 21, 1913, n.p. (*Locke*, 431, p. 106).

92. *Morning Telegraph,* May 22, 1914, n.p. (*Locke*, 431, p. 107).

93. Thomas H. Dickinson, *The Insurgent Theatre* (New York: B. W. Huebsch, 1917). See also Wisner Payne Kinne, *George Pierce Baker and The American Theater* (Cambridge: Harvard University Press, 1954).

94. Eleanor Flexner, Century of Struggle: *The Woman's Rights Movement in the United States* (New York: Atheneum, 1972), pp. 248-275.

95. Casper Names, *Politics in the American Drama* (Washington, D.C.: The Catholic University of America Press, 1960), p. 19.

96. Quoted in Rowell, *The Victorian Theatre*, p. 91.

97. Review of "Votes for Women," *New York Dramatic Mirror*, March 27, 1909, p. 3.

98. Henry James, *Theater and Friendship: Some Henry James Letters*, with commentary by Elizabeth Robins (New York: G. P. Putnam's Sons, 1932), pp. 258-264.

99. Review of "Votes for Women," *Theatre*, IX (May, 1909) n.p. (*Locke*, 431, p. 54).

100. *New York Telegram*, March 31, 1909, n.p. (*Locke*, 431, p. 50).

101. Louis V. Defoe, Review of "Votes for Women," *New York World*, March 21, 1909, n.p. (*Locke*, 431, p. 52).

102. Review of "Votes for Women," *New York Dramatic Mirror*, March 27, 1909, p. 3.

103. Adolph Klauber, "Mary Shaw Superb in 'Votes for Women,'" *New York Times*, March 16, 1909, n.p. (*Locke*, 431, p.n.p.).

104. "Suffragists' Plea in 'Votes for Women,'" *New York Herald*, March 16, 1909, n.p. (*Locke*, 431, n.p.).

105. "A Plea for Equal Suffrage," *Blue Book*, June, 1909, n.p. (*Locke*, 431, pp. 54-55).

106. Ibid.

107. "Votes for Women," *Muncey's* (May, 1909), n.p. (*Locke*, 431, p. 54).

108. Review of "An Impressionistic Sketch of the Anti-Suffragist," *New York Herald*, January 16, 1912, n.p. (*Locke*, 431, n.p.).

109. Ibid.

110. *New York Herald*, January 6, 1912, n.p. (*Locke*, 431, p. 96).

111. Ibid.

112. Ibid.

113. "Suffragette Stock Players," *Toledo News Blade*, February 13, 1913.

114. *Morning Telegraph*, January 25, 1913, n.p. (*Locke*, 431, p. 104).

115. *New Orleans States*, November 7, 1915, n.p. (*Locke*, 431, p. 104).

116. O'Neil, *Everyone Was Brave*, p. x.

117. Aileen Kraditor, *The Ideas of the Woman Suffrage Movement, 1890–1920* (Garden City, New York: Anchor Books, 1971), pp. 38-63.

118. Rose Young, "Suffrage as Seen by Mary Shaw," *Harpers Weekly* (May, 1915), p. 456.

119. *New York Sun*, Octrober 17, 1912, n.p. (*Locke*, 431, p. 104).

120. *New Orleans States*, October 2, 1904, n.p. (*Locke*, 531, p. 115).

121. "Actresses to Have a Club," *New York Times*, May 15, 1913, p. 11.

122. Mary Shaw, "My 'Immoral' Play," p. 694.

123. "Women of the Stage All Desire to Vote," *Billboard*, November 6, 1909, p. 5.

124. "Alice Fischer Unable to Vote," *New York Review*, October 31, 1909, n.p. (*Locke*, 200, p. 92).

125. "Miss Henrietta Crosman Calls Herself 'Militant Suffragist'," *New York Telegram*, October 8, 1910, p. 42.

126. Fola La Follette, "Suffragetting on the Chautauqua," *Ladies Home Journal*, 40, January, 1916, pp. 27, 51.

127. "Trixie Friganza a Suffragette," *Morning Telegraph*, October 27, 1908, n.p. (*Locke*, 220, p. 48).

128. "'The Suffragette Week' Drawing Down No Salary," *Variety*, August 30, 1912, p. 4.

129. Ibid.

130. "Suffragette Bill at 5th Ave. Theatre," *Billboard*, January 6, 1912, p. 11.

131. Israel Zangwill, "Actress Versus Suffraget," *Independent* LXV, December, 1909, p. 1248.

Chapter 6

Lillian Russell: "The American Beauty" as Feminist

riting about the suffragists in 1909, Israel Zangwill said, "The typical suffraget is, even in the popular imagination, no longer the unsexed virago, the unhusbanded surplus, the spectacled bluestocking. Manliness does not go with militancy. Alike on the posters and in the cartoons the suffraget is now a young and pretty girl."[1]

Zangwill's sanguine statement is very different from some earlier thoughts expressed by the British suffragist Mrs. Sarah Grand. A novelist and (according to some historians) author of the phrase "the New Woman,"[2] Mrs. Grand remarked that the vote would have been gained earlier if the suffragists had paid more attention to their appearance and if they had not been so physically "unprepossessing."[3] "If you only saw the harridans, their dress, and their manners, who are agitating for the suffrage, it would be enough. If women are to look like that when they get the suffrage, then defend me from it."[4]

The gap between Zangwill's and Grand's statements indicates just how much the image of the suffragist had changed by the beginning of the twentieth century. The new generation of suffragists came from middle- and upper-class homes and had the manners and appearance that their foremothers did not so much lack as failed to cultivate in their scorn for what they perceived as another element in the oppression of women.[5] Moreover, the adherence of such widely acknowledged beauties as Lillian Russell, Inez Milholland, and Portia Willis to the cause of suffragism obviously helped to change the nineteenth century stereotype.[6]

While a few might have still disputed Zangwill, even these naysayers were probably silenced when Lillian Russell said:

> I am surprised that any American woman should raise a voice against equal enfranchisement, for is it not the fundamental and elementary principle of our boasted democracy based upon the belief that taxation without representation is tyranny? Frankly and firmly, I am not a militant suffragette, nor are most women of intelligence and refinement,

but women believe that the time has come and some drastic action is necessary to awaken the men to the justice and seriousness of our demand.[7]

Indeed, in view of the fact that "the American beauty" had joined their ranks, who could henceforth dare depict the suffragist as a dowdy termagant or condemn feminism for making women mannish?

From the 1890s to her death, Lillian Russell *was* "the American beauty." Though newer styles and fashions in beauty might result in momentary acclaim for women like Anna Held, Edna Wallace-Hopper, and Maxine Elliot,[8] all of whom gained wealth and celebrity, none ever challenged her right to bear that title or equalled her longevity as a star.

Even as she grew older, Lillian Russell's beauty could still draw rapturous praise. After seeing her in the role of Lady Teazle in the 1905 musical version of *School for Scandal*, the New York Journal's drama critic Alan Dale exclaimed: "The point of it was that this was no new beauty, no suddenly discovered prodigality of charm, no novelty of loveliness called from the ranks of youth. This picture that took hold of the eyes and made them wince was none other than—Lillian Russell."[9]

If Lillian Russell at 44 could stir such paeans, it does not seem surprising that, in her heyday, many young men would literally do anything just for a glimpse of her. Novelist Clarence Day (*Life With Father*) remembered how he became an unpaid extra one night during his undergraduate days in New Haven to see her up close.[10] Nor was this attraction confined to men. Although still a young girl, future vaudeville headliner Irene Franklin remembered waiting at her hotel window a whole day just to see Lillian pass and then recalled her many years later as "all the blue-eyed fairy princesses I had ever read about."[11]

Lillian's special fascination lent significance to whatever product, invention, event, idea, or cause she espoused. Her name on cigars and toiletries gave them a special aura. The Columbian Exhibition of 1893 and the first long distance telephone call were incomplete without her attendance or participation, while Thomas A. Edison rushed to record her voice on the newly invented phonograph.[12] Ultimately, this exaltation gave the causes she supported (like exercise for women and, eventually, woman's suffrage) a legitimacy that no other woman could provide, for she made the role of "the American beauty" one that not only carried with it glamour, but also a measure of influence—even power.

The "airy, fairy, Lillian,"[13] as she was called, was born on December 4, 1861, and actually grew up as the "airy, fairy, Nellie," or Helen Louise Leonard, the fifth and youngest daughter of Cynthia Hicks Leonard and Charles Egbert Leonard.[14] Though a child of the middle border, her parents hardly fit the conventional mid-American image. Her mother, Cynthia, was a feminist, suffragist, and a socialist who ran for mayor of New York in 1884.[15] Her father was a publisher and issued the works of the nineteenth century agnostic Col. Robert Ingersoll, whose name was either hissed, whispered, or used as a swear word in American homes.[16]

Lillian always considered her mother her strongest influence. In her memoirs she wrote, "All that we ever became we owe her."[17] Needless to say, the tough, independent Cynthia was an active force throughout Lillian's life. A family anecdote even had her refusing to stay home from church choir practice the day Lillian was born.

The strong-willed Cynthia, who traced her ancestry back to the Pilgrim John Howland,[18] was born outside an Indian reservation near Buffalo, New York. Even before her marriage to Charles Leonard, she became the first woman salesperson to stand behind a counter and a member of Buffalo's first woman's club. In 1852, she married Charles Leonard, who then worked for the *Buffalo Express*. Shortly thereafter they moved to Detroit, and then, in 1856, to Clinton, Iowa, where Leonard began publishing the weekly *Herald*.

Though nurturing a family of five, Cynthia Leonard took time out to nurse wounded Civil War soldiers and became a member of the Sanitary Commission. At her urging in 1863, Charles Leonard sold the *Herald*, and the family moved to Chicago. There Cynthia threw herself into feminist organizing and charitable work. She became a member of Chicago Sorosis and formed a group of women who met at a local ice cream parlor known as the Maison Doree. Supported by these women and some men, she launched a campaign to prevent the Chicago Common Council from licensing prostitutes, and, after the 1871 fire, she worked to establish a home for them. In addition, she also found the time to write two novels, *Lena Rouden, A Rebel Spy* and *Falling Footprints, or The Last of the League of the Iroquois*.[19]

During this period, Helen Louise (nicknamed "Nellie" by her father) grew from a tomboy who liked to swing on trees and pick fights with the local boys in order to prove that women are the equal of men, into a beauty who, at 15, already turned heads. She had a lovely singing voice which provoked the nuns at her school—the Sacred Heart Academy—to warn her parents that "Nellie is talented, dangerously talented; she will require careful watching."[20]

This hardly swayed her parents, who actually encouraged Helen Louise's acting ambitions. After seeing her first opera, *Mignon*, she became convinced she would become an opera star. Shortly thereafter, she made her amateur debut in a pupils' concert at Chicago's Kimball Hall, singing Arthur Sullivan's "Let Me Dream Again" and the aria "Hast Thou E'er Seen the Land" from *Mignon*. Ostensibly to develop this talent, Mrs. Leonard separated from her husband and moved to New York with Helen

Louise and her daughter Susan so that Nellie could study with Leopold Damrosch (father of Walter). However, Cynthia's agenda also included an increasing activism in the cause of suffrage.[21]

Mrs. Leonard and Susan B. Anthony were close friends, the latter staying with the Leonards whenever she was in Chicago.[22] The connection deepened Mrs. Leonard's commitment to the movement, and she ultimately remarked:

> Oh, unholy, grasping power loving man! How long will you continue in your blindness? For more than two hundred years my ancestors have been in America—I had two grandfathers in the Revolutionary Army yet I am not a full fledged citizen. Why? Because man chooses to disinherit me. Because he loves to tyrannize over me. Because (alone) he is incapable to administer justice. Verily men are bringing upon themselves and upon us the flood of Noah, the destruction of Jerusalem. Truly masculine rule is a total failure, your might is not right.[23]

There is no record of Charles Leonard's comments on this or his objecting to their separation; nor is there much information on his background. Nevertheless, this does not mean that his influence on Helen Louise was negligible. Indeed, she owed him that part of her personality which her friends described as easy-going.

Helen Louise was her father's pet, and it was he who nicknamed her "airy, fairy, Nellie,"[24] a name which she kept with one minor alteration throughout her life. Moreover, not for lack of love of his children did he let the hard-driving Cynthia have her way. In fact Marie Dressler, one of Lillian's best friends, points out in her memoirs that he would ride all night by train in later years just to see her perform.[25] His death caused the usually unruffled Lillian one of the seemingly few moral conflicts in her life. This occurred while she was on tour, and for her to attend his funeral meant closing the show and throwing a large number of people out of work. Despite the emotional turmoil it caused her, Lillian decided to continue the tour, because, as she saw it, too many were dependent on her for their livelihood. Although the newspapers excoriated her, she explained that he would have understood.[26]

Needless to say, Lillian's life and personality combined the strong-willed, independent attitudes of her mother with the easy-going, sentimental nature of her father. On one hand, Lillian was very aware of her own best interests and could drive a hard bargain with managers. For instance, impresario Rudolph Aronson of the Casino Theater (where Lillian scored some of the major triumphs of her career) wanted to sign a yearly contract with Lillian for what he saw as a reasonable increase. However, after what he described as a "slight disagreement,"[27] Lillian came by, he assumed, to sign her contract. Instead, she informed him that she had signed with another manager for a larger salary and a percentage of the profits.[28]

On the other hand, Lillian's conduct with friends, fellow actors and actresses, stage hands, and theatrical employees was described as saintly.[29] On one occasion, Lillian's maid, whose job included delivering her mistress's pay envelope, was arrested for helping herself to a little bit of her employer's salary. When told that the maid was putting aside the money for her old age, Lillian refused to press charges and only wondered why the woman had not come to her and told her about it.[30]

Lillian's life style also manifested these contrasting traits of firmness and indulgence, and her sybaritic tastes made her one of the major figures upon whom the "gilded ages" reputation for excess is based. The newspapers unashamedly reported the prices of her gowns, the splendor of her jewelry collection, and the lavishness of her home, while her Chinese porcelain collection was even reported to be the envy of J. P. Morgan.[31] Lillian's relationship with Diamond Jim Brady especially enhanced her reputation for extravagance as Brady's stock and trade was his personal display of diamonds and his championship gastronomic exploits (which Lillian matched forkful for forkful).[32]

Nevertheless, Lillian's luxury-loving, self-indulgent side was balanced by a spartan sense of self-discipline which she employed to maintain her health, figure and beauty, and it is this which accounts for her professional longevity. During one of her frequent periods of stringent dieting, her weight dropped from 186 pounds to 158 pounds, her waist measurement from 27 inches to 22 inches, and her chest measurement from 42 to 38 inches.[33] She accomplished this by a regimen that included bike riding, jogging, tennis, turkish baths, massages, and gymnasium workouts. Her schedule prompted her brother-in-law Fred Ross to comment, "Not many girls, aspirants for stage honors, would be willing to gain success at the cost of so much time, perseverance and physical endurance as is exhibited by Lillian Russell."[34]

Lillian was intense about anything she became interested or involved in. After joining the Professional Woman's League, she figured prominently in its activities, participating in bazaars and fund-raising shows, while extolling its good works to whomever would listen. Her rewards were election as a club officer for many years and selection as the most popular actress at the 1902 Professional Woman's League exhibition at Madison Square Garden.[35]

In fact, Lillian often became so actively involved in an issue or project that she lost sight of other realities. At one point in her career, she was very interested in both Christian Science and the Stoic philosopher Marcus Aurelius. These ideas began to creep into her interviews and the column on beauty, diet and health hints she wrote for the *Chicago Tribune*. Her thesis embodied such epigrams as "I believe that a beautiful physique must contain a broad mind and a sweet spirit of charity"[36] — all of which prompted her exasperated editor to wire, "Write less about soul and more about pimples."[37]

Despite these intellectual interests and commitments, the easygoing side of her nature often exposed Lillian to public criticism and ridicule. In most instances, this revolved around her misadventures with men, primarily those she married. After a youthful marriage to a much older musician and conductor which floundered quickly because of conflicting careers and the death of their infant son, she married the composer Edward "Teddy" Solomon. Following their elopement to England, a brief period in near poverty, and the birth of a daughter, she discovered that Solomon had another wife whom he had never told her about nor legally disposed of. To annul the marriage took all the skill of the notorious nineteenth century lawyer Abe Hummel.[38]

However, it was her third marriage to the tenor Signor Giovanni Perugini (John Chatterton) that made Lillian a laughing stock and the butt of coarse jokes. They met while appearing together in the comic opera *The Princess Nicotine*. Despite onstage shows of passion, Perugini's interest in Lillian was more connected with advancing his own career than with romantic feelings toward her. Concerning their wedding night (most of which Lillian spent playing cards with friends), rumor had it that he refused to sleep with her because he did not want to defile her.[39]

Within a few months their relationship became so hostile that Lillian refused to be alone with him. When they sang on stage together he reportedly said nasty things to her, later spreading vile rumors about her to the press and public. According to Marie Dressler, who appeared with them in the production, so low was his conduct that one evening after overhearing him say something particularly terrible to Lillian, she vowed to brain him with a stage brace if she ever heard him repeat it again.[40]

Lillian and Perugini separated and were later divorced, though not before the newspapers had a field day, even parodying the title of Lillian's comic opera *The Queen of Brilliants* by referring to her as "The Queen of Divorces."[41] Nor were Lillian's friends reticent about her lamentable luck with men. "Aunt Louisa" Eldridge, a venerable old actress and a fellow member of the Professional Woman's League, perhaps summed their slightly amused feelings about Lillian's marital escapades when she remarked after hearing of Lillian's marriage to Perugini: "Good Lord! Just think of it! Her first husband was an orchestra conductor named Braham; her second was Teddy Solomon, the opera composer, and now she has gone and married a tenor singer. If she only keeps divorcing and remarrying, and can get a basso, she will have her own opera outfit complete."[42]

The dichotomy between a woman who was privately known to be intelligent, generous, and gracious with a public image of conspicuous consumption tainted by hints of libertinism was hardly unique and was, in many ways, symbolic of a society and an era noted for even more glaring cultural and economic polarities. These contradictions were not only evidenced by the life style of Lillian Russell, but were also pointed out by American social critics and by visitors to this country in the latter half of the nineteenth century.

One observer, the Englishman James F. Muirhead, who first came to the United States in 1893 to prepare a Baedecker volume for the Columbian Exposition of 1893, also wrote another report of his travels, aptly titled *The Land of Contrasts*.[43] Although not gifted with the political and social insight of his fellow countryman Lord Bryce, his account did show a singular ability to pick out the picturesque detail in daily life that illuminated some of the ambiguities of American society.

Muirhead's anecdotes often shed light on the equivocal nature of American egalitarianism. Thus, while at one moment a porter refers to him and a friend as "you fellows," almost within the same breath the porter says, "The other *gentleman*" will take care of their baggage."[44] He pointed out, too, the irony inherent in a society where the commercial buildings towered above the church steeples. These insights were magnified by the responses of a people who liked to think of themselves as "calling a spade a spade," but blushed when Muirhead somehow incautiously mentioned the temperature of his morning tub.[45]

In addition, Muirhead's keen eye discerned the vivid detail that evoked some of the contradictions in a society which had recently undergone rapid and intense economic, social and cultural change. One of the most perceptive of these vignettes was his description of being whisked from New York to Buffalo on a train going sixty miles an hour, as compared to a California whistlestop tour he made where the engineer shot rabbits from the locomotive and the fireman had the time to jump off the train, pick them up, and still catch the baggage car.[46]

On a deeper level, Muirhead's zany contrasts reflected a society of even more fundamental gaps. Politically, the basic principles of the United States proclaimed equality, yet some states barred Blacks from voting, women were allowed to vote in only three, and a policy of ruthless extermination had been carried out against her Indian population. Culturally, she had hoped to define the democratic spirit but drove some of her leading intellectuals into self-imposed exile or despair. Economically, her promise of boundless opportunity was frequently interrupted by panics, recessions, and depressions, and the individual entrepreneurial zeal, for which she was justly famed, slackened in the face of the growth of huge corporate trusts. Finally, huge fortunes existed side by side with grinding poverty, and the upper class, which called itself the 400, gave lavish balls, while blocks away people literally starved, and elsewhere Pinkertons and National Guardsmen gunned down unarmed workers.[47]

While it hadn't dimmed the essential optimism of the era, the widening gap between rhetoric and reality, promise and performance, and rich and poor fostered disillusion, alienation, and, in some instances, class warfare. This latter problem manifested itself in strikes, the formation of labor unions, and class violence which convinced many Americans that the country was gripped by its severest crisis since the Civil War. People felt that America was at some kind of turning point, and, for those who needed to fix responsibility but refused to look for its source in the economic and social system, the blame fell increasingly on the immigrant and those regarded as his offshoots—the trade unionist, the political bosses, and the radical.[48] Writing in the *Atlantic Monthly*, the Presbyterian clergyman John Denison described the struggle as one between "the lingering type of American and the alien element that surrounds us."[49]

Others not only wrote about this phenomenon they felt was degrading and undermining the American character, but also organized mass movements to protect "the American way" from immigrant deluge. One of these groups (the largest and most influential of the period) found its inspiration and its guiding light in Lillian's home town of Clinton, Iowa, and indirectly provided the impetus for her career.

The organization was the American Protective Association, founded by Henry F. Bowers. Bowers grew up in straitened and despairing circumstances in Maryland. In 1850, he moved to the vicinity of Clinton, Iowa, to take up farming. When his farm failed he got a job as a court official in Clinton and worked there until he passed the bar in 1877. Although there is no direct evidence that he knew the Leonards, it is an ironic twist of fate (in view of Lillian's later symbolic stature and some of her subsequent political opinions) which places them both in the same small town at the same time.

In his youth Bowers became interested in the ideas of the anti-Catholic Know Nothing Party which was strongly represented in his native Baltimore. In 1887, after a close friend lost the Clinton mayoralty election due to the influence of Irish workers affiliated with the Knights of Labor, Bowers and eight others joined forces to organize and promote the semi-secret American Protective Association, whose goals were to thwart Catholics economically and exclude them from American politics. By 1896, the A.P.A. claimed a membership of at least a million throughout much of the West and mid-West, becoming the largest anti-immigrant organization in America between the demise of the Know Nothings and the revival of the Ku Klux Klan.[50]

However, splits among A.P.A. leaders and the economic upturn after 1897 undermined its power and prestige.[51] Nonetheless, the growth and influence of the A.P.A. did indicate a strong desire to find scapegoats for the disruptions in American society in the 1880s and 1890s. Nor did that search end with the eclipse of the A.P.A. In fact, more significant for Lillian Russell than Bowers's mere propinquity was that leadership in the anti-immigrant movement passed from the hands of the working-class-lower-middle-class A.P.A. into the grip of an elite group of New England Brahmins. This group shifted the anti-immigrant rationale from the A.P.A.'s crude and almost archaic obsessions with Popish plots to a more intellectually sophisticated notion of an Anglo-Saxon cult backed up by social Darwinist racial ideas.[52]

In 1894, Prescott Hall, Robert De Courcey Ward and others set up the Immigrant Restriction League, whose immediate goal was passage of congressional legislation to curtail mass immigration. These men were influenced by the thoughts of people like Henry Cabot Lodge and Barrett Wendall, who feared that the new immigrants, strengthened by the power of universal manhood suffrage, would soon inundate the sturdy values and institutions of American society which they nostalgically associated with early New England.[53]

Complementing their romanticization of Old New England was an equal idealization of its historic political roots in Old English traditions, values and institutions. Their ideas were bolstered by the historical research of scholars like Edward A. Freeman, James K. Hosmer, and Herbert Baxter Adams, who believed that American democracy originated in the New England town meeting and could be traced from there to the Teutonic tribes of ancient Germany.[54]

This background, they felt, made the Anglo-Saxons uniquely well qualified to carry the seeds of democracy, and also made their continued dominance of America essential if democracy was to persist. Nor was this authority seen as limited to North America. Some believed that it was merely a prelude to a greater destiny.

Perhaps the best exponent and keenest expression of these ideas came from the Immigrant Restriction League's honorary president, John Fiske. Even before the birth of the League, Fiske stated his grandiose vision of the role of the Anglo-Saxon. In a series of lectures delivered in London in 1885, and then collected under the title *American Political Ideas*, he said:

> The work which the English speaking race began when it colonized North America is destined to go on until every land on the earth's surface that is not already the seat of an old civilization shall become English in its language, in its political habits and traditions and to a predominant extent in the blood of its people. The day is at hand when four fifths of the human race will trace its pedigree to English forefathers, as four fifths of the white people in the United States trace their pedigree today.[55]

Adding intellectual weight to the Anglo-Saxonphiles and their belief in a special American destiny were the new developments in science, particularly the work of biologist Charles Darwin. Although Darwin was himself no racist, the title and some of the implications of his work, *The Origin of the Species: The Preservation of Favored Races in the Struggle for Existence*, lent itself to that interpretation as did his ideas on the survival of the fittest. These ideas struck an especially responsive chord with those who believed in a special Anglo-Saxon mission.[56]

Among the most popular advocates of this position was the Congregational minister and missionary Dr. Josiah Strong. Strong was terrified by the changes that had taken place in American society as a result of industrialization and urbanization.[57] Nevertheless, he still retained his positive faith in the future of the Anglo-Saxon race. He set out these ideas in his widely read 1885 book, *Our Country: Its Possible Future and Its Present Crisis,* in which he envisioned Anglo-Saxon world expansion as the possible solution to America's problems: "If I do not read amiss, this powerful race [the Anglo-Saxon] will move down upon Mexico, down upon Central America and South America, out upon the islands of the sea, over upon Africa and beyond and can anyone doubt that the result of this competition will be the 'survival of the fittest.' "[58]

Strong's beliefs were strengthened by Darwinism, which added to the Anglo-Saxon canon the faith that the North American was in the process of becoming a superior physical being. He wrote, "The higher civilization of the future will not lack an adequate physical basis in the people of the United States."[59]

Other thinkers like Francis Amasa Walker concluded that this change was already in progress. Walker wrote:

> The climate of the United States has been benign enough to enable us to take the English short horn and greatly improve it . . . to take the English race horse and to improve him . . . to take the English man and improve him, adding agility to his strength, and making his eye keener and his hand steadier, so that in rowing, in riding, and in boxing, the American of pure English stock is today the better animal.[60]

Ultimately, Walker's boast came to include the American woman and her unequalled beauty as well. As dress reformer Frances L. Smith noted in her 1885 book, "America is justly styled the land of beauty. No race of men surpass our stalwart sons; no maidens are fairer; in no country is beauty more lasting."[61]

Eventually, these rather abstract affirmations of American racial and physical superiority led to a search for concrete examples of that ascendancy. Just as John D. Rockefeller sought confirmation of the superiority of American business in the metaphoric example of the influence of natural selection on the American Beauty rose, similarly late nineteenth century America found proof of the primacy of its feminine beauty in Lillian Russell (whose emblem *was* the American Beauty rose).[62]

The role of symbolic national beauty was not anything that Lillian craved, nor was its acquisition well planned or gained overnight. In fact, on coming to New York with her mother and sister Susie, Helen Louise settled in for her operatic studies with Professor Damrosch, who was quite lavish in his praise of her potential. However, desiring some stage experience, she secured a job in the chorus of E. E. Rice's production of *H.M.S. Pinafore.*

Shortly thereafter, Tony Pastor overhead Lillian singing at a friend's house, and he invited her to appear at his variety house. Intrigued by the offer of $15 per week and the loan of $50 for a new dress, Helen Louise accepted the job. Not wanting her mama to know of her escapade, she chose the stage name of Lillian Russell, because, as she put it, the numerous L's made it sound musical.[63]

In contrast to the seeming frivolity of her choice of names, there was not anything superficial in Pastor's decision to bill Helen Louise as "Lillian Russell, the English Ballad Singer" at her November 22, 1880 debut, for Pastor was noted for his keen feeling for show business trends. Indeed, Pastor's sensitivity extended into political and social spheres as well, and he composed topical songs and stories, some of which (like the "Alabama Claims" and "Civil Service") were as well known as the issues they addressed. One of his tunes, "What's the Matter with Hewitt"—to which the orchestra replied, "He's All-Right"—was a major factor in the election of that rich merchant as Mayor of New York.[64]

Pastor's sense of an Anglo-Saxon trend and his attempt to fit Lillian into it is apparent in Lillian's own reminiscences. Writing about Pastor's choice of billings, she noted: "I wore my hair in a braid with a bow in the back and it created the effect Mr. Pastor desired when he billed me as 'Lillian Russell, the English Ballad Singer.' I suppose he called me English because English stage people were popular in America at the time."[65]

Pastor knew that Lillian was a perfect physical example of what was generally perceived to be Anglo-Saxon beauty, a beauty typified, according to one specialist, by someone:

> tall, fair and strongly built. Her skin is of dazzling freshness; her features are small and elegantly formed; the oval of her face is marked somewhat heavy toward the lower portion; her hair is fine and silky and charming; and her long and graceful neck imparts to the movements of her head a character of grace and pride.[66]

How closely Lillian answered this description can be seen from her photos of the period or in the words of comedian James T. Powers, who described the 18-year-old Lillian as:

a beautiful blond, graceful, tall and elegant, with the figure of a Venus de Milo and a complexion between a water lily and a rose. Had I the poetic soul of a Browning or a Poe combined I might give a true description of her. To me she looked as if she had flown to us from a fairy conservatory on the back of a butterfly; her eyelashes were about a quarter of an inch long and her neck would have made a robin jealous.[67]

This identification with the Anglo-Saxon was also strengthened by Lillian's initial successes in a number of Gilbert and Sullivan operettas. She appeared as Mabel in Pastor's burlesque version of *The Pirates of Penzance* and in the title role of the first New York performance of *Patience*.[68]

Her career launched by the equation of Anglo-Saxon beauty and art and reviews that called her voice "pure" and "fresh,"[69] Lillian soon found herself well on the way to becoming a national sensation and a source of national pride. Reviewing her performance in Audran's *The Snake Charmer*, *The Dramatic Mirror* said, "There is nothing to compare with her in this country. Paris will have to beg manager McCaull if D'Jemma [Lillian's role in the comic opera] is ever to be ideally represented there."[70]

Lillian's cynosure as a national treasure may have even been enhanced by her elopement to England. In fact, negative reviews of her London performances only seemed to increase the devotion of her American audiences. The *Spirit of the Times* wrote upon receiving word of her notices:

> The London critics like her voice and her pretty face; but objected to her figure, and thought she lacked distinction of manner. We do not need to be informed that Miss Russell can sing and if she be not the figure for London there is plenty of room for her in New York and Boston, in both of which cities she had unfulfilled engagements. Send her home and let Miss St. John [a British prima donna], who has a figure and is very distinguished reign in London without rival.[71]

While this might be viewed as just another example of extreme sensitivity to British criticism, it nevertheless did not hurt Lillian's image to be so closely identified with America's artistic self-esteem. Nor, for that matter, did she suffer by her involvement in comic opera, especially when that form of entertainment grew popular with the upper middle class.[72] This group's views on nationalism, Anglo-Saxon destiny, and art are probably best summarized by Henry James's satiric comment in *Roderick Hudson*: "We were the biggest people and we ought to have the biggest conceptions. The biggest conceptions, of course, will bring forth in time the biggest performances."[73]

For upper middle class Americans who had never attended the theater because of clerical warnings about its depravity, the comic opera represented a good transition from total abstinence to casual participation. Comic opera partook of the high esteem with which grand opera was held in this country.[74] (Respect for opera produced wild acclaim for Jenny Lind in the first half of the century and prompted theatrical managers of minstrelsy and burlesque to call their theaters "opera houses.")[75] Based on pricking the aristocratic pretensions of grand opera, comic opera appealed to the American sense of egalitarianism. Thus, the American musical theater, which grew out of the successes of *The Black Crook* and *Lydia Thompson's British Blondes*, became a national mania with the arrival of the works of Gilbert and Sullivan in the late 1870s and provided the perfect source for the creation of national idols.[76]

Moreover, audience enthusiasm also produced the creation of a high temple of American comic opera, Rudolph Aronson's Casino Theater. Six years in the building, the Casino not only catered to the American upper middle class's desire for entertainment, but also fed their appetite for luxury and lavish spectacle. Its chorus girls were purportedly the loveliest in the world, its productions even included elephants, its board of directors comprised men like J. P. Morgan and Chauncey Depew, and its often glittering first night audiences were made up of celebrities like General William T. Sherman, Mark Twain, and others.[77] For Lillian, who joined the company in 1890, the Casino was a key element in her progress to the rank of "Queen of Comic Opera"[78] and the role of the archetypal American beauty. As the *New York Dramatic News* wrote within a year of her arrival at the Casino: "Lillian Russell easily stands at the head of all the prime donne of the English speaking stage, here and elsewhere. Miss Russell is without peer on the American stage at the present moment, and she is in this country supreme."[70]

Lillian's success in comic operas like Offenbach's antimilitarist, anti-Bismarckian satire *The Grand Duchess of Gerolstein* (in which she set the Casino box office record)[80] confirmed the hold of comic opera on the upper class audience. In addition, she endeared herself to her audience's nationalist sentiments by saying, for example, "American—I should say so. I'm American clear through."[81] Newspapers frequently referred to her as "that American beauty,"[82] and this even gained quasi-eugenic acceptance at the Columbian Exposition of 1893 when showman Florenz Zeigfield spread rumors of the engagement of "The American beauty" Miss Lillian Russell to his protege Eugene Sandow, "The World's Strongest Man."[83]

Lillian's sobriquet soon gained even more widespread acknowledgment when she starred in the 1896 Gustave Kerker comic opera *An American Beauty*. Though the escapades of the title character Gabrielle Chalmont should not detain anyone other than the most enthusiastic collectors of comic opera plots,[84] its program notes are a good example of her growing reputation:

> It would have been a dangerous piece of presumption for any other woman than Lillian Russell to present herself in the title role of an opera having the name "An American Beauty." But it has been so universally acknowledged that Miss Russell is physically magnificent that the public will never think of questioning the taste of the manager in [sic] christening the new piece in which she is now appearing. Just as Cleopatra was an indisputable Egyptian beauty, so Lillian Russell is a self evident example of American loveliness in its most beautiful form and it's natural to speak of her graces as it is to acknowledge the perfume of the rose. The title "An American Beauty" is most well chosen.[85]

Other critics concurred. The *Illustrated American* commented:

> There would I think have been resentment at anyone else who had the temerity to put herself forward in large type and enormous posters as "an American Beauty." But with Miss Russell her claim to physical attractiveness is so generally admitted that her position is unassailable. There are those of course, who have preferences in other directions when it comes to female beauty. They may prefer theirs darker, or slighter, or more willowy, or shorter or taller. But any such predilection is a personal matter, after all everyone acknowledges Miss Russell a beauty and a rare one at that.[86]

The frequency with which her name was associated in rivalries with other national beauties further underscored Lillian's prominence as a symbol of national beauty. One contest (primarily promoted by the newspapers) pitted her against an English rival, the equally beauteous Lilly Langtry. When the two did meet, rather than setting off an international incident, they passed the time playing a friendly round of poker. Nonetheless, the competition could become lethal. In another incident, an American cowboy shot his Spanish counterpart when he dared speak slightingly of Miss Russell's charms in comparison with his own favorite, Lola Montez (whom he mistakenly assumed to be Spanish).[87]

Lillian's reputation did not diminish when she deserted comic opera for the Weber and Field's burlesque company in 1899, a move which was prompted by the decline of her voice and the rather lucrative $3,000 a week salary offered by the two comedians. However, in quitting comic opera and becoming a member of the Weberfieldians, she surrounded herself with luminous artists like David Warfield, Faye Templeton, De Wolf Hopper, and Sam Bernard, and she kept pace with her middle class audience which had moved from comic operas to vaudeville and burlesque. Her celebrity, in fact, was so enhanced by her stay with Weber and Fields that her songs became enormous popular hits and she herself became something of a national institution.[88] The *Morning Telegraph* wrote in 1900: "The beauty of Lillian Russell is as much an institution as Niagara Falls or the Brooklyn Bridge. There is a national flavour about it that is emphatically American. And few of us would admit that America takes second rank with any nation in the matter of beauty."[89]

The equation of American nationalism with the beauty of its women was not new. What was new, however, was the widespread interest in the whole question of national beauty, its embodiment in one woman, and her use of that role as a source of influence.

Even from the early days of the Republic its citizens boasted about the beauty of American women. In one probably apochryphal, although illuminating, anecdote, an English diplomat supposedly commented to an American government official from Connecticut, "Your countrywoman, Mr. Wolcott, would be admired even at St. James," to which the Connecticut Yankee promptly replied, "She is even admired on Litchfield Hill."[90]

The beauty of American women was attested to by some of the nation's severest critics. Mrs. Trollope wrote:

> We attended mass in this church the Sunday after our arrival [in Baltimore] and I was perfectly astonished at the beauty and splendid appearance of the ladies who filled it. Excepting on a very brilliant Sunday at the Tuilleries, I never saw so showy a display of morning costume, and I think I never saw anywhere so many beautiful women at one glance. They all appeared to be in full dress and were really beautiful.[91]

Jacques Offenbach, a veteran of strolls in the Tuilleries, concurred and noted on a visit to this country in 1870: "One must admit that there probably exist no more seductive women in the world than the Americans. In the first place, many more of them are beautiful than in Paris—of one hundred women passing by ninety are ravishing."[92]

Lacking a central hub such as London and its season which united the political and social world,[93] American beauties Betsy Patterson Bonaparte, Theodosia Burr, Peggy Eaton, and Emilie Shoumburg never achieved more than provincial recognition or the approbation of their social peers.[94] Moreover, even the American stage, which numbered among its attractions actress Mary Anderson (who one critic called "the champion beauty of the world")[95], failed to provide a claimant for the title of "The American beauty."

Nevertheless, from the 1870s onward, there was an intense interest in finding a living embodiment of beauty. One of the earliest attempts was circus entrepreneur Adam Forepaugh's 1879 nationwide search that offered a $10,000 prize for the most beautiful girl in America.[96] In addition, as the French novelist Paul Bourget recalled:

> There are two or three [beauties] in every city, and their supremacy is so
> well recognized that you are continually receiving invitations as "Pray
> come to tea tomorrow afternoon to meet Miss _____ the Rich-
> mond beauty." I say Richmond at random; in its place put Savannah,
> Charleston, Albany, Providence, any city north or south that you please.
> Once recognized though she may be no more than twenty years old, she
> enters upon a sort of official almost civic existence. She is, in fact, a
> social actress and a champion of her order, like a master of billiards or
> chess. Let us be more ambitious — like a pugilist — like James Corbett of
> California.[97]

Simultaneous with the attempt to find a national beauty and the
emergence of beautiful women as public symbols was an effort to define
its American essence. And, if as one magazine put it, "Beauty is a result of
race, of circumstances such as personal freedom and mode of life,"[98] then
Americans felt they had just cause for optimism. From the turn of the
century on, as economic and social stability returned and confidence
soared, America not only acclaimed Lillian Russell as its national beauty,
but turned to counting on the melting pot for its influence on the development of a unique national beauty.

Of course the Anglo-Saxon strain was given its due prominence. As
one journalist wrote:

> In the composite American type, with predominant Anglo-Saxon strain,
> the deathless character of the race is attested. From Chicago, born of
> many generations of Americans and of such typically American features
> as never to be mistaken for anything other than an American girl, her
> face need only be compared with those of the Anglo-Saxon type with
> recurrent Anglo strain and previously mentioned Anglo-Saxon-Celtic,
> to see the convincing similarity.[99]

However, writers on the subject agreed that immigration fostered
something new in the realm of American beauty, that the complex mingling of races created a unique American beauty referred to as the com-
posite type:

> From all races we have absorbed characteristics mental and physical.
> From all this composite material is evolving a type which is hoped will in
> time resolve itself into a more fixed standard than we have today, so
> that we may know what it really means when the American type is spo-
> ken of, as we do when the Hungarian, Flemish, or the French is particu-
> larized.[100]

The effort to find and define American beauty was not just confined
to the journalist, the essayist, and the promoter, but was also something

that feminists sought after as well. However, for them, the emergence of a national beauty was less a symbol of nationalism than the awareness that beauty meant power.

Many of these women were taught by the beauty culture books of the period to see that beauty was something practically useful. In one of the most popular volumes, Mrs. Mary E. Haweis's *The Art of Beauty*, beauty is described as the equivalent of an almost Victorian bit of political economy—the exchange value:

> Alas when people complain of men not marrying (even those who are able) they forget how little women offer in *exchange* [italics mine] for all they get by marriage. Girls are so seldom thought to be of any use whatever to a man that I am astonished at the number of men who do marry! Many girls do not even try to be agreeable to look at, much less to live with. They forget how numerous they are, and the small absolute need men have of wives; but nevertheless, men still do marry, and would have oftener could they find mates—women who are either helpful, or amusing, or pleasing to the eye.[101]

Although books and pamphlets stressed dress and grooming, many contained forewords that stressed the historical and philosophical importance of beauty. The anonymously authored *Beauty is Power* even proclaimed grandiosely, "The power of beauty is unconditioned—it is absolute—it is universal."[102]

Mindful of these injunctions and the thought that if Cleopatra's nose had been an inch longer it might have changed history, feminists of the dress reform and physical culture magazine *Jeness-Miller Monthly* looked to the arrival of the American beauty as a source of power:

> American women have within themselves all the possibilities which have made certain of their sisters down the centuries conspicuous as women of beauty and power, but as yet they are indifferent regarding entrance to their kingdoms. They wait for some prophetess to arise and show them the way unto their own, a new Aspasia to teach them the old forgotten truths in a new language and in a new world. When will she appear? Already the time is ripe. Here in this new world, under conditions which no other nation has ever enjoyed, a race of queen ought to arise to outrival all royal predecessors. Is America to have no women of whom the future can write: They quickened enthusiasm for all that was beautiful in nature and art, they inspired men with noble ambition, they stimulated new thought, and gave birth to glorious hopes for all humanity.[103]

The combination of all of these efforts to find a national beauty, to define its unique American qualities, and to foster awareness of the inherent power in the role and its emergence as a public symbol gave Lillian Russell's immense potential influence, an influence of which she was well aware when she commented, "Beauty is unquestionably a great power."[104] Although she referred to some of its limitations, nevertheless she was fully aware of both its financial rewards as well as its cultural significance. Indeed, in what would undoubtedly have delighted the contributors to the *Jeness-Miller Monthly*, she soon brought her immense prestige to bear on issues that were of profound interest to feminists.

Lillian's special power was never more evident than in her energetic embrace of the bicycle and the cause of exercise for women, a campaign that undoubtedly gained special significance since no one was more closely associated with the torturously shaped ideal of the hourglass figure than Lillian Russell.

In the 1890s, the increasing participation of women in tennis and golf was seen as evidence that they might soon begin to escape their physical bondage to inhibiting corsetry and clothes. The invention and perfection of the safety bicycle furthered this move, and those who accepted notions of women's innate passivity and essential frailty were challenged by the bicycle and exercise regimes for women.[105] Clergyman Dr. Asa Blackburn inveighed against the moral consequences of the bicycle and admonished, "You cannot serve God and skylark on a bicycle."[106] In addition, Dr. E. A. Page warned that bicycling would "run the flesh off them [women]."[107]

It was precisely for this latter reason that Lillian Russell took so avidly to the bicycle. Plagued in her late thirties and early forties with a persistent weight problem, Lillian embraced all forms of exercise. According to her friend Marie Dressler, "Every morning rain or shine [she and Lillian] would climb on our wheels, and bending low over the handlebars, give an imitation of two plump girls going some place in a hurry."[108] In defiance of those who condemned cycling, Lillian conspicuously took her gold-plated bicycle (a gift from Diamond Jim Brady) wherever she traveled[109] and, contradicting all conventional dictums, urged women to peddle along furiously:

> Bicycle riding to women usually means peddling along dismounting every five or ten minutes, but this will not do at all if you mean to reduce your weight. You must go along at a brisk gait—not scorch. Riding sitting erect until you are tired. As days go on you will find that you do not tire as easily as at first.[110]

Lillian also gave a boost to those who would do away with severe corsetry by adding: "My wheeling costume consists of the regulation skirt and China silk bloomers with a long woolen shirt. I wear no corsets at all while exercising. Every muscle must be unhampered. This is essential."[111]

Lillian's enlistment in the ranks of the wheelers was just part of her crusade, and she was just as vehement about the positive effects of exercise in general. In her interviews and columns of beauty hints she stressed the importance of exercise, observing, "If you ask me for a panacea for all ills the flesh is heir to, my advice is to throw physic to the wind—and exercise."[112]

Not all the American beauty's energy was used to champion the cause of exercise; it was also linked with social institutions and political causes. After joining the Professional Woman's League, Lillian became one of its most active members and served a number of terms as a vice president. In addition, her name was listed among those American Dreyfusards who vowed to boycott French goods,[113] and she stands as one of the first woman members of the White Rats Vaudeville Union.[114]

All of this was secondary to Lillian's involvement in the suffrage movement. In 1911, true to the spirit of Cynthia Leonard, she said: "If it is true, as we Americans try to make ourselves believe that 'the hand that rocks the cradle is the hand that rules the world' why not let that be one of the hands which places the ballot of intelligence in the voting repository."[115]

Lillian's support of the suffrage movement was prompted by her mother's example and by her own belief in the basic democratic principle that "taxation without representation is tyranny,"[116] a resolve which was strengthened by the passage of the income tax amendment.

Once committed to the cause of suffrage, Lillian's efforts were assiduous. She spoke out at Equal Rights meetings, sold tickets to baseball games to raise money for the suffrage cause,[117] and even marched stalwartly behind the mounted Inez Milholland in the famous 1912 New York suffrage parade.[118] Moreover, her participation in the suffrage campaign was made immeasurably more effective and influential by her fourth marriage to Alexander P. Moore, the publisher of the *Pittsburgh Leader* and a powerful and prominent progressive Republican. Indeed, their marriage coincided with Moore's support of Teddy Roosevelt's 1912 Progressive Party campaign.[119] As a result the newlywed Lillian advocated on political platforms around the country for the eight-hour day and proclaimed that the election of Roosevelt meant "an advancement of 100 years for women in this country and the world. It will mean there will be legislation for women."[120]

Roosevelt's defeat hardly dampened Lillian's enthusiasm, and in 1915, taking a leaf from Cynthia's book and pursuing her own theme, "taxation without representation," she offered herself as a candidate for Mayor of New York. In an interview with the *New York Herald*, she said:

If I were mayor I would do my best to give the city a businesslike administration, conducted on lines of strict economy. As a business woman myself I know what that means. The chief reason why I want to vote is because I pay three kinds of taxes—on my property, my income and my business—and I think I ought to have something to say about what is done with my money.[121]

Lillian's candidacy was not merely shrugged off. *Town Topics* took up her suggestion with an editorial comment:

There is nothing so very grotesque or crazy about the notion of Lillian Russell presiding over our municipal destinies at City Hall. Cases of women occupying the office of mayor are on record in the United States as well as Great Britain and they have shown themselves efficient and honest. Lillian Russell would certainly present an appearance far more pleasing to the eye than most past mayors of New York. Lillian Russell, at any rate, would be a real ornament to our city and if perennial beauty of form and face really constitute "an outward and visible sign of inward spiritual grace" then our municipal affairs ought to go along swimmingly under her reign.[122]

While this did not set off any wild stampedes or bandwagons in support of Lillian, her pronouncements in favor of suffrage did have other positive consequences. For one thing, her image as the American beauty gave her a great deal of credibility in putting to rest the anti-suffrage argument that voting would make women mannish, an idea which was repeated on the floor of the U.S. Senate by Senator George West of Missouri: "For my part I want when I go home—when I return from the arena where man contends with man for what we call the prizes of the paltry world—I want to go back not to be received in the masculine embrace of some female ward politician, but in the earnest loving look and touch of a true woman."[123]

Lillian quickly raised the argument about the mannish reputation of the suffragists and just as quickly dismissed it with long lists of suffragists whom no one could accuse of being unwomanly. Nor, as she told interviewers, did she believe that the vote would make women unwomanly:

I instinctively dislike mannish women with the same abhorrence that I have for effeminate men; but I maintain that the enjoyment of man's prerogative doesn't destroy a woman's womanliness. The mannish woman will be mannish in spite of the denial of her right to vote and the womanly woman will remain womanly even if she drop a ballot into the box. There are types of womankind just as there are types of mankind and these types follow the natural bent of their kind. No manmade law can alter these conditions.[124]

Her belief that the vote would not alter women stemmed from Lillian's faith that suffrage was merely an extension of women's traditional sphere in society as a whole. She argued, in keeping with the rationale for suffrage advocated by Jane Addams and others,[125] that the vote would help women meet their responsibilities of maintaining a clean society for their children's sake:

> A mother wants her son to grow up in clean surroundings. Without clean surroundings you can't be clean politically. That's why I want women to have the vote. They will use it not for themselves, but for the good of their children. She would use her vote to see that men were reared cleanly and to elect men she knows to be clean.[126]

Although resistance to women's suffrage did not collapse overnight, reassuring statements like these certainly gave pause to those who believed that the vote might make women mannish. In addition, Lillian's participation in the movement gave it a luster that few women could match. As one reporter commented when he saw her marching in the 1912 suffrage parade, "Even Lillian Russell who was accustomed to riding in hansome cabs walked the long route for the glory of womanhood."[127]

In acknowledgment of that stature, the United States government enlisted her in its recruiting and Liberty Loan drives during World War I,[128] but her political involvements and activities did not end with the war and the passage of the suffrage amendment. Within a year of the Armistice, Lillian participated in the first Actors Equity strike. Although not an organizer or officer of the union, she served on its negotiating committee and, in the words of Equity president Francis Wilson, "In generosity, loyalty, and inspiration no one exceeded the radiant Lillian Russell."[129]

Along with union activities, Lillian spoke out in the political struggles over the League of Nations (which she denounced), and the election of Warren G. Harding (which she vigorously supported).[130] After the election, Harding appointed her a commissioner to study immigration, and she shortly became involved in an attempt to restrict immigration. She believed that: "Our melting pot has been overcrowded, it has boiled too quickly and is running over. It were better to put out the fires under it and allow its contents to solidify before adding any more raw material. If we don't put up the bars and make them stronger and higher, there will no longer be an America for the Americans."[131]

This response would have gladdened the heart of Henry F. Bowers and the original Immigrant Restriction Leaguers, and it provided a symmetry to the life and times of "the American beauty" (who died the year the report was submitted).[132]

Lillian's attempt to limit immigration punctuated a career that owed some of its earliest impetus to a wave of American nationalism that was a response to the huge influx of immigrants which many Americans saw as the cause of their fin-de-siècle economic and social problems. Ultimately this nationalism was bolstered by social Darwinist, racial ideals that elevated Anglo-Saxon tradition, institutions, and history to first place in the world and sought concrete evidence of that preeminence culturally and physically.

It was Lillian's physical embodiment of the Anglo-Saxon ideal of womanhood that first captured the American imagination and propelled her into the role of "the American beauty." And it was in defense of that Americanness that Lillian later raised her voice against renewed post-war immigration.

Nevertheless her career was not defined by that issue alone. In a professional life that spanned four decades, she became "the American beauty" as a result of her lovely singing voice, her innate and spontaneous expressions of American loyalty, and the affections of an upper middle class audience who identified with her nationalism. Complementing Lillian's ascension to that title was a growing interest in defining the essence of American beauty and the realization that it carried with it great cultural and political influence, an influence on which Lillian Russell capitalized for personal gain and for support of a broad range of issues that ran a gamut from Republican party politics to trade unionism for performers and to feminism.

Lillian's commitment to feminism was, however, preeminent. Based partially on her mother's example, but also on her own belief that, as a taxpayer, she was being denied a basic democratic right and that the vote was merely an extension of women's sphere into the society as a whole, she gave speeches, raised funds and marched for suffrage. Her involvement gave the suffrage movement a legitimacy few other women could bring and rendered dubious the notion that feminism and the desire to vote turned women into harridans and viragos. Finally, to paraphrase the old adage, her activities proved that beauty is as beauty does.

NOTES

1. Israel Zangwill, "Actress Versus Suffraget," *Independent*, LXV (December, 1909), p. 1248.

2. John Higham, *Writing American History: Essays on Modern Scholarship* (Bloomington: Indiana University Press, 1970), p. 85.

3. Sara Grand, "The Duty of Looking Attractive," *Review of Reviews*, VIII (September, 1893), p. 342.

4. Ibid.

5. Aileen S. Kraditor, *The Ideals of the Woman Suffrage Movement 1890–1920* (Garden City, N.Y.: Anchor Books, 1971). William L. O'Neill, *Everyone Was Brave: A History of Feminism in America* (New York: Quadrangle/The New York Times Book Company, 1971). William Henry Chafe, *The American Woman: Her Changing Social, Economic, and Political Roles, 1920–1970* (New York: Oxford University Press, 1972) pp. 3–22.

6. Walter Lord, *The Good Years* (New York: Bantam Books, 1962), p. 259.

7. "Women Should Vote Says Lillian Russell," *Pittsburgh Leader*, May 3, 1911, n.p. (*Locke*, 414, p. 8).

8. Diane Forbes-Robertson, *My Aunt Maxine: The Story of Maxine Elliot* (New York: Viking Press, 1964).

9. Alan Dale, "Lillian Russell Gives Women a Delightful Shock," *New York American*, January 4, 1905, n.p. (*Locke*, 413, p. 32).

10. Clarence Day, "Appearing With Lillian Russell," *Saturday Evening Post*, CVIII (October 26, 1935), p. 90.

11. Irene Franklin, "The American Beauty," *Stage* (October, 1938), pp. 50-51.

12. Parker Morell, *Lillian Russell: The Era of Plush* (New York: Random House, 1940). John Burke, *Duet in Diamonds: The Flamboyant Saga of Lillian Russell and Diamond Jim Brady in America's Gilded Age* (New York: G. P. Putnam's Sons, 1972).

13. Alan Dale, *Familiar Chats with Queens of the Stage* (New York: G. W. Dillingham, 1890), p. 43.

14. Edward T. James, Janet Wilson James, Paul S. Boyer, *Notable American Women 1607–1950* (Cambridge: Belknap Press of Harvard University Press, 1971), III, p. 211.

15. Ibid.

16. James D. Hart, *The Popular Book* (Berkeley: University of California Press, 1961), p. 162.

17. Lillian Russell, "Lillian Russell's Reminiscences," *Cosmopolitan*, 70 (February, 1922), p. 15.

18. Ibid., p. 14.

19. Frances E. Willard and Mary Livermore, *American Women*, 2 vols. (New York: Mast, Crowell, Kirkpatrick, 1897), II, pp. 457-458.

20. Russell, "Reminiscences," p. 18.

21. Ibid.

22. Ibid., p. 16.

23. Morell, *Lillian Russell*, pp. 15-16.

24. Burke, *Duet in Diamonds*, p. 22.

25. Marie Dressler with Mildred Harrington, *My Own Story* (Boston: Little, Brown and Company, 1934), p. 94.

26. Lillian Russell, "Lillian Russell's Reminiscences," *Cosmopolitan* (May, 1922), p. 92. Russell omits the bad press she got but Burke, *Duet in Diamonds*, p. 126, cites it in a footnote.

27. Rudolph Aronson, *Theatrical and Musical Memoirs* (New York: McBride, Nast and Company, 1913), p. 69.

28. Ibid., p. 70.

29. Nat C. Goodwin, *Nat Goodwin's Book* (Boston: Richard G. Badger, The Gorham Press, 1914), p. 197.

30. Burke, *Duet in Diamonds*, p. 28.

31. "Living Up to Her Chinese Porcelain Keeps Lillian Russell Poor," *Morning Telegraph*, September 25, 1910, n.p. (*Locke*, 414, p. 104).

32. Burke, *Duet in Diamonds*, p. 127.

33. "Lillian Russell's Fight With Too Generous Nature," *New York Journal*, September 30, 1899, n.p. (*Locke*, 411, pp. 9-10).

34. "Lillian Russell's Secret," *New York Telegraph*, September 26, 1902, n.p. (*Locke*, 411, p. 55).

35. "The Woman's Exhibition," *New York Dramatic Mirror*, October 25, 1906, p. 16.

36. Morell, *Lillian Russell*, p. 267.

37. Ibid., p. 268.

38. Lillian Russell, "Lillian Russell's Reminiscences," *Cosmopolitan* (March, 1922), p. 126. Russell barely mentions her marriage to Edward "Teddy" Solomon. However, both Morell, *Lillian Russell*, pp. 57-73, and Burke, *Duet in Diamonds*, pp. 34-40 greatly amplify her sparse detail.

39. Morell, *Lillian Russell*, pp. 138-155, Burke, *Duet in Diamonds*, pp. 90-100 detail their marriage. Russell doesn't mention Perugini at all in her "Reminiscences".

40. Dressler, *My Own Story*, p. 90.

41. "Queen of Divorcees," *New York Telegraph*, December 1896, n.p. (*Locke*, 410, pp. 64-69).

42. M. B. Leavitt, *Fifty Years in Theatrical Management* (New York: Broadway Publishing, 1912, p. 529.

43. James F. Muirhead, *The Land of Contrasts* (London: John Lane, 1898).

44. Ibid., p. 20.

45. Ibid., p. 19.

46. Ibid., p. 20.

47. A number of general works analyze this era. Harold U. Faulkner, *Politics, Expansion and Reform* (New York: Harper Brothers, 1959). Samuel P. Hays, *The Response to Industrialism 1885–1914* (Chicago: University of Chicago Press, 1957). Ray Ginger, *Age of Excess* (London: The MacMillan Company, 1955). H. Wayne Morgan, ed., *The Gilded Age: A Reappraisal* (Syracuse: Syracuse University Press, 1963). Also H. Wayne Morgan, *Unity and Culture: The United States 1877–1900* (London: Penguin Books, 1971).

48. John Higham, *Strangers in the Land: Patterns of American Nativism 1860–1925* (New York: Atheneum, 1970) explores the relationship between labor violence and rise of nativism.

49. John H. Denison, "The Survival of the American Type," *Atlantic Monthly*, LXXI (January, 1895), p. 16.

50. John Higham, "The Mind of a Nativist: Henry F. Bowers and the A.P.A.," *American Quarterly*, IV (1952), pp. 16-24.

51. Higham, *Strangers in the Land*, pp. 85-87.

52. Barbara Miller Solomon, "The Intellectual Background of the Immigrant Restriction Movement in New England," *New England Quarterly*, XXV (1952), pp. 47-59.

53. Higham, *Strangers in the Land*, pp. 131-157.

54. Barbara Miller Solomon, *Ancestors and Immigrants: A Changing New England Tradition* (Cambridge: Harvard University Press, 1950).

55. John Fiske, *American Political Ideas: Viewed from the Standpoint of Universal History* (New York: Harper and Brothers Publishers, 1885), p. 143.

56. Richard Hofstadter, *Social Darwinism in American Thought* (Boston: The Beacon Press, 1955).

57. Josiah Strong, *Our Country: Its Possible Future and its Present Crisis*, ed. by Jurgen Herbst (Cambridge: The Belknap Press of Harvard University Press, 1963, originally published in 1886), pp. i-xvi.

58. Ibid., pp. 174-175.

59. Ibid., p. 210.

60. Francis A. Walker, "Immigration and Degradation," *Forum*, XI (1891), pp. 642-643.

61. Frances L. Smith, *Talks with Homely Girls on Health and Beauty; Their Preservation and Cultivation* (New York: A. L. Burt, 1885), p. 16.

62. Hofstadter, *Social Darwinism*, 45, citing William J. Ghent, *Our Benevolent Feudalism* (New York: MacMillan and Company, 1902), p. 29.

63. Russell, "Reminiscences," pp. 10-19.

64. Morell, *Lillian Russell*, pp. 6-8.

65. Russell, "Reminiscences," p. 92.

66. Henry Theophilis Finck, *Romantic Love and Personal Beauty: Their Development, Causal Relation, Historic and National Peculiarities* (New York: MacMillan Company, 1912), p. 532.

67. James T. Powers, *Twinkle Little Star: Sparkling Memories of Seventy Years* (New York: G. P. Putnam's Sons, 1939), p. 159.

68. Morell, *Lillian Russell*, pp. 41-50.

69. "Oily Vet Produced at Tony Pastor's," *New York Spirit of the Times*, March 3, 1881, n.p. (*Locke*, 410, p. 4).

70. Quoted in, Burke, *Duet in Diamonds*, pp. 31-32.

71. "London Critics," *New York Spirit of the Times*, July 28, 1883, n.p. (*Locke*, 410, p. 6).

72. Foster Rhea Dulles, *America Learns to Play: A History of Popular Recreation 1607-1940* (New York: D. Appleton-Century Inc., 1940), pp. 237-238.

73. Henry James, *Roderick Hudson* (New York: Charles Scribner's Sons, 1960), p. 40.

74. Henry C. Lahee, *Grand Opera in America* (Boston: L. C. Page and Company, 1902).

75. Neil Harris, *Humbug: The Art of P. T. Barnum* (Boston: Little, Brown and Company, 1973), pp. 113-141, contains the best discussion and analysis of Jenny Lind's tour and its effects.

76. Cecil Smith, *Musical Comedy in America* (New York: Theatre Arts Books, 1950).

77. Aronson, *Theatrical and Musical Memoirs*, pp. 91-115.

78. Russell, "Reminiscences," (March, 1922), p. 129.

79. "Lillian Russell," *New York Dramatic News*, December 25, 1890, p. 2.

80. Aronson, *Theatrical and Musical Memoirs*, p. 111.

81. "Lillian Russell is an American," *Chicago Times*, February, 1892, n.p. (*Locke*, 410, p. 21).

82. "Lillian Russell," *Robinson Locke Scrapbook Clipping*, Vol. 410, p. 50.

83. Morell, *Lillian Russell*, p. 134.

84. "An American Beauty," *Robinson Locke Scrapbook*, Vol. 410, p. 70.

85. "Program of An American Beauty," *Robinson Locke Scrapbook*, Vol. 410, n.p.

86. "An American Beauty," *The Illustrated American*, January 23, 1897 (*Locke*, 410, n.p.).

87. Amy Leslie, *Some Players* (Chicago and New York: Herbert S. Stone and Company, 1899), pp. 549-562 mentions the poker playing incident. Morell, *Lillian Russell*, pp. 168-169 tells the Lola Montez story.

88. Felix Isman, *Weber and Fields* (New York: Boni and Liveright, 1924).

89. "New York Flooded with Many Beautiful Actresses," *Morning Telegraph*, January

27, 1901, p. 3.

90. Virginia Tatnall Peacock, *Famous American Belles of the Nineteenth Century* (Philadelphia and London: J. B. Lippincott, 1901), p. 290.

91. Frances Trollope, *Domestic Manners of the Americans*, ed. by Donald Smally (New York: Alfred A. Knopf, 1948), p. 207.

92. Jacques Offenbach, *Orpheus in America: The Diaries of Jacques Offenbach of His Trip to the New World*, Translated by A. MacClintock (Bloomington: University of Indiana Press, 1957), p. 82.

93. Leonore Davidoff, *The Best Circles: Society, Etiquette and the Season* (London: Croom Helm, 1973), p. 102.

94. Peacock, *Famous American Belles*, pp. 11-17.

95. Paul Blouët, *John Bull's Womankind* (London: Field and Tuer, 1884), p. 64.

96. William E. Sage, "Passing of the $10,000 Beauty," *Cleveland Leader*, March 29, 1910, p. 28.

97. Paul Bourget, *Outre-Mer: Impressions of America* (New York: Charles Scribner's Sons, 1895), pp. 86-87.

98. "Culture and Physique," *The Spectator*, LXIV (June 28, 1890), p. 896.

99. Broughton Brandenberg, "Racial Traits in American Beauty," *Cosmopolitan,* 41 (May, 1906), p. 63.

100. Gertrude Lynch, "Racial and Ideal Types of Beauty," *Cosmopolitan*, 38 (December, 1904), p. 233.

101. Mrs. H. R. (Mary Eliza) Haweis, *The Art of Beauty* (New York: Harper and Brothers, 1878), p. 263.

102. *Beauty is Power* (New York: G. W. Carleton and Company, Publishers, 1871), p. 21.

103. Laura Giddings, "The Beauty That is Power," *Jeness-Miller Monthly* (March, 1890), pp. 219-220.

104. Lillian Russell, "The Limitation of Beauty," *Theatre Magazine*, IV (December 1, 1904), n.p. (*Locke*, 412, p. 28).

105. Richard Harmond, "Progress and Flight: An Interpretation of the American Cycle Craze of the 1890's," *Journal of Social History*, 5 (1972), pp. 235-257.

106. Quoted in Burke, *Duet in Diamonds*, p. 128.

107. John S. Haller and Robin M. Haller, *The Physician and Sexuality in Victorian America* (Urbana: University of Illinois Press, 1974), p. 182.

108. Dressler, *My Own Story*, pp. 82-83.

109. Russell, "Reminiscences," (May, 1922), p. 94.

110. Lillian Russell, "Lillian Russell Tells What She Did To Regain Her Figure," *New York Herald*, July 9, 1902, n.p. (*Locke*, 411, pp. 49-50).

111. Ibid., p. 49.

112. Ibid.

113. "These Actresses Are Indignant," *Morning Telegraph,* September 12, 1899, p. 1.

114. "Women Can Be White Rats," *Morning Telegraph*, January 22, 1901, p. 1.

115. "Women Should Vote Says Lillian Russell," *Pittsburgh Leader*, May 3, 1911, n.p. (*Locke*, 414, p. 8).

116. Ibid.

117. "Will Sell Tickets for Suffrage Cause," *Pittsburgh Leader*, September 13, 1915, n.p. (*Locke*, 415, p. 36).

118. Burke, *Duet in Diamonds*, p. 223 mentions her marching. Lord, *The Good Years*, p. 259 also indicates she marched.

119. Russell, "Reminiscences," (September, 1922), p. 106. Also in Dorothy Russell, "My Mother, Lillian," *Liberty,* V (November, 1929), p. 58.

120. "Women's Store Aiding Teddy Buyers' Mecca," *Pittsburgh Leader*, October 23, 1912, n.p. (*Locke*, 414, p. 76).

121. Marguerite Mooers Marshall, "If I Were Mayor Says Lillian Russell," *New York World*, March 12, 1915, n.p. (*Locke*, 415, p. 31).

122. "Lillian Russell as Mayor of New York," *Town Topics*, June 26, 1916, n.p. (*Locke*, 415, p. 50).

123. Aileen S. Kraditor, ed., *Up From the Pedestal: Selected Writings in the History of Feminism* (Chicago: Quadrangle Books, 1968), p. 195.

124. "Lillian Russell Utters Words of Great Wisdom," *New York Review*, June 4, 1911, n.p. (*Locke*, 414, p. 18).

125. Kraditor, *Ideas of the Woman Suffrage Movement*, pp. 53-56.

126. "Lillian Russell Favors Clean Politics in Pittsburgh and Points Out the Way," *Philadephia Public Ledger*, September 12, 1917, n.p. (*Locke*, 415, p. 77)

127. Burke, *Duet in Diamonds*, p. 223.

128. "Lillian Russell Moore's Liberty Loan Speech Is Highly Praised," *Pittsburgh Leader*, October 19, 1917, n.p. (*Locke*, 415, p.79).

129. Francis Wilson, *Francis Wilson's Life of Himself* (Boston and New York: Houghton-Mifflin Company, 1924), p. 274.

130. Russell, "Reminiscences," (September, 1922), p. 108.

131. "Is the Melting-Pot Spilling the Beans," *Literary Digest*, 73 (April, 1922), p. 15.

132. James, *Notable American Women 1607–1950*, III, p. 211.

Chapter 7

Ethel Barrymore: "The American Girl" and Women's Emancipation

In his study of *The American Commonwealth*, Lord James Bryce praised the contribution of American women to their society and addressed himself to the condition of the American girl, noting her lack of "fast ways."[1] Underscoring this point, he quoted the remark of a German woman who referred to the American girl as "fruchtbar frei und fruchtbar fromm" (terribly free and terribly respectable).[2] While the duality may not have been apparent to every witness of American social mores, it is nevertheless a reminder that the nature and character of the American girl remained a topic of deepest concern and even controversy for both foreign and domestic observers from the earliest days of the Republic.

The frontier experience in American society and the scarcity of labor provided young women with the possibility of relatively superior economic and social positions than those they had previously occupied in Europe.[3] Similarly, the American Revolution, which stimulated so much debate concerning the nature of the new society, also contributed new ideas about women. Thus, in 1787, Benjamin Rush's widely distributed *Thoughts on Female Education* postulated the young nation's need for a womanhood trained to independence and self-reliance.[4]

The call for an educated womanhood intensified throughout the early days of the nineteenth century, even as industrialism increased socioeconomic pressure on women and relegated them to a rigid domestic sphere. The campaign culminated with the establishment of Emma Willard's Troy Seminary (1821) and Catherine Beecher's Hartford Female Seminary (1823), whose goal (as seen by Beecher) was to educate women so that the interests of the family would be secured.[5]

The quality of female education varied, but the extent of relative freedom enjoyed by American girls was commonly agreed on. Europeans were particularly startled by this freedom and were hardly unanimous in their appreciation of it; they were appalled by the mingling of young men and women, the lack of chaperonage, and the degree of choice allowed women in marriage. As one of our earliest visitors, Fanny Wright, noted in 1821:

The youth of both sexes here enjoy a freedom of intercourse unknown in the older and more formal nations of Europe. They dance, sing, walk and "run in sleighs" together by sunshine and moonshine, without occurrence or even apprehension of impropriety. In this beautiful country, marriages are seldom dreaded or imprudent and therefore no care is taken to prevent the contracting of early engagements.[6]

Other observers like Alexis de Tocqueville were appreciative of the American girl, but more critical. De Tocqueville thought that parental permissiveness in marital selection made the matter more cold and calculating. In addition, he was skeptical about the education of America's young women. While he praised them for learning to avoid evil ("at least knowing what it is"),[7] he also felt their education might make for a precocious, rather than a mature, knowledge of the world.[8]

De Tocqueville's skepticism was echoed by Mrs. Trollope, who believed that the establishment of collegiate institutes for young women was in vain because, after marriage, American women retreated into "insignificance."[9] On the other hand, Frederika Bremer was so impressed by American women that she returned to her native Sweden and urged women there to emulate them.[10]

During the latter half of the nineteenth century, Europeans continued to visit, observe, and analyze American society. By then, a chapter on American women was, for the foreign correspondents, *de rigueur*, and most were enthusiastic about American girls to the point of hyperbole. During his 1870 tour, an impressed Jacques Offenbach wrote that "women and even girls enjoy the greatest liberty here. It seems to me that when Lafayette came to fight for the freedom of America he had only women in view, for they are really free in free America."[11] In the 1890s, Paul Bourget went a step further and proclaimed that "the apotheosis of women, which is the most characteristic feature of 'society' in America, is in the first place and especially the apotheosis of the young girl."[12] Similarly (and less euphorically), James F. Muirhead commented favorably on her frankness, camaraderie, sensitivity, lack of class consciousness, and unconcern for fashion.[13]

In contrast to Offenbach, Bourget, and Muirhead, who wrote on many aspects of American society, some visitors singled out the condition of women in the United States as the sole and central concern of their studies. Charles De Varigny began his book *The Women of the United States* with the comment that "Europe is becoming Americanised" and pinpointed women as the principal source of that Americanization.[14] Writing on the same topic, Madame Th. Bentzon (pseudonym of Thérèse Blanc) was less impressed, and, although she was essentially positive about American women and young girls in *The Condition of Women in the United*

States,[15] she elsewhere raised questions about their lack of humility, obsession with self-development, and "inevitable egotism."[16]

The image of the American girl which so entranced foreign observers was a perception that neither soothed nor was shared by American middle-class women. Despite their freedom, leisure, and education (and, in the eyes of some, because of it), many developed a sense of powerlessness in their youth that could and did (as in the cases of both Jane Addams and Charlotte Perkins Gilman) lead to prolonged periods of nervous depression.[17] By the same token, leisure time could lead to frivolous and often feverish theatre going ("the matinee girl"), bridge playing, or overindulgence in sporting activities.[18]

Unlike Olive Schreiner (*Women and Labour*) and Charlotte Perkins Gilman, who diagnosed this activity as "parasitism" — [19]the feeling of uselessness bred of excessive leisure — others simply saw it as the failure of American women to wholeheartedly embrace their true roles as wives and mothers. The desertion from the domestic sphere prompted writers like Kate Gannet Wells to refer to them as "transitional American women"[20] and charge that "the charm of being simply one's self, apart from having a 'mission' or 'views' is lost in the intensity with which women are seizing upon new fields of usefulness thrown open to them."[21]

Anxiety about American women was also projected onto American girls. Articles with titles like "Squandered Girlhood"[22] and "What Shall We Do With Our Girls"[23] appeared in the periodicals of the day urging parents to encourage their daughters to eschew idle "amusements"[24] and engage in productive activities, as well as providing homilies on the virtues of domesticity. However, some argued that American girls should be trained for remunerative labor. In "The Future of Our Daughters," Helen Ekin Starrett wrote:

> Let us educate them in all the learning of the schools; let us secure for them health and strength of body by careful physical training; let us explain to them the laws of their own being, in its necessities for both physical and mental activity; and let us teach them to regard useful work as the necessity and blessing of their lives. While cultivating all the finer endowments and faculties of their natures, let us seek to find out what productive direction their special talent lies, and, by careful education and training of that talent and endowment, let us fit them to take a high and useful and remunerative place among the workers of the world.[25]

As young women began to assert themselves in higher education, the professions, and the work force, they were taken to task for deserting the domestic sphere. In a *The Ladies Home Journal* article, "What the American Girl Has Lost By an American Mother,"[26] she was criticized for losing all sense of modesty, decency, and purity, and was reminded of her primary responsibility:

> The American girl wants to forget it. She wants to convince the world that she is simply a man in a different body. Half the women's columns published are filled with proofs she can write, paint, reason or vote as well as a man. With all her logic it never oddly enough has occurred to her to put her hand on the man himself and say: "This is my book, my work, my raison d'etre. This is enough for me to have done."[27]

As an example of their concern about the future of the American girl, journals of the period also featured articles creating mythical and fictional confrontations between the "New Woman" and the "Old Lady." In Caroline Ticknor's "The Steel Engraving Lady and the Gibson Girl,"[28] the two stereotypes come face to face. One—"the Gibson Girl"—is assertive, athletic, ambitious, and has a frank and comradely relationship with a man; the other—"The Steel Engraving Lady"—is passive, convinced that a woman's place is in the home nurturing her family, and is placed on a pedestal by her husband. The encounter results in a mutual lack of comprehension, and, although Ticknor maintains a precarious sense of neutrality until the very end of the story, she completes it with the revealing salutation: "Hail the New Woman—behold she comes apace! WOMAN, ONCE MAN'S SUPERIOR, NOW HIS EQUAL!"[29]

Similarly, Anne Warner's "The New Woman and the Old" contrasted the two types of women in a story about an engagement which is made and then broken because the daughter (the new woman) feels that her fiancé is too selfish and does not take her thoughts or needs into consideration in planning their future. Thus, in contrast to her mother (the old woman), who believes that marriage is the highest goal to which any woman could possibly aspire (she is elated when the engagement is announced and then crushed when it is broken off), Emily, the daughter, is depressed when she accepts and relieved when she rejects the proposal.[30]

In an editorial that could have been a commentary on both of these stories, *The Atlantic Monthly* stated: "The old lady must be born again and cannot be made from existing material for in an age of doubt and uncertainty one fact shows clear: the new woman can never grow into the old lady."[31]

How the ever-expanding education, athleticism, ambition and assertiveness of the "New Woman" might be contained within the traditional female role concerned conservative women like the founder and first president of the National Congress of Mothers, Mrs. Theodore Birney.[32] Mrs. Birney sought to create an appropriate model for this new woman in her *Harpers Bazaar* article titled, "The Twentieth Century Girl; What We Expect of Her."[33] She said, "My own conviction is that while the ideal home should by no means absorb all the woman's time and interest, it is there her highest and best thoughts should be concentrated."[34] Along with advocating that parenthood be acknowledged as a vocation and women trained for it, she also accepted the fact that girls should be educated, encouraged in moderate athletic activity and even prepared to earn their own living should the need arise. Nevertheless, Birney emphasized that love, children, and the coming of the girl's "prince"[35] should be the central concerns of her life.

At the moment Mrs. Birney proclaimed her hopes, she probably had no candidate in mind who fit her description. Nonetheless, within a year of the publication of her essay, Ethel Barrymore burst into stardom on the Broadway scene, and, while in many respects she did not fit Mrs. Birney's categories, she was acknowledged and acclaimed for almost a decade as the symbolic "Typical American Girl." However, despite an early identification with that role, Ethel Barrymore used her prestige and fame to encourage American women to a life of greater independence.

Almost concurrently with her first triumph in *Captain Jinks of the Horse Marines*, an article in *Broadway* magazine cast Ethel Barrymore for the part of the typical American girl:

> We are told by art critics of the continent that America is too young to have a type. I throw my glove into the ring and shall be glad to pick a quarrel, for I have found the typical American girl.
>
> Look at these pictures of Miss Ethel Barrymore, and I am certain you will agree with me that Miss Ethel Barrymore, both in the flesh and in photography, represents the idea of that girl.[36]

Indeed, as her career blossomed and she appeared in numerous hit plays (*Carrots, Cousin Kate, Sunday,* and others), her claim to the title grew as well. A sketch in *Frank Leslie's Popular Monthly* called her "a splendid example of the finest type of American girl,"[37] while *Century* magazine referred to her as "the best type of American girl we have today."[38]

Barrymore won this distinction not only due to her abilities as an actress, but also because she was popularly seen as the "ideal American girl in looks" and dress.[39] In words that would clearly placate all but the most die-hard advocates of women's traditional role, newspapers and magazines described her refinement bred of a convent education and her grace which came from an early study of the concert piano. They gushed, too, over Ethel's intelligence and pointed with pride to her taste in art and literature (Rembrandt, Whistler, George Eliot, Robert Louis Stevenson and Henry James), and they proudly proclaimed her skills in tennis and swimming.[40]

The periodicals of the day assuaged any hostility that might have arisen from her professional involvement by allowing Ethel to make a virtue of necessity. Speaking in the defense of the working girl, she said, "Life isn't easy for girls who are thrown on their own. They must earn their living somehow. You're surprised to hear me talk like that. I was thrown on my own when I was sixteen—so I know!"[41] Moreover, indicative of the fact that she had not deserted the traditional sphere of women, they also pointed to her "domesticity in the little home where she and her brothers live together."[42] Consequently, it was no surprise that columnist Vanderheyden Fyles proclaimed her "Our Ethel" and a national treasure:

> She is Ethel to everybody—and that means something. If it were the free and doubtfully respectable Flo and Annabel, that the glittering stars of burlesque win sometimes with applause and notoriety, the something meant would not be pleasant to record, but the beautiful Miss Barrymore is Ethel to us because she is the daughter of every parent in America, the beloved charge of every household. We revere with pride to the regal art of Ada Rehan; we honor the grand achievement of Mrs. Fiske, and gaze with admiration at the beauty of Lillian Russell, but each of us cherishes "Our Ethel" as something sweet and good and loveable, and somehow intimately his own. As fourth in line in a distinguished family, each generation of which has given several players of prominence to the theatre of its day, Miss Barrymore was born to be "daughter of the American stage" but she has made herself "daughter of the American people."[43]

Her stage success, the publicity surrounding her name, and her identification as "the typical American girl" created something of a cult following for Ethel Barrymore. Young girls copied her dress, hairstyle, walk, and even voice mannerisms. Francis Crowninshield, commenting on the conversations one might expect to have with young women at a debutante party, said the topics included "Platonic love, banting, Ethel Barrymore, French dressmaking, John Drew, the relative merits of Harvard and Yale, love at first sight, the football match and the matter of her great charm and beauty."[44]

Not everyone found the Ethel Barrymore cult interesting or amusing. James L. Ford satirized it in "The Ethel Barrymore Following" and described it as "a veritable Frankenstein monster sneering at all worthy ambition and laying waste with vapid laughter and maudlin chatter the whole field of her endeavor." Nevertheless, nothing seemed to diminish her appeal. In fact, it grew to such proportions that, when a ship sank near a yacht she was sailing on, one newspaper headline the next day did not even proclaim the facts of the disaster, but read instead, "Ethel Barrymore Sees Vessel Sink."[45]

Episodes such as these affirmed the distinction of being referred to as the original "glamour girl." Despite the fact that she despised the title, glamour was very much a part of the Barrymore image.[46] Moreover, if glamour, to use John Berger's definition, is "the state of being envied,"[47] then admiration of her social triumphs paved the way for her acclaim as the "typical American girl" and was a key factor in her early stardom. Ethel's social success was in no small part also due to her membership in what would one day be fictionally referred to as the "Royal Family of Broadway,"[48] a lineage which, at the same time, gave her important models of female independence.

Ethel's grandmother was the redoubtable Mrs. John Drew. Writing her memoirs years after her greatest successes, Ethel Barrymore commented that "when in later years I saw royalty abroad, nothing was to surprise me — I had seen grandmother."[49] Indeed, as manager of Philadelphia's renowned Arch Street Theater for almost 42 years and an actress whose Mrs. Malaprop in *The School for Scandal* lifted that role from "low comedy to high comedy,"[50] Mrs. John Drew was one of the most formidable figures in nineteenth century American theater. The former Louisa Lane could trace her theatrical ancestry back to the Elizabethan period, and she herself made her first stage appearance at the age of twelve months. Along with memories of being kissed on the forehead by President Jackson and playing with Forrest, Booth, and Joseph Jefferson, she had three husbands, the last of whom, John Drew, Sr. (himself a well-known comedian), was father of at least three of her four children (Louisa, John Drew Jr., and Georgie).[51]

Hardly a person who knew her was not impressed by her regal manner. One member of her company wrote:

> The Duchess was the familiar sobriquet by which the members of the company permitted themselves to refer to Mrs. Drew — when she was not present. But they all sincerely liked her. Her manner was a blending of the kindliness of Marie Antoinette with the imperiousness of Queen Elizabeth, and she was one of the best hearted women in the business. As manager she was absolutely just, and it was because she was so strict that she was able to maintain discipline for which she was famous.[52]

Mrs. Drew ruled over her family in the same steely manner with which she governed the Arch Street. Over her not too strenuous objections, three of her children (John Drew Jr., Georgie, and Sidney) went on the stage. It was the marriage of her much beloved, beautiful, and talented daughter Georgie to the English actor Maurice Barrymore which produced Lionel (1878), Ethel (1879), and John (1882).

While Ethel got her notion of majesty from her grandmother, her mother gave her wit and beauty. Critics described Georgie Drew Barrymore as "an actress to the tips of her fingers"[53] and said that her "presence in a cast generally means incessant laughter whenever she is upon the stage."[54]

Through her mother, Ethel was also exposed to the influence of another formidable woman, Madame Helen Modjeska. To the young Ethel (who, with her older brother, was allowed to join their parents on tour with the actress in 1882), Modjeska was a "fairy queen,"[55] and such was her adoration that Modjeska recalled, "I often saw her eager eyes watching me from behind the scenes during matinees."[56] Modjeska's influence did not merely extend to acting, for it was Modjeska who convinced Ethel's mother to convert to Catholicism and, with her husband, served as godparents to the rebaptized Lionel and Ethel (much to the chagrin of a scandalized Episcopalian, Mrs. John Drew).[57]

This trio of women clearly exercised a powerful influence on Ethel throughout her life. She remained a devout Catholic, a dedicated and versatile actress, and a woman whose proudest boast was that her grandchildren called her "mum-mum" (the same nickname she and her brothers used for her grandmother).[58]

Maurice Barrymore's influence on his daughter was more problematic and paradoxical. His family were high civil servants in India, and he himself was born during the Sepoy Mutiny. Sent to school in England at a young age, he was apprenticed to a barrister, but found he enjoyed sports (particularly boxing) and acting more. Changing his name from Herbert Blythe to Maurice Barrymore (in order not to embarrass his staunchly Victorian family), he then came to America and, while part of Augustin Daly's company, met and married Georgie Drew.[59]

Theirs was a marriage of two beautiful, witty and, from all accounts, utterly charming people. Anecdote after anecdote reveals their often rapierlike wit. In one particularly famous story, Georgie emerged from the house one morning to go to Mass as Maurice came in from a night on the town. Maurice, with his cape tossed over his shoulder and his top hat askew, tipped his hat and greeted her with a hearty, "Going to Mass, my dear?" to which she replied, "Yes, and you can go to hell."[60] From all reports, it was probably one of the few times anyone got the better of Maurice Barrymore, who was known for his bon mots (some of which were repeated years after his death in actors' clubs and the trade papers), his good fellowship, a tendency to "go up in his lines [forget them]" and improvise, and an over-reliance on his handsome leading-man charm was repeatedly attacked for never fulfilling his potential as an actor.[61]

Maurice, while often heroic and considered brilliant, was hardly noted for his sense of responsibility. Tales of his bohemianism and recklessness abound. However, he was goodhearted and did love his children, though he displayed neither a profound sense of parental authority nor duty. During Ethel's early years, she showed promise of becoming a concert pianist. One evening, she played for her parents, and Maurice was so overcome with awe that he vowed to send her to Vienna in order that she could study with the best European teachers. Unfortunately, after that night, nary a word was ever heard of that promise again.[62]

Brilliant and beautiful though they both were, neither Georgie nor Maurice provided their children with a strong, tightly knit family. Despite this, their children honored, respected, and indeed loved them, as Lionel Barrymore wrote years later philosophically:

> My mother and father, affectionate and generous persons though they certainly were, were actor and actress on the stage, traveling, living in hotels, spending money when they had it, mockingly enduring near poverty when they didn't. The rearing of offspring was not their forte. They did what they could with what they had, which is all that anyone can.[63]

An aura of tragedy and sadness lingered over the Barrymores. Tragedy struck early when the 34-year-old Georgie contracted consumption. Ordered by her doctors to a warm climate as therapy, she was accompanied on her trip to southern California by Ethel, who remembered hearing her cough one night and call out in the dark, "Oh, God, what's going to happen to my three kids!"[64]

At first it seemed that Georgie might recover. However, one day she began hemorrhaging and died. Ethel took the body back East by herself and poignantly remembered saying to herself on the return trip, "Next month I'll be fourteen."[65]

Although terribly bereaved by Georgie's death, Maurice remarried soon afterward. His marriage shocked Ethel, and the depth of her feelings came through even the emotional reticence of her memoirs. She wrote, "I do not want to dwell on this but it was years, really years before I could take it in stride."[66] Nonetheless, it was not Maurice's precipitous remarriage that irrevocably altered Ethel's world as much as the collapse of Mrs. John Drew's fortunes.

Never enormously wealthy, Mrs. Drew saw her theatrical world and her economic future fade before the onslaught of the theatrical syndicate controlled by New York interests which sent out companies to the rest of the country and reduced the role of the old-fashioned theater manager to the status of a hotel clerk. Thus, at the age of 72 when she should have been able to look forward to a respectable and financially secure retirement, Mrs. Drew lost the Arch Street Theater and was forced to start touring again under the economic protection of her devoted son, John Drew.[67]

With neither Mrs. John Drew nor Georgie able to provide even a minimum of economic or familial stability, and with Maurice married and touring, Ethel had to leave her beloved convent school and (since the family knew no other way to earn a living), start work as an actress.[68]

After 1896, when she made her debut in a bit role in her uncle's company's version of *The Bauble Shop*,[69] Ethel's life was filled with exactly the same trials and tribulations of any stage-struck girl (except far from being stage-struck, Ethel hardly even knew if she really wanted to be an actress). She pounded the pavements and climbed stairs to managers' and agents' offices to deliver resumes, and won a series of walkons and bit roles which were the lot of any fledgling actress. In addition, she slept in hall bedrooms the size of closets, cheap boarding houses on the road, and even had to leave her luggage once as collateral for an unpaid hotel bill.[70]

Tragedy dogged her still even when her name went up in lights for the first time in *Captain Jinks*. In the same year, Maurice Barrymore went mad in the last stages of paresis, and had to be institutionalized. Throughout this episode, newspapers seemed to delight in reporting the details of his bizarre behavior and even reported (erroneously) that he had attacked Ethel who, besides paying his hospital bills, visited him dutifully at the Amityville asylum where he remained until his death in 1905.[71]

Although the years 1896 to 1901 were difficult, there were bright spots for Ethel. Ever since a childhood year in England which the whole family spent together as a result of a legacy left to Maurice, England was Ethel's promised land.[72] In 1898, she got a chance to go to London as an understudy and bit player with William Gillette's *Secret Service* company, and this sojourn launched Ethel's claim to the title of "typical American girl."

Ethel's arrival in London came at a particularly propitious moment for actors and actresses. In 1895, the English theatrical world came of age with the knighting of Henry Irving, which raised the profession to the dignity of an art, and, more importantly, irrevocably lifted the age-old social opprobrium against actors and actresses.[73] In addition, even prior to Sir Henry's knighthood, women like the Duchess of Sutherland, whom Disraeli once labelled a "social fairy,"[74] began inviting actors and actresses to their social functions as regular participants in the London season.[75]

After a season with Gillette, Ethel joined Henry Irving's company and she and Irving's son Laurence subsequently became engaged.[76] Though the engagement was short-lived, it seemingly united the theatrical royal families of two continents. Moreover, their romance reminded Americans of other illustrious Anglo-American upper-class unions.[77]

All of this information seeped into the press back home through the publicity genius of manager Charles Frohman, who had taken over guidance of Ethel's career in much the same way he had once determined her mother's, and was then advancing that of her uncle, John Drew. Frohman saw the opportunity of creating another star for a system that already included Maude Adams, Clara Bloodgood, Marie Doro, and others.[78] As Ethel cut a wide swathe through the young manhood of England, becoming engaged to or rejecting the suits of Gerald Du Maurier, Henry Graham, and Winston Churchill,[79] Frohman made sure that her name was splashed across America in headlines which proclaimed Ethel as "The Most Engaged Girl in America."[80]

Despite the dubious aspects of this distinction, Ethel's social exploits were balm to American national pride. Although Americans saw their young women married into some of the most prestigious and aristocratic families in Europe, many still smarted from their characterization in *Daisy Miller*. In fact, often the easiest way to flatter Americans was to tell them that their women were hardly Daisy Millers. This was obviously something that Ellen Terry, Henry Irving's beautiful and brilliant co-star, was aware of when the duo toured America in 1883-1884. She was asked what she thought of American women, and skillfully replied, "I suppose I've seen the nicest ones. And one thing I'll tell you which I haven't seen and never set eyes on—any Daisy Millers." One can almost see the chests of the reporters swelling with pride as they answered, "Of course not; who ever heard or saw a Daisy Miller outside of a book? That's a character you'll find in a James novel—not in America, Miss Terry."[81]

Despite disclaimers to the contrary, it is hard to escape the reality that many American girls, dragged around Europe in the 1870s and 1880s by their mothers or chaperones looking for culture or perhaps marriage to some pedigreed European, were hardly congenial or appreciative of their hosts' world.[82] As a result of the lingering suspicion that Daisy Miller still lurked in many European minds, Ethel's social triumphs particularly exhilarated Americans who now saw Daisy's memory finally erased by Ethel's emergence as an "American princess," even a Cinderella.

Henry James wrote the story of *Daisy Miller* in 1876.[83] The story of a young American girl who, out of innocence and spontaneous feeling, defies social convention and travels unchaperoned with a young Italian and then dies, brought James his first touch of fame and generated a great deal of anger among those who felt that he had denigrated American girls. As the *New York Times* reported, "There are many ladies in and around New York today who feel indignant with Mr. James for his portrait of Daisy Miller and declare it shameful to give foreigners so untrue a portrait of the American girl."[84]

James' friend, William Dean Howells, defended him publicly, saying, "The American woman would [have] none of Daisy Miller because the American woman was too jealous of her own perfection to allow innocence might be reckless and angels in their innocence of evil might not behave as discreetly as worse people."[85] Similarly, commenting privately in a letter to a friend on the uproar caused by the story, Howells wrote:

"Henry James waked up all women with his *Daisy Miller,* the intention of which they misconceive. There has been vast discussion in which nobody felt very deeply, and everybody talked very loudly. The thing went so far that society almost divided itself into Daisy Millerites and anti-Daisy Millerites."[86]

Nor was James' the last word on the American girl. A somewhat whimsical and ironic anonymous ballad in *Scribners Monthly* saluted "An American Girl" with the rhyme:

> She's had a Vassar education,
> > And points with pride to her degree;
> She's studied household decoration;
> > She knows a dado from a frieze,
> And Tell's Corots from Boldini's,
> > A Jacquemart etching, or a Haden;
> A Whistler too, perchance, might please
> > A frank and free young Yankee Maiden.
>
> She does not care for meditation
> > Within her bonnet are no bees;
> She has a gentle animation:
> > She joins in singing simple glee;
> She tries no trills, nor rivalries,
> > With Lucca (now Baronin Rodin,
> With Nilsson or with Gerster): she's
> > A frank and free young Yankee maiden.
>
> I'm blessed above all creation
> > far, far above all other he's;
> I ask you for congratulation,
> > On this the best of Jubilee's;
> I go with her across the seas,
> > Unto what Poe would call an Aiden;
> A frank and free young Yankee Maiden.
>
> > Envoy
> Princes, to you the western breeze
> > Bears many a ship and heavy laden
> What is the best we send in these,
> > A frank and free young Yankee maiden.[87]

Just how much Americans hungered after the praise of Europeans, especially for their women, is probably best exemplified by the popularity of Ludovic Halevy's 1882 novel, *L'Abbe Constantin*. What accounted for the success of this little story (which sold better than Zola's *Nana* or de Maupassant's stories) is the picture it gives of an American woman who is cultivated and sensitive, rather than a soulless, money-grubbing boor.[88]

Despite the contradictory feelings aroused by *Daisy Miller*, the success of the story nonetheless, critic Edmund Wilson pointed out, owed much to "her creator's having somehow conveyed the impression that her spirit went marching on."[89]

The progressive development of James' heroines in his later novels confirms Wilson's insight. His women are more and more able to subject Europe to their needs, until, in the case of Maggie Verver in *The Golden Bowl*, they emerge totally triumphant.[90] It was to this victory that James alluded in his preface to *Wings of the Dove*, wherein he referred to these young women as "that certain sort of young American as more the 'heir of all the ages' than any other young person whatever."[91]

In the last three decades of the nineteenth century, James' image of the American girl as the "heiress of all the ages" began to become progressively true. Indeed, an estimated 90,000 Americans traveled to Europe each year, and in the last thirty years of the century, American fathers established dowries which exceeded $200,000,000. With the weddings of Consuelo Vanderbilt to the Duke of Marlborough, Anna Gould to Count Boni Castellane, Mary Leiter to Marquis Curzon of Kedleston, and Pauline Whitney to Sir Almeric Paget, Baron of Queensborough, these unions seemed to have reached a high water mark.[92]

American social triumphs not only found their way into newspapers and the seldom-read fiction of Henry James, but also appeared in the popular novels of the period. In journalist and travel writer Sara Jeannette Cote's book, *An American Girl in London* (1891), the insouciant and self-conscious Mamie Wicks is sent to Europe alone by her parents. There, she enjoys all the cultural pleasures and social experiences that must have also filled the life of Ethel Barrymore, including rejecting an English lord.[93]

Thus, by the time of Ethel's arrival in London, the image of the American girl had greatly changed. In contrast to Daisy Miller, this girl was not only beautiful and wealthy, but supremely and almost arrogantly self-assured. Like her predecessor, she had an artistic embodiment (though not from literature) in the fine arts, where she took the name "The Gibson Girl" from her creator, Charles Dana Gibson.[94] Although Ethel Barrymore could claim no direct credit as the physical model for the "Gibson girl," she knew Gibson well enough to have served as one of the actual inspirations for his girls, and became her embodiment on the American stage and in the American mind.

Ethel's connection to Gibson came through her life-long friendship with Richard Harding Davis. Long neglected, the counterpart of the "Gibson girl" was the "Gibson man," tall, square-jawed, broad-shouldered, clean-shaven, and absolutely heroic.[95] His model, both in life as well as art, was Richard Harding Davis. Davis, the son of two outstanding Philadelphia writers, Clarke Davis, editorialist for the *Philadelphia Inquirer*, and novelist Rebecca Harding Davis (*Life in the Iron Mills*) was a journalist, war correspondent, and novelist. Like the characters in his novels, Davis led a life of adventure and romance which took him to the four corners of the world and made him a fixture in international society. Davis' stories of Gallagher and the copy boy and Van Bibber the man about town gave illustrator Gibson his first opportunities to draw the "Gibson girl."[96]

Davis was also a close friend of the Barrymores and a particular friend of Ethel's. Writing of their relationship, his brother Charles Belmont Davis said:

> I can remember Mrs. Barrymore [Georgie Drew] at the time very well — wonderfully handsome and a marvelously cheery manner. Richard and I loved her greatly, even though it was a secret. Her daughter Ethel I remember best as she appeared in the beach, a sweet long-legged child in a scarlet bathing suit running toward the breakers and then dashing madly back to her mother's open arms. A pretty figure of a child but much too young for Richard to notice at the time. In after years the child in the scarlet bathing suit and he became great pals. Indeed, during the latter half of his life, through the good days and bad days there were few friends who held so close a place in his sympathy as Ethel Barrymore.[97]

"Dick" Davis sometimes served as Ethel's escort in London, and, with her, had an adventure which served as the basis of one of his short stories.[98] In addition, Ethel served as the only bridesmaid at his first marriage. Moreover, through him Ethel met Charles Dana Gibson and, as a result of his persuasiveness with her uncle, was allowed to go to Gibson's wedding (where, according to Davis, she made a big hit).[99]

Despite the fact that she never actually modeled for Gibson, magazines recognized Ethel's identification with his image of the American girl. However, it was not until her success in *Captain Jinks* that she became widely acknowledged as the representative of that girl.[100]

Even by the standards of 1901, *Captain Jinks* was a fluff play. A period light comedy set in the 1870s, it concerned the romantic adventures of prima donna Madame Trentoni (really Aurelia Johnson), who returns home to make an artistic conquest, only to fall victim to the charms of Captain Jinks.[101] More than likely the play would have closed in Philadelphia after its initially poor tryout if it had not been for its author, Clyde Fitch. One of the most successful playwrights of the day, Fitch wanted to make some kind of record by having three plays running simultaneously on Broadway, and he convinced manager Charles Frohman to bring it to New York. As Ethel admitted, "Thank God Clyde Fitch had vanity."[102]

Fitch's ego aside, the critics generally were divided over the play, but they liked Ethel. The Hearst critic Alan Dale wrote: "As the prima donna in the play, she was quite a surprise. There was a good deal of natural charm in her work, and in spite of her lack of experience, she made a pleasing impression. She was judged as an actress and she was not applauded until she had done something good."[103]

Dale hinted that Ethel's previous claim to fame rested primarily on her social success. Needless to say, this element in her life increased markedly after *Captain Jinks*. One reporter wrote, "While others climb, Ethel leaps,"[104] and another asked, "How Does She Do It?" and then described how she "watches the cup races from the deck of Mrs. John Jacob Astor's yacht; she automobiles with the Goelets; she dines at Sherry's with Mrs. Herman Oelrichs, with Mrs. Stuyvesant Fish, with Mrs. Cooper-Hewitt."[105]

Despite working as an actress and taking up with the English aristocracy, Ethel retained an air of wholesomeness and lack of pretense. As an interviewer for the *Theater* magazine remarked: "Miss Ethel Barrymore is a wholesome American girl, independent, because of her inherent strength, intellectual in her interests, refined in her sensibilities, and an arch enemy of humbug and sham."[106] Ethel greatly appealed to Americans alarmed by the picture of their young women reflected in anxious headlines that proclaimed "The Unrest of Modern Women,"[107] or, as novelist Margaret Deland said about them, "this young person . . . she occupies herself passionately with everything except the things that used to occupy the minds of young girls. Restlessness, Restlessness!"[108]

Therefore, to see and read about Ethel Barrymore—successful, talented, independent, and self-assured, yet continuously referring with filial piety to her grandmother, parents, and uncle, while reminding people of her devotion to her brothers ("My income is their income"),[109] and remarking with total innocence that she did not even own a string of pearls—was a tonic to Americans worried over the future of their daughters. Consequently, it is not difficult to see why, when she and her friend Alice Roosevelt (another contemporary model for American girls) went riding one day, a reporter (taking note of it) wrote, "It is a strong healthy ideal these girls illustrate."[110]

Nevertheless, the American girl epitomized by Ethel Barrymore was hardly without a disruptive effect on these conventional values. As Josephine Gibson Knowlton, Charles Dana Gibson's sister and sometime model, said about his creation:

> My brother wanted to portray a totally American type. The Gibson girl was symbolic of a wholesome, healthy, utterly American girl. She liked sports, was a little ahead of her time, definitely athletic. Importantly she carved out a new type of femininity suggestive of emancipation.[111]

Ethel Barrymore helped foster an image of womanhood with a greater sense of autonomy.

Initially, Ethel Barrymore inclined her efforts toward the stage, and what little effort she made in any other direction was a consequence of her desire to advance her career, rather than the struggle for women's emancipation. Most particularly, Barrymore wanted to escape the cloying definition of herself as a society actress who depended on her "personality,"[112] rather than the skills of the artist. As a result, she began to attempt more difficult roles. Ethel chose Ibsen's Nora in *The Doll's House* as her first major dramatic role, and her approach to the part stressed the psychological, rather than the sociological, elements of the character. One critic who reviewed her interpretation of the part said:

> Miss Barrymore was not filled with the importance of Nora as a missionary light. She emphasized, perhaps too much that she was more a woman than a tract and her girlish manner throughout was a sardonic comment on those who read sociological meanings into the lines, for Nora was as willful in the end as she was in the beginning.[113]

Ethel did, however, evince some interest in the women's movement and was even noted to attend suffragist meetings, a fact which garnered the headlines—as almost all her comings and goings at the time did— "Ethel Barrymore Is a Suffragist."[114] However, her support of suffrage was rather casual and became even less evident after her 1909 marriage to Russell Griswold Colt, son of the president of the rubber trust.[115] Within a year of the marriage, she celebrated the birth of her first child, and probably gladdened the hearts of the enemies of feminism by allowing magazines to take publicity shots which showed her in bed with an old-fashioned nursing cap on her head, embracing the child.[116]

Despite the image of a devoted wife and mother, Barrymore did not lead a traditional woman's life. She continued in her career and did not sway from her desire to escape association with light comedy parts. Even before her marriage and Nora, Ethel took parts that went against her image, namely, the scrub woman in John Galsworthy's *The Silver Box*. After only two years, her marriage began to progressively deteriorate, and there were already rumors of impending divorce.[117] Basic disagreements arose over different interests, her desire to continue her career, and reports of Colt's eye for other women. These created a pattern of estrangement, reconciliation, and estrangement that continued for the eleven years they lived together until their formal divorce in 1923.[118]

As a result of the strains in her marriage and in order to support herself and her children, Ethel expanded her acting involvement beyond her Broadway roles. In 1912, much against the wishes of her manager Charles Frohman, she began to tour the vaudeville circuits in J. M. Barrie's one-act play *The Twelve Pound Look*, a playlet that was to become as much identified with her as her famous and often imitated curtain speech, "That's all there is, there isn't anymore."[119]

Described by one critic as Barrie's most bitter play, *The Twelve Pound Look* is certainly a departure from the fantasy of *Peter Pan* or the romanticism of *The Little Minister.*[120] Performed even today by feminist theatre groups, *The Twelve Pound Look* concerns the meeting of Kate, a typist who comes unawares to the house of her ex-husband, the soon-to-be-knighted Sir Harry, who wants to dictate an acceptance speech for the upcoming ceremony. Startled by her unexpected return, Sir Harry is even further disrupted when he learns that Kate left him, not for another man as he assumed, but when she had saved up the twelve pounds necessary to buy a typewriter and leave his arrogance, stupidity and bullying. As Kate exits, Barrie's stage directions report the same look coming into the eyes of Sir Harry's present wife, whom he treats in the same way he treated Kate.[121]

In its portrayal of a woman who refuses to accept subservience (albeit in a gilded cage) and opts for freedom, *The Twelve Pound Look* gave women a sense of the importance and possibility of economic independence. These ideas caused Ethel Barrymore to approach the play with almost missionary zeal. Her former status as the typical American girl and her current position as a society matron gave the script a special meaning and pungency. As she candidly told one interviewer, "Don't think me gushing or sentimentalizing. On the contrary, I'm the most practical of persons. But when I speak those lines of Barrie I feel as if I were preaching a sermon to every married man and woman in the world. I just have to get that message across."[122]

Barrymore was not alone in her feeling that everyone should see the play. Writing in the *Chicago Record*, critic Walter Prichard Eaton said, " 'The Twelve Pound Look' ought to be seen in every city and village in the land."[123] Although it was not seen everywhere, millions, drawn by Ethel's name and fame, came to see it as she toured it on the vaudeville circuits. Such was its popularity that she twice broke the house record at the Palace.[124]

Its impact on women was phenomenal. One critic reported:

"The Twelve Pound Look" rudely woke up about a million husbands from a deep sleep of complacence, it galvanized an equal number of weary wives into economic freedom. And it boomed the typewriter trade.

Men who for fat successful years . . . in the proud belief that said spouses were supremely happy and envied of other women glanced hastily into the faces of their mates to see if "The Twelve Pound Look" was there.[125]

If it didn't quite move women to seek economic independence or change men's attitudes toward their wives, the play did make them think. Summarizing this phenomenon in her classic study of vaudeville, Caroline Caffin wrote, "It is a play which makes plenty of demand on the audience, for it holds more than mere words. It is a piece of modern life in touch with modern feeling."[126]

The Twelve Pound Look proved to be a significant shift in Barrymore's career on other levels, for she irrevocably changed her image from that of a society actress and a young girl to that of an actress of range and depth. Critic Alan Dale acknowledged and applauded this when he wrote:

> It was "The Twelve Pound Look" by J. M. Barrie that lifted Ethel Barrymore to the position that she now occupies—a position in which girlhood plays no part. In "The Twelve Pound Look" all her latent emotionalism emerged. How many times I saw that admirable little sketch! Night after night I used to watch it, just as much for the sake of Ethel Barrymore as for its intrinsic value. No trace of the old ingenue now remained.[127]

With her stage girlhood thus behind her, Ethel began to portray older and more complicated women such as *The Second Mrs. Tanqueray* and the wealthy but unhappily married Zoe Blundell in *Mid-channel*.[128]

The Twelve Pound Look also opened Ethel to her social responsibilities, a circumstance which culminated in her support for the Actors Equity strike of 1919. Indeed, her commitment to the actors and actresses, as one reporter wrote, could have been predicted from her appearance in *The Twelve Pound Look*. Robert Cole of the *New York Times* said:

> Perhaps the most curious fact of the revolution is the presence of the traditional aristocrat, whose interests would seem to lie with the establishment. This woman, who speaks so earnestly for the actor, is an aristocrat of the stage. Those who saw her in Barrie's "Twelve Pound Look" however, find nothing strange in her present attitude. If she ever seemed to be playing herself, speaking out of her heart from the stage, it was in the character of the woman who left every comfort to become a poor stenographer, because she hated the world where material success was everything, where invisible realities were despised. In the same accents she despises the man who can see nothing but money in the theater.[129]

Cole was right, and Ethel's joining the strikers had an electrifying effect on them. As Ethel described it when she came down to strike headquarters to show them her support, "I was practically carried along the steps and into the house. I found myself up on a table. People were crying and kissing my hands and even the hem of my dress and saying, 'It's all right, we've won, we've won.' "[130]

Doubtless her family's great reputation as well as her own premier status in the theater had something to do with the way the strikers treated Ethel. However, in her memoirs, she described herself as feeling like Joan of Arc.[131] The comparison to the maid of Orleans is an interesting one since it highlights another reason for the reverence of the actors and actresses: her former status as "the typical American girl" gave her adherence to the strike a special prestige in the eyes of other actors, managers, the press, and the rest of America.

The early cries of victory were a bit premature and the strike went on for almost a month. After her little speech at Equity headquarters where she pledged to support the strike, Ethel was indefatigable in her efforts on behalf of the union. She performed at benefits, contributed and raised money, wrote letters to the newspapers, and gave supportive interviews to reporters. In addition, she helped Marie Dressler and others organize the mostly female Chorus Equity, where she gave one of the most well-remembered speeches of the strike, a rather wistful but faith-filled oration in which she said, "I don't know how to make a speech really, but I am with you heart and soul, and more than that. Don't be discouraged. Stick! It's all coming out just the way it ought to for us."[132]

Following the victorious Equity strike, if there was any further evidence needed of Ethel Barrymore's transformation, it came in her starring role in Zoë Akins' *Déclassé*. A smash hit of the early twenties, *Déclassé* seemed in one respect almost a case of art following life, for it cast Ethel Barrymore in the role of a rich and titled Englishwoman who gives up her status and class. This part inspired a generation of actresses, among them Tallulah Bankhead, who saw it literally dozens of times.[133]

The success of *Déclassé* was a clear sign that the "typical American girl" had come of age. Moreover, although this maturity may not have lived up to everyone's expectations of what she should become (a fact that caused so much anxiety and aroused so much interest), it did go beyond the simplicities of *Daisy Miller* and the "Gibson girl" and gave us a sense of an American girl who was more akin to Henry James' astute comment that "to be an American is a complex fate."[134]

NOTES

1. James Bryce, *The American Commonwealth* (New York: MacMillan and Company, 1895), pp. 736.

2. Ibid.

3. Arthur W. Calhoun, *A Social History of the American Family: From Colonial Times to the Present.* (3 Vols. New York: Barnes and Noble, 1947).

4. Linda K. Kerber, "Daughters of Columbia: Educating Women for the Republic, 1787-1805," in *Our American Sister: Women in American Life and Thought*, ed. by Jean E. Friedman and William G. Shade (Boston: Allyn and Bacon, Inc., 1976), pp. 76-92.

5. Eleanor Flexner, *Century of Struggle: The Woman's Rights Movement in the United States.* (New York: Atheneum, 1972), pp. 23-40.

6. Frances Wright, *Views of Society and Manners in America*, ed. by Paul R. Baker (Cambridge: The Belknap Press of Harvard University Press, 1963), pp. 24-25.

7. Alexis de Tocqueville, *Democracy in America*, ed. by J. P. Mayer (Garden City, N.Y.: Anchor Books, Doubleday and Company, Inc., 1969), p. 591.

8. Ibid.

9. Frances Trollope, *Domestic Manners of the Americans*, ed. by Donald Smally (New York: Alfred A. Knopf, Inc., 1948), p. 285.

10. William Wasserstom, *Heiress of All the Ages: Sex and Sentiment in the Gilded Age* (Minneapolis: University of Minnesota Press, 1959), p. 9.

11. Jacques Offenbach, *Orpheus in America: Offenbach's Diary of His Journey to the New World*, translated by Lander MacClintock (Bloomington, Ind.: University of Indiana Press, 1957), p. 82.

12. Paul Bourget, *Outre-Mer: Impressions of America* (New York: Charles Scribner's Sons, 1895), p. 80.

13. James F. Muirhead, *The Land of Contrasts* (London: John Lane, 1898), pp. 45-62.

14. Charles De Varigny, *The Women of the United States.* (New York: Dodd, Mead and Company, 1895), p. 1.

15. Th. Bentzon (Marie Thérèse Blanc), *The Condition of Women in the United States* (Boston: Roberts Brothers, 1895).

16. Th. Bentzon (Marie Thérèse Blanc), "Family Life in America," *Forum*, XXI (March, 1896), p. 17.

17. Christopher Lasch, *The New Radicalism in America 1889–1963* (New York: Vintage Books, 1965), pp. 3-37. See also Carl N. Degler, ed., "Introduction to the Torchbook Edition," in Charlotte Perkins Gilman, *Women and Economics: The Economic Factor between Men and Women as a Factor in Social Evolution* (New York: Harper Torchbooks, 1966), pp. vi-xxxv.

18. Elliot Gregory, "Our Foolish Virgins," *Century*, LXIII (November, 1901), pp. 3-15.

19. Lasch, *The New Radicalism*, p. 46.

20. Kate Gannett Wells, "The Transitional American Woman," *Atlantic Monthly*, XLVI (December, 1880), pp. 817-823.

21. Ibid., p. 820.

22. Edith Lyttleton Gell, "Squandered Girlhood," *Nineteenth Century*, XXXII (December, 1892), pp. 930-937.

23. F. M. Edselas, "What Shall We Do With Our Girls," *Catholic World*, LXI (July, 1895), pp. 538-545.

24. Sarah M. Amos, "The Evolution of the Daughters," *Contemporary Review*, LXI (April, 1894), pp. 515-520.

25. Helen Ekin Starrett, "The Future of Our Daughters," *Forum*, X (October, 1890), pp. 85-196.

26. "What the American Girl Has Lost By An American Mother," *Ladies Home Journal*, 17 (May, 1900), p. 17.

27. Ibid.

28. Caroline Ticknor, "The Steel Engraving Lady and the Gibson Girl," *Atlantic Monthly*, LLXVIII (July, 1907), pp. 105-108.

29. Ibid., p. 108.

30. Anne Warner, "The New Woman and the Old," *Century*, XLVII (November, 1909), pp. 85-92.

31. "The Passing of the Old Lady," *Atlantic Monthly*, CIX (June, 1907), p. 874.

32. Mrs. David O. Means, "A Tribute to Mrs. Theodore Birney," *The New York Public Library.*

33. Mrs. Theodore Birney, "The Twentieth-Century Girl: What We Expect of Her," *Harpers Bazaar*, XLII (May, 1900), pp. 224-227.

34. Ibid., p. 224.

35. Ibid., p. 227.

36. Allen J. Saunders, "The Typical American Girl," *Broadway* (February, 1901) n.p. (*Locke*, 34, p. 8).

37. DeLancey M. Albert, "Ethel Barrymore: A Sketch," *Frank Leslie's Popular Monthly* (May, 1903), p. 60.

38. "Ideal Type of American Girl, Portrayed by Ethel Barrymore," *Century* (April, 1908), n.p. (*Locke*, 36, p. 20).

39. Charles E. Laughlin, "How Ethel Barrymore Thinks a Young Girl Should Dress," *Ladies Home Journal*, 25 (May, 1908), pp. 13, 73.

40. Gustav Kobbe, "The Girlishness of Ethel Barrymore," *Ladies Home Journal*, 20 (June, 1903), p. 4.

41. "Ideal Type of American Girl," (*Locke*, 36, p. 20).

42. Kobbe, "The Girlishness of Ethel Barrymore," p. 4.

43. Vanderhyden Fyles, "Our Ethel," *Gunter's* (October, 1906), n.p. (*Locke*, 35, pp. 57-58).

44. Francis Crowninshield quoted in James Kotsilibas-Davis, *Great Times, Good Times: The Odyssey of Maurice Barrymore* (Garden City, N.Y.: Doubleday and Company, Inc., 1977), p. 474.

45. James L. Ford, "The Ethel Barrymore Following," *Appleton's* (November, 1908), pp. 546, 550.

46. Ethel Barrymore, *Memories: An Autobiography* (New York: Harper and Brothers, 1955), p. 103.

47. John Berger, *Ways of Seeing* (New York: Viking Press, 1972), p. 132.

48. Julia Goldsmith Gilbert, *Ferber, A Biography* (Garden City, N.Y.: Doubleday and Company, 1978).

49. Ethel Barrymore, *Memories*, p. 8.

50. Brander Matthews, *Rip Van Winkle Goes to Play and Other Plays and Players* (Port Washington, N.Y.: Kennikat Press, 1967), p. 202.

51. Mrs. John Drew, *Autobiographical-Sketch* (New York: Charles Scribner's Sons, 1899).

52. A. Frank Stull, "Where Famous Actors Learned Their Act," *Lippincott's*, LXXV (March, 1905), pp. 373.

53. "The Senator" review, *New York Spirit of the Times*, August 9, 1891, n.p. (*Locke*, 39, p. 129).

54. Alan Dale, *Familiar Chats with the Queens of the Stage* (New York: G. W. Dillingham, Publishers, 1890), p. 311.

55. Ethel Barrymore, "My Reminiscences, The Life Story of America's Foremost Character Actress." *The Delineator* (October, 1923), p. 7.

56. Helena Modjeska, *Memories and Impressions of Helena Modjeska: An Autobiography* (New York: The Macmillan Company, 1910), p. 464.

57. Ethel Barrymore, *Memories*, p. 13.

58. Ibid., p. 301.

59. Kotsilibas-Davis, *Great Times, Good Times*, pp. 3-115.

60. Ibid., pp. 266-270.

61. Ibid., pp. 389-390.

62. Ethel Barrymore, *Memories*, p. 17.

63. Lionel Barrymore as told to Cameron Shipp, *We Barrymores* (New York: Appleton-Century-Crofts, Inc., 1951), p. 85.

64. Ethel Barrymore, *Memories*, p. 32.

65. Ibid., p. 34.

66. Ibid., p. 37.

67. Hollis Alpert, *The Barrymores* (New York: Dial Press, 1964), pp. 41-44.

68. Ethel Barrymore, *Memories*, p. 37.

69. Ibid., p. 49.

70. Ibid., p. 39.

71. Kotsilibas-Davis, *Great Times, Good Times*, pp. 492-495.

72. Ethel Barrymore, *Memories*, p. 66.

73. Michael Baker, *The Rise of the Victorian Actor* (London: Croom Helm, 1978), pp. 160-174.

74. Leonore Davidoff, *The Best Circles: Society, Etiquette and Season* (London: Croom Helm, 1973), p. 54.

75. Ibid., p. 64.

76. Ethel Barrymore, *Memories*, pp. 84-86.

77. Dixon Wecter, *The Saga of American Society: A Record of Social Aspiration 1607-1937* (New York: Charles Scribner's Sons, 1937), p. 181.

78. Isaac F. Marcosson and Daniel Frohman, *Charles Frohman: Manager and Man* (New York: Harper and Brothers, 1916), pp. 276-289.

79. Ethel Barrymore, *Memories*, p. 125.

80. "Ethel Barrymore 'Most Engaged Girl' in America," *Morning Telegraph*, December 16, 1899, n.p. (*Locke*, 34, p. 5)

81. Henry Irving, *Impressions of America* (Boston: James R. Osgood and Company, 1884), p. 320.

82. See as an example Julia Newberry, *Julia Newberry's Diary*, with an Introduction by Margaret Ayers Barnes and Janet Ayer Fairbank (New York: W. W. Norton, 1933).

83. Leon Edel, *Henry James: The Conquest of London 1870–1891* (Philadelphia: J. B. Lippincott and Company, 1962), p. 301.

84. Ibid., p. 312.

85. Ibid., p. 312.

86. Ibid., p. 312.

87. "An American Girl" (Ballade), *Scribner's Monthly*, XXI (December, 1880), p. 296-297.

88. James D. Hart, *The Popular Book: A History of America's Literary Taste* (New York: Oxford University Press, 1950), p. 186.

89. Edmund Wilson, "The Ambiguity of Henry James," in *The Question of Henry James*, ed. by F. W. Dupee (New York: Octagon Press, 1973), p. 176.

90. Philip Rahv, *Image and Idea: Twenty Essays on Literary Themes* (New York: A New Direction Paperbook, 1957), pp. 51-76.

91. Henry James, *The Art of the Novel: Critical Prefaces*, with an Introduction by R. P.

Blackmur (New York: Charles Scribner's Sons, 1934), p. 292.

92. Wecter, *Saga of American Society*, p. 181.

92. Sara Jeanette Cotes (Duncan), *An American Girl in London* (New York: D. Appleton and Company, 1891).

94. Fairfax Downey, *Portrait of an Era as Drawn by Charles Dana Gibson* (New York: Charles Scribner's Sons, 1936).

95. Edmund Vincent Gillor Jr., ed., *The Gibson Girl and Her America: Best Drawings of Charles Dana Gibson* with an introductory essay by Henry C. Pitz (New York: Dover, 1969), p. xi.

96. Lazar Ziff, *The American 1890's: The Life and Times of a Lost Generation* (New York: The Viking Press, 1966), pp. 173-184.

97. Charles Belmont Davis, ed., *Adventures and Letters of Richard Harding Davis* (New York: Charles Scribner's Sons, 1917), p. 8.

98. Fairfax Downey, *Richard Harding Davis: His Day* (New York: Charles Scribner's Sons, 1933), p. 140.

99. Ibid., p. 175.

100. Allen J. Saunders, "Typical American Girl," (*Locke*, 34, p. 20).

101. Eric Bentley, ed., *From the American Drama*, the Modern Theatre Series, Vol. 4 (Garden City, N.Y.: Doubleday Anchor Books, 1956), pp. 1-119.

102. Ethel Barrymore, *Memories*, p. 119.

103. Alan Dale, "Fitch's New Play, 'Capt. Jinks' is Splendid, Says Alan Dale," *New York Journal*, February 5, 1901, n.p. (*Locke*, 34, pp. 8-9).

104. "Little Ethel Barrymore's Amazing Social Triumphs, How Does She Manage to Do It?" *New York Journal*, May 31, 1903, p. 13.

105. Ibid.

106. W. De Wagstaffe, "Ethel Barrymore An Impression: Chat with Players, No. 12" *Theatre*, II (November, 1902), p. 23.

107. Susanne Wilcox, "The Unrest of Modern Woman," *Independent*, LXVII (July, 1909), pp. 62-66.

108. Margaret Deland, "The Change in the Feminine Ideal," *Atlantic Monthly*, CV (March, 1910), p. 291.

109. Rennold Wolf, "Ethel Barrymore," *Smith's* (November, 1907), n.p. (*Locke*, 35, pp. 44-46).

110. Idah M'Glone Gibson, "Just Two Girls," *Toledo Blade,* October 26, 1904, n.p. (*Locke*, 34, p. 94).

111. Woody Gelman, *The Best of Charles Dana Gibson* (New York: Bounty Books, 1969), p. ix.

112. Bijou Fernandez, "What I Think of Ethel Barrymore, Her Acting, Her Personality and Her Ideals," *Designer* (February, 1909), n.p. (*Locke*, 36, p. 44).

113. "Measuring Off Stage Center: Miss Barrymore's Experiment with Nora of the Doll's House," no title given, May 3, 1905, n.p. (*Locke*, 35, p. 15).

114. "Ethel Barrymore is a Suffragist," *Morning Telegraph,* February 11, 1910, p. 12.

115. Ethel Barrymore, *Memories*, p. 167.

116. David Gray, "Ethel Barrymore's Little Son," *Ladies Home Journal*, 30 (April, 1911), p. 23.

117. "Miss Barrymore is a Happy Wife," *New York Herald*, November, 17, 1910, n.p. (*Locke*, 37, p. 5).

118. Ethel Barrymore, *Memories*, p. 231.

119. Ethel Barrymore, *Memories*, p. 148.

120. Janet Dunbar, *J. M. Barrie: The Man Behind the Image* (Boston: Houghton-Mifflin Company, 1970).

121. Alpert, *The Barrymores*, p. 157.

122. Zoe Beckley, "Has Your Own True Wife That Twelve-Pound Look Tru Dr. Barrie's Remedy," *New York Mail,* August 26, 1914, n.p. (*Locke,* 38, p. 10).

123. Walter Prichard Eaton, "Walter P. Eaton's New York Letter," *Chicago Record*, n.p. (*Locke,* 37, p. 21).

124. Ethel Barrymore, *Memories*, p. 177.

125. Zoe Beckley, *"Has Your Wife That Twelve-Pound Look,"* (*Locke,* 38, p. 10).

126. Caroline Caffin, *Vaudeville* (New York: Mitchell Kennerley, 1914), p. 124.

127. Alan Dale, "The Most Interesting People of the Theater, No. 1: Ethel Barrymore," *Green Book* (December, 1915), p. 1072.

128. Ethel Barrymore, *Memories*, p. 171.

129. Ibid., pp. 223-224.

130. Ibid., p. 221.

131. Ibid.

132. Alfred Harding, *Revolt of the Actors* (New York: William Morrow and Company, 1929), p. 115.

133. Tallulah Bankhead, *Tallulah, My Autobiography* (New York: Harper and Brothers, Publishers, 1952), p. 85.

134. Van Wyck Brooks, *The Pilgrimage of Henry James* (New York: E. P. Dutton and Company, 1925).

Chapter 8

Conclusion

By the 1920s, the theater's influence on American mass consciousness was on the wane, the most important reasons for its decline being the popularity of the movies and the proliferation of the motion picture theater. From a high of 392 companies touring the United States in 1900, the number dropped to 42 in 1920.[1] In addition, the number of theaters playing live drama and musical comedy fell from 1,549 in 1910 to 674 in 1925.[2] Meanwhile, the average weekly attendance at movies reached 40 million in 1922,[3] and the number of theaters showing films increased to 15,000 throughout the country.[4]

As a consequence of these changes, Hollywood, rather than Broadway, became the center of American popular culture, and the actress became the star. Instead of merely creating characters that produced some sort of catharsis, the actress became, in the words of French critic Edgar Morin, "the provender of dreams" who, he also added, "provoke only partial catharsis and foster fantasies which for all their yearning cannot release themselves in action."[5]

These shifts reflected a significant change from the situation which existed between 1890 and 1920, when the Broadway theater and actress exercised a large influence on American society and culture. Their influence had grown slowly and had overcome severe social, economic, and ideological obstacles. Nevertheless, as a result of the work of the Hallams, William Dunlop, and Edwin Forrest, the theater became firmly rooted in American society. Among the theatrical pioneers, women like Mercy Otis Warren, Susanna Rowson, Charlotte Cushman, and Anna Cora Mowatt gave evidence of the quality of native female theatrical talent and by their professional stands and social standing added immeasurably to the stature of the American theater.[6]

Women found their greatest opportunity for professional equality in the theater during the first half of the nineteenth century. The freedom that resulted from their social and economic independence permitted some actresses to form personal and social relationships with other women seeking to redefine women's position in society. While connec-

143

tions between Adah Isaacs Menken and George Sand, and Fanny Kemble and Catherine Sedgewick rarely strayed beyond the personal, the actress-writer Abbey Sage Richardson not only created social ties to feminists, but her tragic marriage also became a cause célèbre in their battle for equal rights. Ultimately, these links allowed the actress-activist Olive Logan to speak out publicly for equal rights and provided her with an audience for her book *Apropos of Women and Theatres* (1869), which points to the theater as a place where women could achieve equality with men.[7]

Coinciding with Logan's eloquent pleas was a burgeoning American industrial economy which would fulfill her ideas in ways Logan had not foreseen. As America's industrial strength grew, so did its entertainment industry. Along with it, too, came an increase in the number of actresses and women entertainers, not to mention a swelling number of female theatergoers. This latter group continued to grow as the number of women in higher education rose, as more women entered the work force, and as women began to find increased leisure time. Indicative of this development was the social phenomenon of the "matinee girl," whom some considered the backbone and others the bane of the theater. Furthermore, critics noted and commented upon the "feminization of the theater," for women occupied a stellar position among the players of the day.

Actresses became prominent in other ways as well. Among the most striking examples of their power was the actress-led excoriation of renowned British critic Clement Scott. Their response to his scurrilous attacks on the morals of women in the theater eventually led to his resignation as critic for the influential London *Daily Telegraph*. In addition, by the turn of the century women of the theater topped their male counterparts in the size of their salaries and their popularity.

This period also saw the appearance of "stagestruck girls" who, enamored with the theater, besieged the profession. A far cry from the early entrants to the profession who were recruited mainly from actor-families and the poor, these new arrivals came from the middle class, and their influx prompted a debate in the theatrical community over methods of training (acting schools vs. stock companies). Moreover, they provoked a host of articles intended to dash rose-colored expectations about the profession.

Though life in the theater could be economically rewarding, emotionally gratifying, and glamorous, it was nevertheless filled with hardship. While wages for women were generally higher in the theater than other occupations, actresses faced the economic hardships of long periods of unemployment and the heavy burden of providing their own wardrobe (or, in the case of vaudeville, their own fresh material). Touring presented the physical discomforts of bad food and even worse accommodations, physical danger (train wrecks, theater fires, unhealthy dressing rooms), loneliness, and even sexual harassment. In addition, actors and actresses continued to be socially ostracized throughout most of the nineteenth century.

By the end of the century, the theater had reached its peak in prosperity and prestige. However, its growth and development was but one way in which the fortunes of the theatrical profession reflected and influenced the rest of American cultural life.

Although isolated from the rest of American society by virtue of the conditions of their labor (touring, late hours), the acting profession nevertheless experienced the major changes convulsing the nation. One of the most significant of these social changes was the rise of the "New Woman." While she was a consequence of the same transformations that created the "matinee girl" and the "feminization of the theater," the "New Woman" also sought to achieve equal rights, especially the right to vote. This campaign was soon shared and supported by actresses who contributed to it the power of the drama and their celebrity.

As America experienced the rise of the "New Woman" it underwent also a corresponding growth of economic, social and political organizations. Professional groups like the American Medical Association and academic associations grew rapidly and gave people a source of stability in a period of intensified social change. In the theater, this took the form of the Actors Fund and the Players Club. Following on the heels of these male groups, actresses founded the Twelfth Night Club and the Professional Woman's League.

The Twelfth Night Club was primarily a social group, but the Professional Woman's League was very much in the mold of the women's intellectual, social and self-help organizations pioneered by Sorosis and the New England Woman's Club. Like these groups, the Professional Woman's League provided women with a network of supportive social relations, a vehicle for the discussion of political and social issues (including feminism), and an opportunity to extend their organizational and leadership skills.

Among the many beneficiaries of this experience was Mary Shaw, who used the lessons learned at the League in activities that went beyond the confines of the acting profession. Seizing on the possibilities of the stage as a consciousness-raising tool, she led a life of artistic and political activism which included advancing the cause of the new realist dramatists Ibsen and Shaw (whom she regarded as particularly sensitive to women) and writing and acting in suffragist sketches and plays intended to mobilize women's support for the equal rights campaign.

Mary Shaw's overt feminism and her use of the stage as a weapon in the struggle for the vote was but one way that the actress helped the movement. Another, Lillian Russell, lent her name and the celebrity often attached to it — sometimes as a national cultural symbol — to aid women's rights.

Lillian Russell's activities on behalf of suffrage are generally cited as a mere footnote to her career. Nevertheless, politics were intrinsically bound up with Lillian's life and career. Both her parents were active in political and culturally radical causes, her mother as a feminist, suffragist, and socialist, and her father as the publisher of radical literature. Lillian's own career benefitted from her identification with Anglo-Saxon physical beauty when Anglo-Saxon racial hegemony was seen as the solution to late nineteenth century America's social, economic, and cultural problems. As a result of her remarkable conformity to the Anglo-Saxon ideal, a highly regarded vocal talent, and the esteem with which she was regarded by the newly entertainment-oriented and nationalistic American middle class, she became the embodiment of American beauty.

Aware of her importance as a national cultural symbol and the power it brought, Lillian Russell promoted the causes she espoused: Christian Science and health, and beauty culture. Her enthusiastic belief in the value of the bicycle and strenuous physical activity for women helped break restrictions on women's physical activities and undermined the myth of their essential passivity. Additionally, her reputation as the American beauty and her attacks on the canard that feminism made women mannish helped lay that argument to rest.

Lillian Russell also gave her outspoken support to the suffrage campaign. As she had in Teddy Roosevelt's political campaign in 1912 and subsequently in the debates over the League of Nations and the Presidential campaign of Warren G. Harding, Russell worked energetically as a speaker and fund raiser for the suffrage movement. The most illustrious actress in America to lend her name in support of equal rights, her high salary and taxes underlined the fact that denying women the vote violated the fundamental American principle of equal representation.

Not every actress who aided in the struggle for women's rights and emancipation was as self-consciously militant and direct as Mary Shaw and Lillian Russell. Some supported the women's cause by appearing in plays that advocated women's need for self-determination and autonomy, or used their prestige to help actors and actresses fight for greater professional and economic dignity. It was Ethel Barrymore who made such a contribution.

The scion of an acting family that extended back three centuries, Ethel Barrymore possessed fine models of feminine independence and achievement in her grandmother, Mrs. John Drew, and her mother, Georgie Drew Barrymore. Entering the acting profession by necessity rather than choice, she soon found herself exalted as the embodiment of the typical American girl. Her popularity at home resulted from her glittering social triumphs in London, which were seen as particularly spectacular to Americans who welcomed them as a way of erasing some of the anxiety and concern about the "American girl" which had arisen with the dawn of the American republic and had reached a high pitch after the publication of Henry James' controversial *Daisy Miller.*

Ethel Barrymore's social success, coupled with her equation with the self-assured "Gibson girl" and her Broadway stage acclaim, gave her immense popularity and prestige. However, despite these achievements, Barrymore sought greater stage fulfillment, escape from her role as a "personality" and a "society actress," and some surcease from the economic anxieties of an unstable marriage by attempting more complex and demanding roles. A key to Barrymore's search was her national vaudeville tours in James M. Barrie's *The Twelve Pound Look*—a serious dramatic piece which gave a resounding call for women's economic independence. Seen by millions, the issues it dealt with were an important element in women's demands for self-determination and autonomy, which gained greater credibility by dint of Barrymore's association with them. Furthermore, its socially relevant message was a factor in prompting Barrymore to link her name and fortunes with the actors and actresses in the momentous Actors Equity strike of 1919.

Actresses like Mary Shaw, Lillian Russell, and Ethel Barrymore showed how the stage and celebrity was used both wittingly and unwittingly in the struggle for women's rights and women's emancipation in the period between 1890 and 1920, and their lives underscored the importance of the actress in the American cultural life of that period. Ultimately, the stage actress gave way in influence before the Hollywood star, though not before she had made as much of an impact on our social and political lives as the star has subsequently had on our psyches.

NOTES

1. Jack Poggi, *Theater in America: The Impact of Economic Forces, 1870-1967* (Ithaca, New York: Cornell University Press, 1968), p. 30.

2. Ibid., p. 29.

3. Garth Jowitt, *Film, the Democratic Art: A Social History of American Film* (Boston: Little, Brown and Company, 1976), p. 475.

4. Ibid., p. 60.

5. Edgar Morin, *The Stars: An Account of the Star-System in Motion Pictures* (New York: Grove Press, Inc., 1960), p. 166.

6. Glenn Hughes, *A History of the American Theatre, 1700-1950* (New York: Samuel French, 1951).

7. Olive Logan, *Apropos of Women and Theatres, with a Paper or Two on Parisian Topics* (New York: Carleton, Publisher, 1869).

Bibliography

ARCHIVES:

Museum of the City of New York, Theater Collection.
New York Historical Society Library.
New York City Public Library, Lincoln Center for the Performing Arts, Billy Rose Theater Collection.
New York City Public Library, Main Research Collection.
Players Club, Library, New York City.

THEATRICAL SCRAPBOOKS, CLIPPINGS, PROGRAMS AND PHOTOGRAPHS:

Ethel Barrymore, Robinson Locke Scrapbooks, Vols. 34-39 and portfolios complete.
Nora Bayes, Robinson Locke Scrapbooks, Vols. 46-47 and portfolios complete.
Amelia Bingham, Robinson Locke Scrapbooks, Vols. 70-71 and portfolios complete.
Emma Carus, Robinson Locke Collection complete.
Henrietta Crosman, Robinson Locke Scrapbooks, Vols. 136-138 and portfolios complete.
Alice Fischer, Robinson Locke Scrapbook, Vol. 200 and portfolios complete.
Trixie Friganza, Robinson Locke Scrapbook, Vol. 220 and portfolios complete.
May Irwin, Robinson Locke Scrapbooks, Vols. 297-298 and portfolios complete.
Lillian Russell, Robinson Locke Scrapbooks, Vols. 410-415 and portfolios complete.
Mary Shaw, Robinson Locke Scrapbok, Vol. 431 and portfolios complete.
Eva Tanquay, Robinson Locke Scrapbook, Vol. 450 and portfolios complete.
Faye Templeton, Robinson Locke Scrapbook, Vol. 453 and portfolios complete.
Cited in Footnotes as (*Locke,* Vol. Number, Page Number).

NEWSPAPERS:

Billboard
Figaro (San Francisco)

New York Amusement Gazette
New York Clipper
New York Dramatic Chronicle
New York Dramatic Mirror
New York Dramatic News and Times
New York Morning Telegraph
New York Spirit of the Times
New York Times
Variety

UNPUBLISHED MANUSCRIPTS:

Blair, Karen. "The Clubwoman as Feminist: The Woman's Culture Movement in the United States, 1855-1914." Unpublished Ph.D. dissertation, State University of New York at Buffalo, 1976.

Brumm, Beverly M. "A Survey of Professional Acting Schools in New York City, 1870-1970." Unpublished Ph.D. dissertation, New York University, 1973.

Erenberg, Lewis Allan. "Urban Nightlife and the Decline of Victorianism: New York City's Restaurants and Cabarets, 1890-1918." Unpublished Ph.D. dissertation, University of Michigan, 1974.

Harper, Charles Harold. "Mrs. Leslie Carter: Her Life and Acting Career." Unpublished Ph.D. dissertation, University of Nebraska, 1978.

Irving, John D. "Mary Shaw, Actress, Suffragist, Activist (1854-1929)" Unpublished Ph.D. dissertation, Columbia University, 1978.

May, Larry Linden. "Reforming Leisure: The Birth of Mass Leisure and the Motion Picture Industry, 1896-1920." Unpublished Ph.D. dissertation, University of California, Los Angeles, 1977.

Melder, Keith. "The Beginnings of the Women's Rights Movement in the United States, 1800-1840." Unpublished Ph.D. dissertation, Yale University, 1964.

Ryan, Pat. "A.M. Palmer, Producer: A Study of Management, Dramaturgy and Stagecraft in the American Theater, 1872-1896." Unpublished Ph.D. dissertation, Yale University, 1959.

Wills, Jr., J. Robert. "The Riddle of Olive Logan: A Biographical Profile." Unpublished Ph.D. dissertation, Case Western Reserve University, 1971.

MAGAZINE AND JOURNAL ARTICLES:

Allen, Viola. "On the Making of An Actress." *Cosmopolitan*, XXXL (August, 1900), pp. 409-414.

Amos, Sarah M. "The Evolution of the Daughters." *Contemporary Review*, LXV (April, 1894), pp. 515-520.

Barrymore, Ethel. "The Young Girl and the Stage." *Harpers Bazaar*, XL (December, 1906), pp. 999-1001.

———"My Reminiscences: The Life Story of America's Foremost Character Actress." *Delineator*, (October–February, 1924).

Belasco, David. "Advice to the Girl with Dramatic Ambitions." *Woman's Home Companion*, XXXI (October, 1904), p. 7.

Bell, Archie. "What Woman Has Done for the Stage." *Theatre*, VII (August, 1907), pp. 216-217.

Bentzon, Th. (Marie Therese Blanc) "Family Life in America." *Forum* XXL (March, 1896), pp. 1-20.

Bernheim, Alfred L. "The Facts of Vaudeville." *Equity*, VIII-IX (September, 1923-January, 1924).

Birney, Mrs. Theodore. "The Twentieth Century Girl: What We Expect of Her." *Harpers Bazaar*, XLII (May, 1900), pp. 224-227.

Bok, Edward, "The Young Girl at the Matinee," *Ladies Home Journal*, 20 (June, 1903), p. 16.

Brandenberg, Broughton. "Racial Traits in American Beauty." *Cosmopolitan*, XLI (May, 1906), pp. 57-64.

Burnham, James C. "The Progressive Era Revolution in American Attitudes Toward Sex." *Journal of American History*, LIX (March, 1973), pp. 885-908.

Cowl, Jane. "Why a Reputation for Beauty is a Handicap." *American*, LXXIV (August, 1917), pp. 50-51, 90, 92.

Dale, Alan. "Why Women are Greater Actors Than Men." *Cosmopolitan*, LI (September, 1906), pp. 517-524.

———"The Most Interesting People of the Theater, Number 1: Ethel Barrymore." *Green Book*, XXX (December, 1915), pp. 1065-1072.

Davis, Charles Belmont. "On the Road with Players." *Outing*, LII (August, 1908), pp. 529-541.

———"The Young Girl and the Stage." *Colliers*, 44 (October, 1909), pp. 22-23, 26.

Davis, Hartley. "The Business Side of the Theatre." *Everybody's*, XXL (November, 1905), pp. 665-674.

———"The Business Side of Vaudeville." *Everybody's*, XXV (October, 1907), pp. 527-537.

Day, Clarence. "Appearing with Lillian Russell." *Saturday Evening Post*, CVIII (October, 1935), p. 90.

Deland, Margaret. "The Change in the Feminine Ideal." *Atlantic Monthly*, CV (March, 1910), pp. 289-302.

Denison, John. "The Survival of the American Type." *Atlantic Monthly*, LXXI (January, 1895), pp. 16-28.

De Wagstaffe, W. "Ethel Barrymore: An Impression." *Theatre*, II (November, 1902), pp. 24-26.

Eaton, Walter Prichard. "Women as Theater-Goers." *Woman's Home Companion*, XXXVII (October, 1910), p. 13.

Edselas, F.M. "What Shall We Do With Our Girls." *Catholic World*, LXI (July, 1895), pp. 536-545.

Ferguson, Katherine. "Shall We Go to the Theater?" *Woman's Home Companion*, L (January, 1917), p. 23.

Ford, James L. "The Ethel Barrymore Following." *Appleton's*, (November, 1908), pp. 546-550.

Franklin, Irene. "The American Beauty." *Stage*, (October, 1938), pp. 50-51.

Gell, Edith Lyttelton. "Squandered Girlhood." *Nineteen Century*, XXXII (December, 1892), pp. 930-937.

Giddings, Laura. "The Beauty that is Power." *Jeness-Miller Monthly*, (March, 1890), pp. 217-220.

Grand, Sara. "The Duty of Looking Attractive." *Review of Reviews*, VIII (September, 1893), pp. 342-343.

Grau, Robert. "The Amazing Prosperity of the Vaudeville Entertainer." *Overland Monthly*, LVII (June, 1911), pp. 608-609.

Gray, David. "Ethel Barrymore's Little Son." *Ladies Home Journal*, 20 (April, 1911), p. 23.

Green, Helen. "One Day in Vaudeville." *McClures*, XXXIX (October, 1912), pp. 637-647.

Gregory, Elliot. "Our Foolish Virgins." *Century*, LVIII (November, 1901), pp. 3-15.

Halbert, Delancey M. "Ethel Barrymore: A Sketch." *Frank Leslie's Popular Monthly* (May, 1903), pp. 60-61.

Harbin, Billy J. "The Role of Mrs. Hallam in the Hodgkinson-Hallam Controversy, 1794-1797." *Theatre Journal*, XXXII (May, 1980), pp. 212-222.

Harmond, Richard. "Progress and Flight: An Interpretation of the American Cycle Craze of the 1890's." *Journal of Social History*, 5 (1972), pp. 235-257.

Higham, John. "The Mind of a Nativist: Henry F. Bowers and the A.P.A." *American Quarterly*, IV (1952), pp. 16-24.

————"The Reorientation of American Culture in the 1890's." In *Writing American History: Essays in Scholarship* by John Higham. Bloomington: Indiana University Press, 1970.

Hutcheson, Maud MacDonald. "Mercy Otis Warren, 1728-1814." *William and Mary Quarterly*, X (July, 1953), pp. 379-402.

Irwin, May. "The Business of the Stage as a Career." *Cosmopolitan*, XXVIII (April, 1960), pp. 655-660.

Johnson, Claudia D. "That Guilty Third Tier: Prostitution in Nineteenth Century American Theater." *American Quarterly*, XXVI (December, 1975), pp. 575-584.

Kent, Christopher. "Image and Reality: The Actress and Society." *A Widening Sphere*. Edited by Martha Vicnus. Bloomington: Indiana University Press, 1977, pp. 94-116.

Kerber, Linda K. "Daughters of Columbia: Educating Women for the Republic, 1787-1805." In *Our American Sisters: Women in American Life and Thought*. Edited by Jean E. Friedman and William G. Shade. Boston: Allyn and Bacon, pp. 76-92.

Kobbe, Gustave. "The Girlishness of Ethel Barrymore." *Ladies Home Journal*, 20 (June, 1903), p. 4.

Kolb, Deborah S. "The Rise and Fall of the New Women in American Drama." *Educational Theatre Journal*, XXXVII (May, 1975), pp. 149-160.

La Follette, Fola. "Suffragetting on the Chautauqua." *Ladies Home Journal*, 40 (January, 1916), pp. 27, 51.

Laughlin, Charles E. "How Ethel Barrymore Thinks Young Girls Should Dress." *Ladies Home Journal*, 25 (May, 1908), pp. 13, 73.

Lerner, Gerda. "New Approaches to the Study of Women in American History." In *The Majority Finds its Past: Placing Women in History*, Gerda Lerner. New York: Oxford University Press, 1981, pp. 3-14.

————"Women's Rights and American Feminism." in *The Majority Finds its Past: Placing Women in History*, Gerda Lerner. New York: Oxford University Press, 1981, pp. 48-62.

Lynch, Gertrude. "Racial and Ideal Types of Beauty." *Cosmopolitan*, XXXVIII (December, 1904), pp. 223-233.

Mawson, Henry P. "The Truth About Going on the Stage." *Theatre*, II (August, 1902), pp. 10-12.

McGovern, James R. "The American Woman's Pre-World War I Freedom in Manners and Morals." *Journal of American History*, LV (September, 1963), pp. 315-333.

Means, Mrs. David O. "A Tribute to Mrs. Theodore Birney." *New York Public Library*.

Page, William A. "The Stage Struck Girl." *Woman's Home Companion*, XLIII (September, 1916), p. 19.

Repplier, Agnes. "The Repeal of Reticence." *Atlantic Monthly*, CIX (March, 1914), pp. 297-304.

Richardson, Anna Steese. "A Women-Made Season." *McClures*, LVII (April, 1908), pp. 22-23, 65-67.

Royale, Edwin Milton. "The Vaudeville Theater." *Scribner's*, XXVI (October, 1899), pp. 485-495.

Russell, Annie. "What it Really Means to be an Actress." *Ladies Home Journal*, 26 (January, 1909), p. 17.

Russell, Dorothy. "My Mother, Lillian Russell." *Liberty*, VI (October-November, 1929).

Russell, Lillian. "Lillian Russell's Reminiscences." *Cosmopolitan*, LXX (February-September, 1922).

Saxton, Alexander. "Blackface Minstrelsy and Jacksonian Ideology." *American Quarterly*, XXVII (March, 1975), pp. 3-28.

Shaw, Mary. "Actresses on the Road." *McClures*, XXXVII (July, 1911), pp. 263-272.

————"My 'Immoral' Play: The Story of the First American Production of Mrs. Warren's Profession!" *McClures*, XXVIII (April, 1912), pp. 684-694.

Sheridan, E. V. "Manners Among Stage People." *Theatre*, VII (August, 1890), pp. 28-29.

Sherlock, Charles R. "Where Vaudeville Holds the Boards." *Cosmopolitan*, XXXII (February, 1902), pp. 411-420.

Smith, Daniel Scott. "Family Limitation, Sexual Control and Domestic Feminism in Victorian America." *Clio's Consciousness Raised*. Edited by Mary Hartman and Lois W. Banner. New York: Harper and Row, 1974, pp. 119-136.

Solomon, Barbara Miller. "The Intellectual Background of the Immigrant Restriction Movement in New England." *New England Quarterly,* XXV (1952), pp. 47-59.

Starrett, Helen Ekin. "The Future of Our Daughters." *Forum,* X (October, 1890), pp. 185-196.

Stern, Madelaine B. "Trial by Gotham 1870: The Career of Abby Sage Richardson." XXVIII *New York History* (July, 1947), pp. 271-287.

Stull, A Frank. "Where Famous Actors Learned Their Art." *Lippincott's,* LXXV (March, 1905).

Ticknor, Caroline. "The Steel Engraving Lady and the Gibson Girl." *Atlantic Monthly,* LCVIII (July, 1907), pp. 105-108.

Tompkins, Juliet Wilbor. "The Brutality of the Matinee Girl." *Lippincott's* (November, 1907), pp. 687-689.

Tyrell, Henry. "Mary Shaw—A Woman of Thought and Action." *Theatre,* II (August, 1902), pp. 21-23.

Walker, Francis A. "Immigration and Degradation." *Forum,* XI (July, 1891), pp. 634-644.

Warner, Ann. "The New Woman and the Old." *Century,* XLVII (November, 1909), pp. 85-92.

Wells, Kate Gannett. "The Transitional American Woman." *Atlantic Monthly,* XLVI (December, 1880), pp. 817-823.

Wilcox, Susanne. "The Unrest of Modern Woman," *Independent,* LXVII (July, 1909), pp. 62-66.

Wilson, Edmund. "The Ambiguity of Henry James." *The Question of Henry James.* Edited by F. W. Dupre. New York: Octagon Press, 1973, pp. 160-190.

Wolf, Rennold. "Ethel Barrymore." *Smith's* (November, 1907) n.p. (Locke, 35, pp. 44-46).

—————— "The Salary of Actors—When They Get It." *American,* LXII (September, 1916), pp. 32-33.

Yellis, Kenneth A. "Prosperity's Child: Some Thoughts on the Flapper." *American Quarterly,* XXI (Spring, 1969) pp. 44-63.

Young, Rose. "Suffrage as Seen by Mary Shaw." *Harpers Weekly* (May, 1915), p. 456.

Zangwill, Israel. "Actress Versus Suffraget." *Independent,* LXV (December, 1909), pp. 1248-1250.

Zellers, Parker. "The Cradle of Variety: The Concert Saloon." *Educational Theatre Journal,* XX (December, 1968), pp. 578-585.

UNSIGNED ARTICLES:

The American Girls Damaging Influence on the Drama." *Current Opinion,* XLIII (December, 1907), p 673.

"As An Actor Sees Women." *Ladies Home Journal,* 25 (November, 1908), pp. 26-27.

"Culture and Physique." *Spectator,* LXIV (June 28, 1890), p. 896.

"Decay of Vaudeville." *American,* LXIX (April, 1910) pp. 840-848.

"How I Became an Actor, A Girl's Actual Experience on the Stage and What Happened After She Gets On." *Ladies Home Journal,* 28 (May, 1911), pp. 13-14, 30.

"Injustices to Actresses." *Theatre,* VII (May-June, 1892), pp. 167-168.

"Is the Melting Pot Spilling to Beans." *Literary Digest,* 73 (April, 1922), p. 15.

"Matinee Girl." *Munsey's,* XVIII (October, 1900), pp. 34-42.

"The Passing of the Old Lady." *Atlantic Monthly,* CIX (June, 1907), p. 874.

"Tights and the Stage." *Theatre,* VIII (May-June, 1892), pp. 176-177.

"Trend of Vaudeville." *Independent,* LIII (May, 1901), pp. 1092-1093.

"What the American Girl Has Lost, By an American Mother." *Ladies Home Journal,* 17 (May, 1900), p. 17.

"Women and the Theater." *Nation,* CVI (January, 1918), p. 665.

BOOKS:

Addams, Jane. *The Spirit of Youth and the City Streets.* New York: MacMillan Company, 1910.

Allen, Frederick Lewis. *Only Yesterday: An Informal History of the Nineteen Twenties.* New York: Harper and Brothers, 1931.

Alpert, Hollis. *The Barrymores.* New York: Dial Press, 1964.

Armstrong, Margaret. *Fanny Kemble: A Passionate Victorian.* New York: MacMillan Company, 1938.

Aronson, Rudolph. *Theatrical and Musical Memoirs.* New York: McBride, Nast and Company, 1913.

Astaire, Fred. *Steps in Time.* New York: Harper and Brothers, Publishers, 1959.

Baker, Michael. *The Rise of the Victorian Actor.* London: Croom Helm, 1978.

Bankhead, Tallulah, *Tallulah: My Autobiography.* New York: Harper and Brothers, Publishers, 1952.

Barnes, Eric Wollencott. *The Lady of Fashion: The Life and the Theatre of Anna Cora Mowatt.* New York: Charles Scribner's Sons, 1954.

Barrymore, Ethel. *Memories: An Autobiography.* New York: Harper and Brothers, 1955.

Bentley, Eric. ed. *From the American Drama.* The Modern Theatre Series, Vol. 4. Garden City, N.Y.: Doubleday Anchor Books, 1956.

Bentzon, Th. (Marie Therese Blanc) *The Condition of Women in the United States.* Boston: Roberts Brothers, 1895.

Berger, John. *Ways of Seeing.* New York: Viking Press, 1972.

Bernheim, Alfred L. *The Business of the Theater.* New York: Actors Equity Association, 1932.

Binns, Archie. *Mrs. Fiske and the American Theatre.* New York: Crown Publishers, 1955.

Blake, Nelson Manfred. *The Road to Reno: A History of Divorce in the United States.* New York: MacMillan Company, 1962.

Blouët, Paul. *John Bull's Womankind.* London: Field and Tuer, 1884.

Bourget, Paul. *Outre-Mer: Impressions of America.* New York: Charles Scribner's Sons, 1895.

Brooks, Van Wyck. *The Pilgrimage of Henry James.* New York: E. P. Dutton and Company, 1925.

Bryce, James. *The American Commonwealth.* New York: MacMillan and Company, 1895.

Burggraff, Winfield. *Walter Edmund Bentley: Actor-Priest, Missionary,* No publisher.

Burke, John. *Duet in Diamonds: The Flamboyant Saga of Lillian Russell and Diamond Jim Brady in America's Gilded Age.* New York: G. P. Putnam's Sons, 1972.

Caffin, Caroline. *Vaudeville.* New York: Mitchell Kennerly, 1914.

Calhoun, Arthur W. *A Social History of the American Family: From Colonial Times to the Present.* 3 Vols. New York: Barnes and Noble, 1947.

Carroll, David. *The Matinee Idols.* New York: Arbor House, 1972.

Collier, Jeremy. *A Short View of the Immorality and Profaneness of the English Stage Together with the Sense of Antiquity upon this Argument.* London: S. Kebler, 1697-1698.

Chafe, William Henry. *The American Woman: Her Changing Social, Economic and Political Roles.* New York: Oxford University Press, 1972.

Chinoy, Helen Krich and Jenkins, Linda Walsh. *Women in American Theater.* New York: Crown Publishers, 1981.

Cotes (Duncan), Sara Jeanette. *An American Girl in London.* New York: D. Appleton and Company, 1891.

Cott, Nancy F. *The Bonds of Womanhood: "Woman's Sphere" in New England, 1780–1835.* New Haven: Yale University Press, 1977.

Crowther, Bosley. *The Lion's Share: The Story of an Entertainment Empire.* New York: E.P. Dutton and Company, 1957.

Dale, Alan. *Familiar Chats with Queens of the Stage.* New York: G.W. Dillingham, 1890.

Dardis, Tom. *Keaton: The Man Who Wouldn't Lie Down.* New York: Charles Scribner's Sons, 1979.

Davidoff, Leonore. *The Best Circles: Society, Etiquette and the Season.* London: Croom Helm, 1977.

Davies, Cecil W. *Theater for the People: The Story of the Volksbühne.* Austin: University of Texas Press, 1977.

Davis, Charles Belmont, ed. *Adventures and Letters of Richard Harding Davis.* New York: Charles Scribner's Sons, 1917.

Davis, Michael M., Jr. *The Exploitation of Pleasure: A Study of Commercial Recreation in New York City.* New York: Department of Child Hygiene of the Russell Sage Foundation, 1911.

De Beauvoir, Simone. *The Second Sex.* New York: Bantam Books, 1961.

Degler, Carl. *Out of Our Past: The Forces That Shaped Modern America.* New York: Harper Colophon Books, 1959.

Dempsey, David with Baldwin, Raymond P. *The Triumphs and Trials of Lotta Crabtree.* New York: William Morrow and Company, Inc., 1968.

De Tocqueville, Alexis. *Democracy in America.* Edited by J.P. Mayer. Garden City, N.Y.: Anchor Books, 1969.

De Verigny, Charles. *The Women of the United States.* London: John Lane, 1898.

Dexter, Elizabeth A. *Colonial Women of Affairs: Women in Business and Professions in America Before 1776.* Boston: Houghton, Miflin and Company, 1931.

———*Career Women of America, 1776-1840.* Francistown, N.H.: Marshall Jones Company, 1950.

Dickinson, Thomas H. *The Insurgent Theater.* New York: B. W. Huebsch, 1917.

Douglas, Anne. *The Feminization of American Culture.* New York: Avon Books, 1977.

Downey, Fairfax. *Richard Harding Davis: His Day.* New York: Charles Scribner's Sons, 1933.

———*Portrait of an Era as Drawn by Charles Dana Gibson.* New York: Charles Scribner's Sons, 1936.

Dreiser, Theodore. *Sister Carrie.* New York: New American Library, 1961.

Dressler, Marie as told to Harrington, Mildred. *My Own Story.* Boston: Little, Brown and Company, 1934.

Drew, Mrs. John. *Autobiographical Sketch.* New York: Charles Scribner's Sons, 1899.

Dulles, Foster Rhea. *America Learns to Play: A History of Popular Recreation 1607-1940.* New York: Appleton-Century, Inc., 1940.

Dunbar, Janet. *J. M. Barrie: The Man Behind the Image.* Boston: Houghton, Mifflin Company, 1970.

Eaton, Walter Prichard. *Plays and Players: Leaves From a Critic's Scrapbook.* Cincinnati: Stewart and Kidd, 1916.

Edel, Leon. *Henry James: The Conquest of London 1870-1891.* Philadelphia: J. B. Lippincott and Company, 1962.

Ervine, St. John. *Bernard Shaw, His Life, Work and Friends.* London: Constable and Company, 1956.

Faulkner, Harold U. *Politics, Expansion and Reform.* New York: Harper Brothers, 1959.

Feldheim, Marvin. *The Theater of Augustin Daly: An Account of the Late Nineteenth Century American Stage.* Cambridge: Harvard University Press, 1956.

Finck, Henry Theophilis. *Romantic Love and Person Beauty; Their Development Causal Relations, Historic and National Peculiarities.* New York: MacMillan Company, 1912.

Findlater, Richard. *The Player Queens.* New York: Taplinger Publishing Company, 1977.

Fiske, John. *American Political Ideas: Viewed From the Standpoint of Universal History.* New York: Harper and Brothers, Publishers, 1885.

Flexner, Eleanor. *Century of Struggle: The Woman's Rights Movement.* New York: Atheneum, 1972.

Forbes-Robertson, Diane. *My Aunt Maxine: The Story of Maxine Elliot.* New York: The Viking Press, 1964.

Foster, William Trufort. *Vaudeville and Motion Picture Shows.* Portland, Oregon: Reed College Record No. 16, 1914.

Foy, Eddie and Harlow, Alvin F. *Clowning Through Life.* New York: E. P. Dutton and Company, 1928.

Gelman, Woody. *The Best of Charles Dana Gibson.* New York: Bounty Books, 1969.

Gerson, Noel. *Lilly Langtry.* London: Robert Hale and Company, 1971.

Gilbert, Douglas. *American Vaudeville: Its Life and Times.* New York: Dover Publications, Inc., 1940.

Gilbert, Julia Goldsmith. *Ferber, a Biography.* Garden City, N.Y.: Doubleday and Company, 1978.

Gilder, Rosamund. *Enter the Actress: The First Women in the Theatre.* New York: Theatre Arts Books, 1931.

Gillor, Jr., Edmund Vincent, ed. *The Gibson Girl and Her America: Best Drawings of Charles Dana Gibson.* With an Introduction by Henry C. Pitz. New York: Dover, 1969.

Gilman, Charlotte Perkins. *Women and Economics: The Economic Factor Between Men and Women as a Factor in Social Evolution.* Edited with an Introduction by Carl Degler. New York: Harper Torchbooks, 1906.

Ginger, Ray. *Age of Excess: The United States from 1877-1914.* London: The MacMillan Company, 1965.

Gish, Lillian with Pinchot, Anne. *The Movies, Mr. Griffith and Me.* New York: Avon, 1969.

Goodwin, Nat C. *Nat Goodwin's Book.* Boston: Richard G. Badger, The Gorham Press, 1914.

Grau, Robert. *The Businessman in the Amusement World.* New York: Broadway Publishing Company, 1910.

Green, Abel and Laurie, Jr., Joe. *Show Biz: From Vaude to Video.* Garden City, N.Y.: PermaBooks, 1953.

Grimstead, David. *Melodrama Unveiled: American Theatre and Culture 1800-1850.* Chicago: University of Chicago Press, 1968.

Gusfield, Joseph. *Symbolic Crusade: Status Politics and the Temperance Movement.* Urbana, IL.: University of Illinois Press, 1972.

Haller, John S. and Haller, Robin M. *The Physician and Sexuality in Victorian America.* Urbana: University of Illinois Press, 1974.

Harding, Alfred. *Revolt of the Actors.* New York: William Morrow and Company, 1929.

Harris, Neil, ed. *Land of Contrasts,* 1880-1901. New York: George Braziller, 1970.

Harris, Neil. *Humbug: The Art of P. T. Barnum.* Boston: Little, Brown and Company, 1973.

Hart, James D. *The Popular Book.* Berkeley, CA.: University of California Press, 1961.

Haweis, Mrs. H. R. (Mary Eliza) *The Art of Beauty.* New York: Harper and Brothers, Publishers, 1878.

Hayner, Norman S. *Hotel Life.* Chapel Hill: University of North Carolina Press, 1936.

Henderson, Archibald. *George Bernard Shaw: Man of the Century.* New York: Appleton-Century Crofts, 1956.

Henderson, Mary C. *The City and the Theater: New York City Playhouses from Bowling Green to Broadway.* Clifton, NJ: James T. White and Company, 1927.

Hewitt, Barnard. *Theatre U.S.A., 1668-1957.* New York: McGraw-Hill Company, 1959.

Higham, John. *Strangers in the Land: Patterns of American Nativism 1860-1925.* New York: Atheneum, 1970.

Hodge, Francis. *Yankee Theatre: The Image of America on the Stage, 1825-1850.* Austin: University of Texas Press, 1964.

Hofstadter, Richard. *Social Darwinism in American Thought.* Boston: The Beacon Press, 1955.

Hooks, Janet M. *Woman's Occupations Through Seven Decades.* Women's Bureau Bulletin No. 218. Washington, D.C.: U.S. Government Printing Office, 1947.

Hopper, Hedda. *From Under My Hat.* Garden City, N.Y.: Doubleday and Company, Inc., 1952.

Hughes, Glenn. *A History of the American Theatre, 1700-1950.* New York: Samuel French, 1951.

Irving, Henry. *Impressions of America.* Boston: James Osgood and Company, 1884.

Isman, Felix. *Weber and Fields.* New York: Boni and Liveright, 1924.

James, Edward T.; James, Janet W.; and Boyer, Paul S., eds. *Notable American Women, 1607-1950.* 3 Vols. Cambridge: Belknap Press of Harvard University Press, 1971.

James, Henry. *The Art of the Novel: Critical Prefaces.* With an Introduction by R. P. Blackmur. New York: Charles Scribner's Sons, 1934.

——— *Roderick Hudson.* New York: Charles Scribner's Sons, 1960.

——— *Theatre and Friendship: Some Henry James Letters.* With a Commentary by Elizabeth Robins. New York: G. P. Putnam's Sons, 1932.

Jowitt, Garth. *Film: the Democratic Art.* Boston: Little, Brown and Company, 1976.

Kemble, Frances Anne. *Journal of a Residence in America.* Philadelphia: Carey, Lea and Blanchard, 1835.

——— *Records of Later Life.* 3 Vols. New York: Henry Holt and Company, 1884.

Kendall, Elizabeth. *Where She Danced.* New York: Alfred A. Knopf, 1976.

Kennedy, David C. *Birth Control in America: The Career of Margart Sanger.* New Haven: Yale University, 1970.

Kinne, Wisner Payne. *George Pierce Baker and the American Theater.* Cambridge: Harvard University Press, 1954.

Kirkland, Edward Chase. *Industry Comes of Age: Business, Labor and Public Policy, 1860-1897.* Chicago: Quadrangle Books, 1961.

——— *Dream and Thought in the Business Community, 1860-1900.* Chicago: Quadrangle Books, 1964.

Knepler, Henry. *The Gilded Stage: The Years of the Great International Actresses.* New York: William Morrow and Company, Inc., 1965.

Kobbe, Gustave, *Famous Actors and Actresses and Their Homes*. Boston: Little, Brown and Company, 1903.

Koht, Holvdan. *Life of Ibsen*. New York: Benjamin Bloom, Inc., 1971.

Kotsilibas-Davis, James. *Great Times, Good Times: The Odyssey of Maurice Barrymore*. Garden City, N.Y.: Doubleday and Company, 1977.

Koster, Donald Nelson. *The Theme of Divorce in American Drama, 1871-1939*. Philadelphia: University of Pennsylvania Press, 1942.

Kraditor, Aileen. *The Ideas of the Woman Suffrage Movement, 1890-1920*. Garden City, N.Y.: Anchor Books, 1971.

—— *Up From the Pedestal: Selected Writings in the History of Feminism*. Chicago: Quadrangle Books, 1968.

Lahee, Henry C. *Grand Opera in America*. Boston: L. C. Page and Company, 1902.

Lasch, Christopher. *The New Radicalism in America 1889–1963*. New York: Vintage Books, 1965.

Laurie, Jr., Joe. *Vaudeville: From the Honky Tonks to the Palace*. New York: Henry Holt and Company, 1953.

Leach, Joseph. *Bright Particular Star: The Life and Times of Charlotte Cushman*. New Haven: Yale University Press, 1970.

Leavitt, M B. *Fifty Years in Theatrical Management*. New York: Broadway Publishing, 1912.

Lerner, Gerda. *The Majority Finds its Past: Placing Women in History*. New York: Oxford University Press, 1981.

Leslie, Amy. *Some Players*. Chicago and New York: Herbert S. Stone and Company, 1899.

Lesser, Allen. *Enchanting Rebel: The Secret Life of Adah Isaacs Menken*. New York: Beechhurst Press, 1947.

Lauchtenberg, William E. *The Perils of Prosperity, 1914-1932*. Chicago: University of Chicago Press, 1958.

Lewis, Paul. *Queen of the Plaza: A Biography of Adah Isaacs Menken*. New York: Funk and Wagnalls Company, 1964.

Lockridge, Richard. *Darling of Misfortune, Edwin Booth 1833-1893*. New York: Century Company, 1932.

Logan, Olive. *Apropos of Women and Theatres, with a Paper or Two on Parisian Topics*. New York: Carleton Publishers, 1869.

—— *Before the Footlights and Behind the Scenes, A Book about the "Show Business" in all its Branches*. Philadelphia: Parmalee and Company, 1870.

Lord, Walter. *The Good Years*. New York: Bantam Books, 1962.

Lynd, Robert S. and Lynd, Helen M. *Middletown: A Study in Contemporary American Culture*. New York: Harcourt Brace and Company, 1929.

Marcosson, Isaac F. and Frohman, Daniel. *Charles Frohman: Manager and Man*. New York: Harper and Brothers, 1916.

Marston, William Moulton and Fuller, John Henry. *F. F. Procter: Vaudeville Pioneer*. New York: Richard R. Smith Publisher, 1943.

Martineau, Harriet. *Society in America*. 2 Vols. Paris: Baudry's European Library, 1842.

Matthews, Brander. *Rip Van Winkle Goes to the Play and Other Essays on Plays and Players.* Port Washington, N.Y.: Kennikat Press, 1967.

May, Henry F. *The End of American Innocence: A Study of the First Years of Our Time 1912-1917.* Chicago: Quadrangle Paperbacks, 1961.

———— *Protestant Churches and Industrial America.* New York: Harper Torchbooks, 1967.

McLean, Jr., Albert F. *American Vaudeville as Ritual.* Lexington, KY.: University of Kentucky Press, 1965.

Meyer, Michael. *Ibsen.* New York: Doubleday and Company, 1971.

Modjeska, Helena. *Memories and Impressions of Helena Modjeska: An Autobiography.* New York: The MacMillan Company, 1910.

Moody, Richard. *Astor Place Riot.* Bloomington: Indiana University Press, 1958.

———— *Edwin Forrest: First Star of the American Stage.* New York: Alfred A. Knopf, 1960.

Mooney, Michael MacDonald. *Evelyn Nesbit and Stanford White: Love and Death in the Gilded Age.* New York: William Morrow and Company, Inc., 1976.

Morehouse, Ward. *George M. Cohan: Prince of the American Theater.* Philadelphia: J. B. Lippincott Company, 1943.

Morell, Parker. *Lillian Russell: The Era of Plush.* New York: Random House, 1940.

Morgan, H. Wayne. *The Gilded Age: A Reappraisal.* Syracuse: Syracuse University Press, 1963.

———— *Unity and Culture: The United States, 1877-1900.* London: Penguin Books, 1971.

Morin, Edgar. *The Stars: An Account of the Star-System in Motion Pictures.* New York: Grove Press, 1960.

Morris, Clara. *Stage Confidences: Talks About Players and Play Acting.* Boston: Lothrop Publishing Company, 1902.

———— *The Life of a Star.* New York: McClure, Phillips and Company, 1905.

Moses, Montrose and Brown, John Mason, eds. *The American Stage as Seen By its Critics, 1752-1934.* New York: Cooper Square Publishers, Inc., 1967.

Muirhead, James F. *The Land of Contrasts.* London: John Lane, 1898.

Names, Caspar. *Politics in the American Drama.* Washington, D.C.: The Catholic University of America Press, 1960.

Newberry, Julia. *Julia Newberry's Diary.* Edited with an Introduction by Margaret Ayer Barnes and Janet Ayer Fairbank. New York: W. W. Norton, 1933.

Nye, Russell Blaine. *The Cultural Life of the New Nation, 1776-1830.* New York: Harper Torchbooks, 1960.

———— *The Unembarrassed Muse: The Popular Arts in America.* New York: Dial Press, 1970.

Offenbach, Jacques. *Orpheus in America: The Diaries of Jacques Offenbach of His Trip to the New World.* Translated by Lander MacClintock. Bloomington: University of Indiana Press, 1957.

O'Neill, William L. *Divorce in the Progressive Era.* New Haven: Yale University Press, 1971.

———— *Everyone was Brave: A History of Feminism in America.* New York: Quadrangle/New York Times Book Company, 1971.

Peacock, Virginia Tatnall. *Famous American Belles of the Nineteenth Century.* Philadelphia and London: J. P. Lippincott, 1901.

Perry, John. *James A. Herne, The American Ibsen.* Chicago: Nelson-Hall, Inc., Publishers, 1978.

Pickford, Mary. *Sunshine and Shadow.* Garden City, N.Y.: Doubleday and Company, Inc., 1955.

Powers, James T. *Twinkle Little Star: Sparkling Memories of Seventy Years.* New York: G. P. Putnam's Sons, 1939.

Rahv, Phillip. *Image and Idea: Twenty Essays on Literary Themes.* New York: A New Directions Paperback, 1957.

Rankin, Hugh F. *The Theater in Colonial America.* Chapel Hill: The University of North Carolina Press, 1955.

Ranous, Dora Knowlton. *Diary of a Daly Debutante.* New York: Duffield and Company, 1910.

Richardson, Dorothy. *The Longest Day: The Story of a New York Working Girl, as Told By Herself.* New York: Century Company, 1905.

Rosen, Roth and Davidson, Sue, eds. *The Maimie Papers.* Old Westbury, N.Y.: The Feminist Press, 1977.

Rowell, George. *The Victorian Theater: A Survey.* London: Oxford University Press, 1956.

Ruggle, Eleanor. *Prince of Players, Edwin Booth.* New York: W. W. Norton and Company, Inc., 1953.

Ryan, Mary P. *Womanhood in America: From Colonial Times to the Present.* New York: New Viewpoints, 1975.

Sanger, William W. *The History of Prostitution: Its Extent, Causes, and Effects Throughout the World.* New York: Harper Brothers, Publishers, 1858.

Shaw, Bernard. *The Quintessence of Ibsenism.* New York: Hill and Wang, 1962.

Simon, Louis M. *A History of the Actors Fund of America.* New York: Theatre Arts Books, 1972.

Sinclair, Andrew. *The Emancipation of the American Woman.* New York: Harper Colophon Books, 1965.

Sklar, Kathryn Kish. *Catherine Beecher.* New Haven: Yale University Press, 1973.

Sklar, Robert. *Movie-Made America: How the Movies Changed American Life.* New York: Random House, 1975.

Smith, Cecil. *Musical Comedy in America.* New York: Theatre Arts Books, 1950.

Smith, Frances L. *Talks with Homely Girls on Health and Beauty; Their Preservation and Cultivation.* New York: A. L. Burt, 1885.

Solomon, Barbara Miller. *Ancestors and Immigrants: A Changing New England Tradition.* Cambridge: Harvard University Press, 1950.

Stagg, Jerry. *The Brothers Shubert.* New York: Ballantine Books, 1969.

Strong, Josiah. *Our Country: Its Possible Future and Its Present Crisis.* Edited by Jurgen Herbst. Cambridge: The Belknap Press of Harvard University Press, 1963.

Toll, Robert C. *Blacking Up: The Minstrel Show in Nineteenth Century America.* New York: Oxford University Press, 1974.

Trollope, Frances. *Domestic Manners of the Americans.* Edited by Donald Smally. New York: Alfred A. Knopf, 1948.

Tucker, Sophie. *Some of these Days: The Autobiography of Sophie Tucker.* Garden City, N.Y.: Doubleday, Doran and Company, 1945.

Twain, Mark (Samuel L. Clemens) *Mark Twain's Autobiography.* 2 Vols. New York: Harper and Brothers, 1924.

———— *The Adventures of Huckleberry Finn.* New York: Washington Square Press, 1962.

Van Vorst, Bessie. *The Woman Who Toils: Beginning Experiences of Two Ladies as Factory Girls.* New York: Doubleday, Page and Company, 1902.

Wasserstom, William. *Heiress of All the Ages: Sex and Sentiment in the Gilded Age.* Minneapolis: University of Minnesota, 1959.

Waxman, Samuel M. *Antoine and the Theatre-Libre.* New York: Benjamin Bloom, 1926.

Wecter, Dixon. *The Saga of American Society: A Record of Social Aspiration 1607-1937.* New York: Charles Scribner's Sons, 1937.

Weibe, Robert. *The Search for Order, 1877-1920.* New York: Hill and Wang, 1967.

West, Mae. *Goodness Had Nothing to Do With It.* New York: MacFadden-Bartell Book, 1970.

Willard, Frances E. and Livermore, Mary. *American Women.* 2 Vols. New York: Mast, Crowell, Kirkpatrick Company, 1897.

Williamson, Jefferson. *The American Hotel: An Anecdotal History.* New York: Alfred A. Knopf, 1930.

Wilson, Francis. *Francis Wilson's Life of Himself.* Boston and New York: Houghton-Mifflin Company, 1924.

Wilson, Garff B. *A History of American Acting.* Bloomington: Indiana University Press, 1966.

Winter, William. *The Wallet of Time.* 2 Vols. New York: Moffat, Yard and Company, 1913.

Wolfe, Albert Benedict. *The Lodging House Problem in Boston.* Boston: Houghton-Mifflin and Company, 1906.

Woolf, Virginia. *A Room of One's Own.* New York: A Harvest/HBJ Book, 1929.

Wright, Constance. *Fanny Kemble and the Lovely Land.* New York: Dodd, Mead and Company, 1972.

Wright, Frances. *Views of Society and Manners in America.* Edited by Paul R. Baker. Cambridge: The Belknap Press of Harvard University Press, 1963.

Wyndham, Horace. *Chorus to Coronet.* London: British Technical and General Press, 1951.

Young, Miriam, *Mother Wore Tights*. New York: McGraw-Hill, 1944.

Zeidman, Irving. *The American Burlesque Show*. New York: Hawthorn Books Inc., Publishers. 1967.

Zellers, Parker. *Tony Pastor: Dean of the Vaudeville*. Ypsilanti, Michigan: Eastern Michigan University Press, 1971.

Ziff, Lazar. *The American 1890's: The Life and Times of a Lost Generation*. New York: The Viking Press, 1966.

UNSIGNED BOOKS AND REPORTS:

"The Amusement Situation in the City of Boston." *Being a Report of the Drama Committee of the Twentieth Century Club*. Boston: Twentieth Century Club, 1910.

Beauty is Power. New York: G. W. Carleton and Company, Publishers, 1871.

New York State Courts: Court of General Sessions. *The Trial of Daniel McFarland for the Shooting of Albert D. Richardson the Alleged Seducer of His Wife*. By a Practical Law Reporter. New York: W. E. Hilton Publishers, No. 128 Nassau Street, 1870.

The Seamy Side: A Story of the True Conditions of Things Theatrical by One Who Has Spent Twenty Years Among Them. Boston: Percy Ives Publishing Company, 1906.

U.S. Department of Commerce and Labor. Bureau of the Census. *Marriage and Divorce 1887-1906*. Washington, D.C.: Government Printing Office, 1908.

U.S. Department of Commerce and Labor. *Special Reports: Occupations at the Twelfth Census*. Washington, D.C.: Government Printing Office, 1901.

Index

Actors' Alliance of America, 82
Actors-Church Alliance, 33, 75
actors' clubs, 67-70
Actors Equity strike of 1919, 111,
    136, 137, 147
Actors' Fund, 67, 68-69, 71, 145
Actors Order of Friendship, 67
actresses' clubs, 70-75
Adamless Eden, 73
Adams, Herbert Baxter, 99
Adams, Lucille, 68
Adams, Maude, 4, 40, 53, 129
Addams, Jane, 37-38, 39, 53, 78,
    111, 121
Adventures of Huckleberry Finn, The, 2
airy, fairy, Nellie. See Russell, Lillian
Akins, Zoe, 137
Aldrich, Thomas Bailey, 69
Allen, Viola, 50
amateur night, 37, 53
American Academy of Dramatic Arts,
    51
American beauty, 92
American Beauty, An, 103, 104
American beauty rose, 101
American Commonwealth, The, 119
American Company, 13
American girl, image of, 119-122,
    147
American Girl in London, An, 131
American Ibsen, 77
American Magazine, 39
American Medical Association, 145
American Music Hall, 38
American nationalism and beauty,
    105-108

American national theater, 52
American Political Ideas, 99
American Protective Association,
    98-99
American Revolution, 119
*American Vaudeville, Its Life and
    Times,* 34
American Vaudeville as Ritual, 3
American Woman's Suffrage
    Association, 21, 70
Anderson, Mary, 17, 105
Anthony, Susan B., 5, 21, 22, 24, 26,
    73, 84, 94
Antoine, Andre, 76
Apollo Hall, 22
Apropos of Women and Theatres, 25,
    144
Arch Street Theater, 33, 125, 127
Aronson, Rudolph, 94-95, 103
Arthur, T. S., 77
Art of Beauty, The, 107
Astaire, Adele, 54
Astaire, Fred, 54
Astor, Mrs. John Jacob, 133
Astor Place riot of 1849, 14-15
Atlantic Monthly, The, 22, 98, 122
audiences, women in, 39-42
Augustin Daly Company, 75
Aurelius, Marcus, 95
autonomy for women, 7, 11, 26, 146

Baker, Colgate, 80
Baker, George Pierce, 81
bands, all-women, 73
Bankhead, Tallulah, 137
Banks, Maud, 73

Barnum, P. T., 33
Barrett, Lawrence, 69
Barrie, James M., 40, 134, 136, 147
Barrymore, Ethel, 7, 40, 49, 50, 52, 54, 61-62, 119-141; American girl, as images of, 146-147; American girl, as images of, 132-133; ancestral heritage, 125-127; career, 123-124, 128-129, 132-134, 135-137; Gibson girl, 131-133, 147; marriage, 134; suffragette, 134
Barrymore, Georgie Drew, 126-127, 132, 146
Barrymore, John, 125
Barrymore, Lionel, 125, 127
Barrymore, Maurice, 5, 37, 59, 125, 126-127, 128
Basselin, Olivier, 34
Bateman, Victory, 72
Bauble Shop, The, 128
Bayes, Nora, 37
Beauty is Power, 107
Beck, Martin, 44
Beecher, Catherine, 19, 119
Beecher, Henry Ward, 21, 22, 24
Before the Footlights and Behind The Scenes, 25
Behn, Aphra, 12
Belasco, David, 49, 50, 52, 78
Bell, Alexander Graham, 31
Bell, Archie, 42
Belmont, August, 59
Benedict, E. C., 69
Bennett, Richard, 5
Bentley, Walter E., 33
Bentzon, Madame Th. See Blanc, Therese
Berger, John, 125
Berkeley, Victor Emmanuel, 19
Bernard, Sam, 104
Bernhardt, Sarah, 4, 5, 37, 38
Bijou Theater (Boston), 35
Billboard, 56, 60, 85
Bingham, Amelia, 73-74
bird and bottle supper, 58
Birney, Mrs. Theodore, 122-123

Blackburn, Asa, 108
Black Crook, The, 25, 103
Blacking Up, 3
Blackwell, Elizabeth, 73
Blanc, Therese, 120
Blanch, Belle, 37
Blatch, Harriet Stanton, 81
Bloodgood, Clara, 40, 129
blue material, 55
Blundell, Zoe, 136
Blythe, Herbert. See Barrymore, Maurice
boardinghouse, 52, 56-57
Bok, Edward, 39
Bonaparte, Betsy Patterson, 105
Booth, Edwin, 22, 23, 69, 125
Booth, Junius Brutus, 69
Booth family, 50
Booth's Theater, 17
Boston Museum Company, 75
Bourget, Paul, 105-106, 120
Bowers, Henry F., 98-99, 111
Bozenta, Count, 75
Brady, Diamond Jim, 59, 95, 108
Brady, William, 61
Brahm, Otto, 76
Bremer, Frederika, 120
Brieux, Eugene, 5
British Blondes, 25
Broadway, 5, 37, 77, 81, 123, 143, 147
Bronte, Charlotte, 25
Brook Farm, 75
Brooklyn Eagle, 14
Browning, Mrs., 25
Browning, Robert, 102
Bruce, Lord, 97
Bryce, Lord James, 119
Buffalo Express, 93
Burhardt, Lillian, 37
Burke, Billie, 40
burlesque, 34, 103, 104
Burnham, James, 3
Burr, Theodosia, 105
Bushnell, Horace, 32
Businessman in the Amusement World, The, 33

Butler, Pierce, 19-20
Byron, Lord, 12

Caffin, Caroline, 136
Calhoun, Laura, 23, 27
Callaghan, Delia, 50
Calvin, John, 12, 32
Cameron, Beatrice. *See* Mansfield, Mrs.
Candida, 79
Captain Jinks of the Horse Marines, 62, 123, 128, 132, 133
Carrie, Sister, 27, 31, 40
Carrots, 123
Carter, Leslie, 54
Carter, M., 2
Carus, Emma, 86
Casey, Pat, 44
Casino Theater, 94, 103
Castellane, Boni, 131
catholicism, 98, 126
Catholic Know Nothing Party, 98
Catiline, 77
Cato, 2
Catt, Carrie Chapman, 81
Century, 123
Chamberlain, Lord, 79
Charlotte Temple, 16
Chicago Common Council, 93
Chicago Record, 135
Chicago Sorosis, 93
Chicago Sunday Tribune, 78
Chicago Tribune, 96
Chicago World's Fair Auxiliary Woman's Congress, 76
Child Wife, A, 77
Chinoy, Helen Krich, 1, 2
Chorus Equity, 137
chorus girl, 50
Christian Science, 95, 146
Christy Minstrels, The, 15
Churchill, Winston, 129
Civil War, 40; post, 32
Clemens, Samuel, 2, 25, 69, 103
Cleopatra, 104, 107
Cobbe, Frances, 20
Cohan, George M., 61

Cole, Robert, 136
Colfax, Schuyler, 22
Collier, Jeremy, 32
Colonial Theater, 86
Colt, Russell Griswold, 134
Columbian Exposition of 1893, 92, 97, 103
comic opera, 34, 103-104
commedia del'arte, 12
Comstock, Anthony, 79
Condition of Women in the United States, 120-121
Congress, U.S., 81
Contented Wife, A, 81
Continental Army, 2, 16
Continental Congress, 13
Cooper-Hewitt, Mrs., 133
Corbett, James, 106
Coriolanus, 13
Cosmopolitan, 37, 42
costume, importance of, 54
Cote, Sara Jeannette, 131
Cousin Kate, 123
Cowl, Jane, 53
Crabtree, Charlotte Mignon, 71-72
Crabtree, Lotta. *See* Crabtree, Charlotte Mignon
Croly, David, 70
Croly, Jennie "June", 70
Croly, Vida, 70
Crosman, Henrietta, 86
Crowninshield, Francis, 124
Crummle Family, 50
Cummings, Ellen, 59
cup and saucer plays, 76
Current Opinion, 41
Currie, Jim, 59
Curzon, Marquis, 131
Cushman, Charlotte, 16-17, 18, 21, 27, 143

Daily Telegraph (London), 40, 144
Daisy Miller, 129, 130, 131, 137, 147
Daisy Millerites, 130
Dale, Alan, 42, 92, 132, 136
Daly, Arnold, 79

Daly, Augustin, 2, 5, 23, 51, 55, 69, 77, 126
Daly, Joseph, 70
Daly company, 59
Daly's Debutantes, 51
Damaged Goods, 5
Damnation of Theron Ware, The, 43
Damrosch, Leopold, 94
Darwin, Charles, 32, 99, 100, 112
Davenport family,, 50
Davis, Charles Belmont, 51, 132
Davis, Clarke, 132
Davis, Rebecca Harding, 132
Davis, Richard Harding, 131-132
Day, Clarence, 92
De Beauvoir, Simone, 1, 7
Declaration of Independence, 21, 22, 84
Declaration of Sentiments, 21
Declasse, 137
DeFoe, Louis V., 82
Deland, Margaret, 133
DeMaupassant, Guy, 130
Denison, John, 98
Depew, Chauncey, 103
DeVarigny, Charles, 120
Devine, Sarah, 12
Dexter, Elizabeth, 1
Dickens, Charles, 18, 70
Dickinson, Anna, 24, 26
Dickson, Charles, 36
Disraeli, Benjamin, 128
Divine One, 38
Divorce, 77
divorce, 21-23, 60-61
Dixey, Harry, 2
Dolls House, A, 77, 78, 134
Doro, Marie, 40, 129
Douglass, David, 13
Douglass, Frederick, 24
Douglass Company, 16
Douglass-Hallam troupe, 13
drama, American: declining standards of, 40-41; writing of original, 13-14
drama school, 51-52, 53
Dramatic Mirror, 69, 73, 74, 77, 102

Dreiser, Theodore, 2, 11, 39
dress, importance of, 53-54
dressing rooms, conditions of, 55-56
Dressler, Marie, 50, 60, 94, 96, 108, 137
Drew, Ethel, 33
Drew, Georgie. *See* Barrymore, Georgie
Drew, John, 33, 124, 125, 127, 128
Drew, Lionel, 33
Drew, Louisa, 125
Drew, Mrs. John, 33, 125, 126, 127-128, 146
Drew, Sidney, 125
Dudevant, Louis, 19
Dudevant, Madame, 25
Dumas, Alexandre, 18
DuMaurier, Gerald, 129
Duncan, Isadora, 7
Dunlop, William, 13, 143
Duse, Eleanora, 5
Dwight family, 19

Eaton, Peggy, 105
Eaton, Walter Prichard, 40, 135
Edison, Thomas A., 92
education of women, 119-122
Eldridge, "Aunt Louisa," 96
Eliot, George, 123
Elliot, Maxine, 92
emancipation of women, 119-137
Emmett, Dan, 15
Enter the Actress, 1
entertainment, new forms of, 34
Equal Rights Convention of 1869, 24
equal rights for woman. *See* women's rights
Erlanger, Abraham, 4, 34
Eugenie, Empress, 23
Evesson, Isabelle, 72

F.A.D. Club, 70
Falling Footprints, 93
Fashion, 18
Father of the American Drama, 13
Father of Vaudeville, 33
Faucit, Helen, 25

Faust, 38
feminization of the theater, 11, 17-18, 25-26, 43, 80-81, 144, 145
Fernandez, Bijou, 52
film industry, 34, 35, 53, 143
Fischer, Alice, 70
Fish, Mrs. Stuyvesant, 133
Fiske, Harrison Grey, 68
Fiske, John, 99
Fiske, Minnie Maddern, 4, 50, 72, 77, 124
Fitch, Clyde, 40, 132
Floradora sextette, 55
Follies of 1909, 55
Forbes-Robertson, Johnston, 5
Ford, James L., 124
Forepaugh, Adam, 105
Forrest, Edwin, 13-14, 17, 67, 125, 143
Frank Leslie's Popular Monthly, 123
Franklin, Irene, 37, 38, 92
Frederic, Harold, 43
Free Love and Fourierism, 22
Freeman, Edward A., 99
Freie Volksbuhne, 76-77, 78
Friday Morning Club (Los Angeles), 81
Frigenza, Trixie. *See* Callaghan, Delia
Frohman, Charles, 4, 40, 128-129, 132, 134, 142
fundamentalism, 32
Furry, Elda. *See* Hopper, Hedda
Fyles, Vanderheyden, 124
Fynes, J. Austin, 36

Galsworthy, John, 134
Gamut Club, 74, 85
General Federation of Woman's Clubs (GFWC), 70, 73
George, Grace, 61
Gerry, Eldridge P., 22
Ghosts, 78, 80
Gibson, Charles Dana, 41, 131, 132, 133
Gibson girl, 122, 131, 132, 133, 137, 147

Gibson man, 131
Gilbert, Douglas, 34
Gilbert, Sir William Schwenck, 102, 103
Gilder, Rosamund, 1
Gillette, William, 128
Gilman, Charlotte Perkins, 121
Gish, Dorothy, 51
Gish, Lillian, 50-51
Gladden, Washington, 32
Gladiator, The, 13
golden age of players, 4
Golden Bowl, The, 131
Gould, Anna, 131
Graham, Henry, 129
Graham, Martha, 7
Grand, Sarah, 91
Grand Duchess of Gerolstein, The, 103
Grau, Robert, 33, 36
Greatest Show on Earth, 33
Great Thoughts, 43
Greeley, Horace, 18, 21, 22
Grein, J. T., 76
Grey, Prudence, 53, 58
Grimstead, David, 3
Grundy, Sydney, 81-82
Guilbert, Yvette, 5
Gumpertz, Samuel, 80
Gwynne, Nell, 12

Hale, Sarah Josepha, 19, 21
Halevy, Ludovic, 130
Hall, Prescott, 99
Hallam, Lewis, Jr., 16
Hallam, Lewis, Sr., 13
Hallam, Mrs. Lewis, 16
Hallam, Mrs. Lewis, Jr., 16
Hallam, William, 13
Hallam Company, 13, 16
Hallam-Douglass, Mrs., 13
Hammerstein, William, 36, 37
Harcourt, Alice Fischer, 86
Harding, Warren G., 111, 146
Harpers Bazaar, 122
Hartford Female Seminary, 119
Harvard playwrighting workshop, 81
Harvard University, 51, 124

Haweis, Mary E., 107
Haymen and Frohman, 34
Hazlitt, William, 12
Hearst, William Randolph, 42
Heart's Ease, 72
Held, Anna, 92
Hepburn, Dr. Thomas, 5
Herald (Clinton, Iowa), 93
Herne, James A., 77
Higham, John, 3
High Hat bills, 41
historical dramas, 76
History of Prostitution, 105
History of the American Theater, 13
Hodge, Francis, 3
Hollywood, 47, 62, 143
Holy Roman Emperor, 12
Home, Dorothea Dix, 75
Hope Leslie (1827), 19
Hopkinson, John, 16
Hopper, De Wolf, 104
Hopper, Hedda, 62
Hosmer, James K., 99
Hotel Astor, 83
hotels and show business, 56
Howe, Marie Jenney, 83
Howells, William Dean, 41, 78,
    129-130
How He Lied to Her Husband, 79
Howland, John, 93
How the Vote Was Won, 86
Hoyt, Charles, 81-82
Hrothvithsa, 12
Hubbard, W. L., 78
Hull House, 78
Hummel, Abe, 96
Hutton, Lawrence, 69

Ibsen, Henrik, 76, 77, 78, 79, 80,
    81, 134, 145
Illustrated American, 104
Immigrant Restriction League, 99
Immigrant Restriction Leaguers, 111
Independent, 36
Independent Theater (London), 76
Ingelow, Jean, 25
Ingersoll, Margaret, 73

Ingersoll, Robert, 93
International Woman's Congress
    (1899), 76
Irving, Henry, 128, 129
Irving, Laurence, 128
Irwin, Flo, 36
Irwin, May, 36, 43, 58, 67

Jackson, Andrew, 15, 125
Jacobs, Jennie, 44
James, Henry, 82, 102, 123, 129,
    130, 137, 147
James, Henry, Sr., 21
Janauschak, Fanny, 70
Janis, Elsie, 37
Jefferson, Joseph, 2, 4, 125
Jefferson, Thomas, 16
Jeness-Miller Monthly, 107, 108
Jenkins, Linda Walsh, 1, 2, 0
Jesuits, 85
Joan of Arc, 137
John Bull's Other Island, 79
Johnson, Aurelia, 132
Journal, 42
*Journal of a Residence on a Georgia
    Plantation,* 20

Kean, Mrs., 25
Kean, Thomas, 12
Keaton, Buster, 61
Keith, B. F., 4, 33, 34, 35, 36, 38,
    86
Keith's Union Square Theater (New
    York), 36
Kellerman, Annette, 44
Kemble, Fanny, 19, 20, 27, 144
Kemble, John Phillip, 19
Kennedy, David, 3
Kerker, Gustave, 103
Kimball Hall (Chicago), 93
Klauber, Adolph, 82
Klaw, Marc, 34
Knights of Labor, 98
Knowlton, Dora, 59
Knowlton, Josephine Gibson, 133
Kraditor, Aileen, 84
Ku Klux Klan, 98

L'Abbe Constantin, 130
Ladies Home Journal, 39, 40-41, 55, 121
Lady Teazle Company, 61
La Follette, Fola, 79, 86
La Follette, Robert, 79
La Maire, George, 55
Lambs' Club, 69
Land of Contrasts, The, 99
Lander, Mrs., 25
Langtry, Lillie, 5, 58
Last of the League of the Iroquois, The, 93
League of Nations, 111, 146
leg business, the, 25
legitimate stage, 36-37, 86
Leiter, Mary, 131
Lena Rouden, A Rebel Spy, 93
Leonard, Charles Egbert, 92-93
Leonard, Cynthia Hicks, 92-94, 109
Leonard, Helen Louise. *See* Russell, Lillian
Leonard, Susan, 94, 101
Lerner, Gerda, 1, 6
Les Avaries, 5
Lewes, Mrs., 25
Lewisohn, Jesse, 59
Liberty Loan drives, 111
Life in the Iron Mills, 132
Lincoln, Abraham, 2
Lind, Jenny, 102
Lippincott's, Packard Monthly, 25
Little Minister, The, 135
Little Nell, 72
Lloyd, Alice, 44
Lloyd, Marie, 5
Lodge, Henry Cabot, 99
Lowe, Marcus, 34, 44
Lowe's Circuit, 44
Lowe's chain, 34
Loftus, Cissie, 37
Logan, Cornelius, 23
Logan, Olive, 23-27, 53, 144
London Company of Comedians, 13
Lorne, Dolores, 51
Lotta Gallop, 72

Lotta Polka, 72
Louisa Lane. *See* Drew, Mrs. John
Lyceum Theater School, 51
Lydia Thompson's British Blondes, 103
Lynd, Helen M., 3
Lynd, Robert S., 3

MacAuley, Rachel, 73
Macbeth, 13
McClellan, George, 79
MacFarland, Abby Sage. *See* Richardson, Abby Sage
MacFarland, Daniel, 21-22, 22, 23
McGovern, James R., 3
MacGuire, Tom, 71
MacKaye, Steele, 51
McLean, Albert F., Jr., 3
McTwobucks, Lillian, 34
Macready, William, 14, 16
Madison Square Garden, 73
Maguire, Tom, 33
Maison Doree, 93
Man of Destiny, The, 79
Mansfield, Mrs. Richard, 77
Mansfield, Richard, 4
Margaret Fleming, 77
Mark Twain. *See* Clemens, Samuel
Marlborough, Duke of, 131
Marlowe, Julia, 61
Martineau, Harriet, 70
mashes, 58
matinee, 42
Matinee girl, 39, 40, 41, 49, 121, 144, 145
matinee idol, 40
May, Henry, 3
Mazeppa, 18
melodramas, 76
Melodrama Unveiled, 3
Menken, Adah Isaacs, 18-19, 20, 27, 144
Metamora, 13
Mid-channel, 136
Middletown, 3
Midwest Stair, 4
Mignon, 93

Milholland, Inez, 91, 109
Miller, Daisy, 129, 131
minstrel show, 15-16, 33, 40, 103;
   all-female, 72
Mirror, 41, 68
Modjeska, Helena, 4, 55, 75-76, 77,
   126
Modjeska Company, 78
Montague, Harry, 40
Montez, Lola, 71, 104
Moore, Alexander P., 109
Morgan, J. P., 95, 103
Morgan Bank, 34
Morin, Edgar, 143
Morning Telegraph, 105
Morris, Clara, 17, 54, 59, 70
Morris, William, 44
Morse, Samuel F. B., 31
Most Engaged Girl in America, The,
   129
motion pictures. *See* film industry
Mott, Lucretia, 21, 24, 73
Mowatt, Anna Cora, 17-18, 21, 27,
   51, 143
Mowatt, James, 17
Mrs. Warren's Profession, 2, 74, 79,
   80, 81, 85
Muirhead, James F., 97, 120
Munsey, 39
Murray, Walter, 12
musical comedy, 34

Napoleon of Managers, 33
Nation, 43
National Congress of Mothers, 122
National Women's Suffrage
   Association, 21, 70
natural rights, 84
Nesbitt, Evelyn, 59
New England Tale (1822), 19
New England Women's Club, 70, 145
Newton, Eliza, 68
New Woman, 5, 6, 81-82, 91, 122,
   145
New Woman, The, 81
New York Clipper, 51, 82
New York Dramatic Mirror, 6, 33, 39,

   41, 43, 49, 68
New York Dramatic News, 103
New York Evening Post, 34
New York Herald, 68, 78, 79,
   109-110
New York Herald Tribune, 51-52
New York Press Club, 70
New York suffrage parade (1912),
   109, 111
New York Sun, 57, 79, 84-85
New York Telegram, 59
New York Times, 72, 79, 129, 136
New York Tribune, 17, 18, 21
New York World, 82
Nixon and Zimmerman, 34
Norton, William, 68
Nude Drama, The, 25, 26
Nugent, Elliot, 61

Oelrichs, Mrs. Herman, 133
Offenbach, Jacques, 103, 105,
   120
Ogden, Anna Cora, 17
Oliver's Optics, 25
Olympia Theater, 36
Olympic Theatre, 12
Oneida, 69
O'Neill, William, 84
opera, 103
Origin of the Species, The, 100
Orpheum Circuit, 35, 44
Osborn, Howell, 59
Othello, 13
*Our Country: Its Present Crisis and
   Possible,* 100
Owen, Robert Dale, 21

Packard's Monthly, 25
Page, E.A., 108
Paget, Sir Almeric, 131
Palace, 135
Palmer, A. M., 68
Palmer, Mrs. A. M., 71, 72, 73
Pankhurst, Christabel, 5, 83
Parisian Theatre Libre, 76
Park Theater, 13
Parrot Cage, The, 83

Pastor, Antonio "Tony," 33, 35, 36, 101, 102
Patience, 102
Paul, Alice, 81
Perugini, Signor Giovanni. *See* Chatterton, 0
Philadelphia Inquirer, 132
Philadelphia Ledger, 15
Pickford, Mary, 50
Pillars of Society, 77
Pinero, Sir Arthur Wing, 59
Pinzer, Maimie, 38
Pirates of Penzance, The, 102
Pittsburgh Leader, 109
Playboy of the Western World, 2
Players, 69
Players Club, 145
playwrights, American, 14
Poe, Edgar Allen, 18, 102
Porter, Ben, 59
Powers, James T., 101-102
Prentiss, Isabell, 52
Princess Nicotine, The, 96
problem plays, 39
Proctor, F. F., 35, 36, 86
professional clubs, 67-86
Professional Woman's League (PWL), 71, 72-73, 74, 75, 83, 95, 96, 109, 145
Progressive Party Campaign (1912), 109
propagandist drama, 82
protestantism, 32-33
Provincetown Players, 81

Queen of Brilliants, The, 96
Queen of Comic Opera, 103
Queen of Divorces, 96
Quintessence of Ibsenism, The, 79
Quo Vadis, 75

railroad and show business, 55
Ranous, Dora Knowlton, 51, 55
Rauschenbush, Walter, 32
realistic drama, 76-81
Redwood (1824), 19
Reicher, Emmanual, 78

Rembrandt, van Rijn, 123
repertory company, 51, 52, 53, 55
Republican party, 112
Revolution, 24
Rice, E. E., 101
Rice, T. D., 15
Richardson, Abby Sage, 21, 22, 23, 27, 144
Richardson, Albert D., 21, 22
Richardson, Anna Steese, 42
Richardson, Dorothy, 38
Ristori, Rachel, 25
Robertson, Tom, 76
Robins, Elizabeth, 82
Robson, Anna, 59
Rockefeller, John D., 100
Roderick Hudson, 102
Roosevelt, Alice, 133
Roosevelt, Theodore, 109, 146
Ross, Fred, 95
Rowson, Susanna, 16, 143
Rush, Benjamin, 119
Russell, Anna, 54, 58
Russell, Lillian, 7, 36, 58, 59, 61, 73, 74, 91-117, 145-146, 147; American beauty, 92, 101-108; American Protective Association, 98-100; exercise program, 108-109; marriages, 96, 109; parental influence, 93-94; singing career, 101-105; suffrage movement, 109-111; Theodore Roosevelt campaign, 109; union activities, 111
Russell Sage Foundation, 38

Sacred Heart Academy, 93
Sage, Abby, 21-22
St. Denis, Ruth, 7
St. Leger, Harriet, 20
Salt Cellar, The, 37
Sand, George, 18-19, 20, 27, 144
Sandow, Eugene, 103
San Francisco Chronicle, 80
Sanger, William W., 12
Sappho, 3
Sargeant, Franklin, 51, 52, 78

School for Scandal, 92, 125
Schreiner, Olive, 73, 81, 121
Schuberts chain, 34
Scott, Clement, 43, 144
Scribners Monthly, 130
Seamy Side, The, 53, 58
Second Mrs. Tanqueray, The, 136
Second Sex, The, 1
Secret Service, 128
Sedgewick, Catherine, 19, 27, 144
Senate, U.S., 110
Sepoy Mutiny, 126
sexual harassment and actresses, 59-60
Shakespeare, Wiliam, 2, 13, 43, 72
Shaw, George Bernard, 2, 76, 79, 80, 84, 85, 145, 0
Shaw, Mary, 7, 44, 54, 59, 67-90, 73, 145, 146, 147; Professional Woman's League, 74-75; realistic drama, 76-81; women's suffrage, 81-86
Shay, Arthur, 5
Sheridan, Emma V., 58
Sheridan's School for Scandal, 61
Sherman, William T., 69, 103
Shook, Sheridan, 68
Shore Acres, 77
Shoumburg, Emilie, 105
show business: boardinghouse, 52, 56-57; growth in leisure time, 32, 34; industrialization and, 31-32; minstrel show. *See* minstrel show; new forms of entertainment, 34; suffragette shows, 82-86; urbanization and, 31-32; women and the growth of, 31-48. *See also* burlesque; theater; vaudeville
Siddons, Sarah, 12, 19, 25
Sienkiewiecz, Henry, 75
Sigourney, Lydia, 19, 21
Silver Box, The, 134
Sister Carrie, 2, 11
Sklar, Robert, 7
Smith, Frances L., 100
Smith, Sidney, 13
Snake Charmer, The, 102

Social Feminism, 70, 84
Social Gospel, 32
Solomon, Edward, 96
Sorosis, 70, 71, 72, 145
Sothern, E. H., 4, 61
Spirit of the Times, The, 102
Spirit of Youth and the City Streets, 37-38
stagedoor johnnies, 58
Stage Struck Girl, The, 39, 53, 62
Standard Oil, 4
Stanton, Elizabeth Cady, 5, 21, 22, 23, 26, 27, 84
Starret, Helen Ekin, 121-122
Steel Engraving Lady, The, 122
Stevenson, Robert Louis, 123
stock company, 52, 53
Stone, Lucy, 21, 73
Stowe, Mrs., 25
Strong, Josiah, 100
suffrage movement, British, 82
suffragete shows, 82-86
suitcase romances, 60
Sullivan, Arthur, 93, 102, 103
Sunday, 123
Surf, 23
Sutherland, Duchess of, 128
Swinborne, Algernon, 18
Synge, John Millington, 2

Tammany, 80
Tanguay, Eva, 37, 44, 54, 55
Templeton, Faye, 50, 59, 104
Ten Nights in a Barroom, 5, 77
Terry, Ellen, 5, 129
Thaw, Harry, 59
Theater, 133
theater: beauty vs. talent, 52-53; children in, 50-51, 52, 61; colonial period, 16; costume, importance of, 54; drama schools, 51-52; dress, importance of, 53-54; economic lives of women in, 11, 36, 37, 49-62; equality in, 23, 25-26, 44, 143; European, 12-13, 14; evolution in America, 11-27; female domination of stage, 42-43;

growth of entertainment industry, 31-48; life on road, grievances of, 55-56, 144-145; politics of American society and, 14-15; realism, development of, 76-77; social classes and, 15; social lives of women in, 11, 49-62; stage business, etiquette, and tradition, 54-55; stage discipline, 55. vaudeville. *See* vaudeville; women as economic backbone of, 80-81; women of, and literature, 18-20; women of, influence in, 11, 17-18, 43, 144

Theatre, 49

Theatre Libre, 76-77

Theatre Magazine, 42, 52, 53

Theatrical Enterprises, 34

Thompson, Denman, 5

Thompson, Lydia, 25

Thoughts on Female Education, 119

Ticknor, Caroline, 122

Tocqueville, Alexis de, 67, 120

Toll, Robert, 3

Town Topics, 110

Trentoni, Madame. *See* Johnson, Aurelia

Trollope, Frances, 20, 105, 120

Troy Seminary, 119

tuberculosis, 56

Tucker, Dora, 37

Tucker, Sophie, 37, 50, 53, 54, 55, 60, 61

Tuke, Sarah, 16

Twelfth Night Club, 70, 86, 145

Twelve Pound Look, The, 134, 135, 136, 147

Two Orphans, 69

Typical American Girl, 123, 124

Tyrell, Henry, 75

Under Gaslight, 2

Union Square Hotel, 68

Union Square Theater, 35

Upchurch, Janet, 77

Vanderbilt, Consuelo, 131

Van Vorst, Bertha, 38

Variety, 43, 52, 56, 60, 86

vaudeville, 33, 34-39, 42, 48-49, 53-54, 73, 86, 104, 136; amateur night, 37; audience, women in, 39-42; salaries, 36, 37, 53-54; women in, 37-39

venereal disease, 5

Venus de Milo, 102

Verver, Maggie, 131

Vestris, Madame, 1, 12

vice plays, 5

Victorianism, 11, 57-58

Victoria Theater, 86

Virginia Minstrels, 15

Votes for Women, 82, 83

Walker, Francis Amasa, 100

Wallace-Hopper, Edna, 92

Wallack, Lester, 33, 68

Wallack family, 50

Ward, Robert De Courcey, 99

Warfield, David, 104

Warner, Anne, 122

Warren, Mercy Otis, 16, 143

Warsaw Imperial Theater, 75

Washington, George, 2

Wayburn, Ned, 54

Welby, Bertha, 73

Wells, Kate Gannet, 121

Wendall, Barrett, 99

West, George, 110

West, Mae, 37

Westford, Suzanne Leonard, 74

White, Stanford, 58, 69

White Rats Vaudeville Union, 109

Whitman, Walt, 14, 18

Whitney, Pauline, 131

Wicks, Mamie, 131

Widower's House, The, 79

Willard, Emma, 119

William Lloyd Garrison Equal Suffrage League, 86

Williams, Percy, 34, 86

Willis, Portia, 91

Wilson, Edmund, 131

Wilson Francis, 111

Wings of the Dove, 131
Winter, Wales, 52
Winter, William, 17, 78, 79
Wolfe, Georgia, 53
Woman's Home Companion, 40, 43, 52
Woman's National Theater, 75, 81
Woman's Suffrage Party, 83
Women and Labour, 121
Women in American Theater, 1
Women of the United States, The, 120
Women's Christian Temperance Union (WCTU), 5, 77
women's rights, 6, 7, 20-21, 23-27, 82-84
Women's Rights Convention, 21
women's suffrage movement, 5, 22, 82; Ethel Barrymore, 134; Lillian Russell, 109-111; Mary Shaw, 67-90; new image of, 91; Olive Logan, 23-27
Woolf, Virginia, 12
World Magazine, 61
Wright, Fanny, 119-120

Yale, 124
Yankee Theater, 3
You Can Never Tell, 79
Young, Miriam Burt, 55
Young, Myrtle MacKinley, 55

Zangwill, Israel, 86, 91
Zeigfield, Florenz, 103

About the Author

Albert Auster is a Professor of Television and Radio at Brooklyn College. He earned his PhD in History from the State University of New York at Stony Brook.

Dr. Auster has published widely in the area of film and history. His articles have appeared in the Radical History Review, Social Policy Midstream, The Chronicle of Higher Education, and The Nation. He is an associate of *Cineaste* Magazine and is coauthor of *American Film and Society Since 1945.*